# WESLEY'S

# CHRISTOLOGY

# *WESLEY'S*

# CHRISTOLOGY

## *AN*
## *INTERPRETATION*

## *JOHN DESCHNER*

**FRANCIS ASBURY PRESS**
*of Zondervan Publishing House*
Grand Rapids, Michigan

WESLEY'S CHRISTOLOGY: An Interpretation
Copyright © 1960, 1985 by Southern Methodist University Press

The Francis Asbury Press is an imprint of Zondervan Publishing House, 1415 Lake Drive S.E., Grand Rapids, Michigan 49506.

This edition published 1988 by special arrangement with Southern Methodist University Press, Dallas, Texas.

**Library of Congress Cataloging in Publication Data**
Deschner, John.
    Wesley's Christology : an interpretation / John Deschner : with a new foreword by the author.
        p.     cm.
    Reprint. Originally published: Dallas : Southern Methodist University Press, 1960.
    Originally presented as the author's thesis (doctoral)—University of Basel.
    Bibliography: p.
    Includes index.
    ISBN 0-310-36861-8
    1. Jesus Christ—History of doctrines—18th century. 2. Wesley, John, 1703–1791—Contributions in Christology. I. Title.
[BT198.D4        1988]
232'.092'4—dc19                                                              87-30272
                                                                                      CIP

*Printed in the United States of America*

88   89   90   91   92   93 / EP / 10   9   8   7   6   5   4   3   2   1

# Contents

# *Foreword to the Reprint Edition*

THE CRITICAL RESPONSE TO THIS BOOK, and the years since it was written, have taught me a good deal about how to read Wesley, although the way he is read here seems to me to point to a question which still needs answering. Therefore, when the SMU Press proposed a reprint edition to mark its observance of the United Methodist Bicentennial, I was grateful.

The book was originally written in the world of post-war continental theology, with its lively interest in recovering the creative impulses of the Protestant Reformation. The hermeneutical horizon of its "Interpretation" was marked by Luther, Calvin, the radical reformers, and especially Protestant Orthodoxy; and in this respect the book was not unlike other serious Wesley interpretations of the time, such as those of Cell or Lindström or Hildebrandt, which attempted to assess Wesley's place in that company.

It was the work of Albert C. Outler which in my case challenged this approach. He has shown us how deeply Wesley's mind was rooted not only in the theologies of the sixteenth to the eighteenth centuries, but, equally important, in "Christian antiquity," and especially in the patristic tradition of *theosis* as the goal of the Christian life. "Thus it was that the ancient and Eastern tradition of holiness as *disciplined* love became fused in Wesley's mind with his own Anglican tradition of holiness as *aspiring* love, and thereafter was developed in what he regarded to the end as his own most distinctive doctrinal contribution."[1] We have learned with Outler's help how limiting it can be to understand Wesley simply as a Protestant, and how insistent he himself was upon the ecumenical tradition as the foundation and interpretative context for the Methodist message of salvation.

When the American Methodists set about to transform his renewal movement into a church, Wesley characteristically sent
them as a standard of doctrine not only his own Sermons and
Notes, but his version of the Anglican Thirty-Nine Articles and
basic liturgies of the Church of England as well—that is, not
merely a summary of his evangelical message, but also the best
compendium he knew of the ecumenical tradition of apostolic
faith. Wesley's deepest intent was to be not simply a Methodist
or a Protestant or even an Anglican, but a Christian minister of
the one catholic church.

To acknowledge that is to recognize the importance of the
attempt to recover "the historical Wesley." But just here, it is
also important to draw a distinction. My book is not, strictly
speaking, an historical study; it rather intentionally focuses upon
something else: upon "the standard Wesley," that is, on the
christological teaching of the Methodist standards of doctrine, all
of which of course derive in one way or another from John
Wesley's own hand as either author or editor. But it is the teaching of these documents, not the developing mind of John Wesley
himself or his place in the history of doctrine, which is the primary focus of this study. It is with this in mind that it aims to
investigate rather more a problem in symbolics than in the history
of doctrine (p. 9). That is a necessary distinction, for neither Wesley himself nor his theology is the United Methodist standard of
doctrine. Strictly construed, that standard consists, rather, of
several documents recognized as such in the *ecclesial* decision to
adopt the Constitution and Restrictive Rules of the Methodist
Church (1808). Within those limits, the decisive materials for
this christological study became the Articles of Religion, the
Standard Sermons and, for reasons explained in the book,
especially the Notes on the New Testament.

Nevertheless, among the interpreters of that standard of doctrine, John Wesley himself deserves first place, and the historical
problem of what he himself thought, how that thought developed
throughout his life, and the intricate question of how that de-

veloping thought was related to its historical contexts and to sources which in some cases were historically and geographically remote—that quest for what Richard Heitzenrater with an appropriate sense of reserve calls "the 'real' Wesley"—can raise salutary questions about how we today should interpret "the standard Wesley."

And I think that is the right way to put it. Historical inquiry by itself cannot give us authoritative church doctrine. Ecclesial magisteria do that. But historical inquiry can question our understandings of authoritative church doctrine, and indeed without its unsettling probings into our received understandings of "the Christian tradition," those understandings themselves are all too vulnerable to the unrecognized distortions of our own historical situation and its development.[2] Wesleyan perfectionism is an instructive example. We are being pressed to recover this theme from moralistic and puritanical misinterpretations by the historians' insistence that John Wesley himself found its key in patristic notions of union with God. Does that mean that the historian in so doing gives us the adequate or even decisive context for understanding Wesleyan perfectionism? No, but it does acknowledge that under the pressure of the historians' questioning, we are discovering afresh the decisive context to which "the standard Wesley" itself points, for example in "the witness of the Spirit" understood not simply as a religious experience but as an indication of the Trinitarian presupposition for holiness of heart and life.

Therefore, it is highly appropriate to acknowledge here the importance of the rigorous new historical-critical edition of Wesley's works for just such a study of Methodist symbolics as this book aims to be. This initiative, well begun, and promising to claim the labors of a generation to come, should provide us with a body of historical-critical research in which fresh understandings of "the standard Wesley" can flourish. The historical-critical edition of Wesley's Notes on the New Testament, called for in the first edition of this book, is now well under way and should yield much new insight on the problems investigated here.

It is the encounter with liberation theology, and with the consequent effort to work out an adequate theory of practical theology, which has opened my eyes to the importance of yet another way of reading Wesley. Wesley expressed his theology on several levels. There are the articulated theology of his writings, the presupposed theology behind the writings, and the enacted theology of his praxis. Those three are not simply the same theology in three different modes. Each has its own foci and interests, and an adequate reading of Wesley requires attention to all three. Wesley's articulated theology is the most accessible and therefore the most studied. The Wesleyan message of salvation as formulated in the Sermons would be its most characteristic expression. His presupposed theology is for the most part the source-theology which underlies the Sermons: especially the ecumenical traditions of the Articles, but also to some degree the patristic, Anglican, puritan, pietist, and mystical influences which shaped his mind. It is important to recognize that this presupposed theology is not Wesley's unconscious theology, or some speculation on our part about what he might have thought, but a quite intentional level of Wesley's considered and settled theological understanding: the level of his Trinitarianism, of his christology, of his ecclesiology—themes which were absolutely fundamental in his theology, but which he did not emphasize when he preached at street corners. This book is best understood as an exploration of one of the crucial themes in Wesley's presupposed theology, and it can illustrate the interesting methodological problems and some of the solutions which can arise in any serious attempt to explore it.

But it is Wesley's enacted theology which seems to me to be a new frontier for Wesley studies. Here, too, superficial notions must be set aside. The focus is not simply Wesley's "organizing genius"; nor is it simply his version of a *praxis pietatis*; and it certainly is not the work of a practical left hand which knew not what the theological right hand was doing. It would be more accurate to say: the focus is the theology which Wesley "wrote" or enacted in his praxis quite deliberately, and as a fully intentional aspect of the theological renewal to which he devoted his life. That enacted theology asks for much more reflection from students of Wesley's theology than it has yet received, and it may be that a liberation theology schooled in praxis-reflection methodologies will have the insight and will to undertake it.

To give only two examples: Such an inquiry might help us understand the significance of the fact that Wesley devoted most of his active ministry to creating a nurturing *ecclesial* context for those conversions and sanctifications which his articulated theology spoke about, even though his articulated theology leaves us rather poorly informed about how Wesley understood that enacted ecclesiology. Again, such research could open our eyes to the significance of the fact that Wesley opted quite deliberately to address this gospel of personal salvation to the *poor* of his day. To the rich he preferred, as he sometimes said, to preach the law. Other examples could be cited, but the drift of his enacted theology as a whole is to point to the "location" of the Wesleyan message, first of all in the ecclesial community—in fact, the enacted theology is our best source for Wesley's ecclesiology —and then among the disadvantaged of the human community as such. It is not enough to let the former be represented by his occasional remarks about the means of grace and the latter by what we tend to study as his social ethics. In general, Wesley's enacted theology confirms the basic insight of his presupposed theology about the importance in his mind of a wider horizon for understanding the articulated theology: namely, a theologically illumined ecclesial and secular context which fundamentally challenges any individualistic perversion of the Wesleyan message of salvation.

Here, too, the warning must be sounded: Wesley himself is not a standard of doctrine, not even in his praxis. But a "reading" of Wesley's theological intentions at these levels belongs to any genuine recovery of "the historical Wesley" and shares in the function of that enterprise for our understanding of "the standard Wesley"—the function, that is, of providing a privileged source of questions about how the church today should understand its constitutional authoritative standards of faith and practice, and not simply in United Methodism.

Against that background, we can ask again what specific claim the present book might have upon our renewed attention today. As suggested earlier, I believe that this book points to a question which still deserves an answer. Briefly, that question is this: If the interpretation presented here (in spite of its unavoidable eighteenth-century terminology) accurately represents the christological *emphases and tensions* of the Methodist "standards," what does such an interpretation allow us to discern about the fundamental ecumenical issues involved: namely, the reception of the apostolic faith in Methodist churches, and conversely, the reception of Methodist traditions in the one, holy, catholic and apostolic church? For the intention of this study is, by translating the Wesleyan message of salvation into christological terms, to facilitate just such an ecumenical encounter at the most basic level. And note: such an encounter is not merely a meeting with other churches, but with the one apostolic faith as attested in scripture—which is acknowledged in every Methodist standard to be the *primary* rule of faith, but which is, as the *Discipline* says, "illumined by tradition," that is, by "the Christian tradition" within which Nicaea and Chalcedon are recognized to have expressed good ecumenical symbols of that same apostolic faith.[3]

At least two preliminary questions arise concerning such an encounter. The first is a somewhat formal one. Why make this detour through a presupposed and reconstructed Methodist christology? Why not face the ecumenical dialogue on much more visible ground: on the ground of the articulated Methodist tradition of the doctrine of salvation? Such a prudent procedure has much to recommend it, and of course it has been followed repeatedly, although the ecumenical use of the results is still in its infancy. It needs to be noted, however, that this procedure has tended to focus attention on ecumenical discussion within Protestantism, where the doctrine of salvation—God's grace and human freedom, justification and sanctification, faith and works— has been historically the center of interest. And this focus has tended to obscure the "evangelical catholicism" of the Wesleyan tradition which recent research has been bringing more and more to the fore, with its question about how far it is fruitful to understand Wesley simply as a Protestant. But even where this Wesleyan "catholicism" has been recognized for what it is, the conceptualization of issues in soteriological terms has tended to promote the discovery of similarities rather more than the clari- fication of ecumenical issues, as recent phases of the Roman Catholic–Methodist bilateral conversations demonstrate, or even as Outler's researches into Wesley's patristic roots show.

In other words, there is reason to think that the translation of the ecumenical dialogue into terms of the classic christological issue might serve two purposes: it could facilitate dialogue within "the Christian tradition," where the christological issue has classically provided the focus of discourse for the theological articulation of inter-church issues; and it would at the same time have the advantage of directing attention to the fundamental thing we have in common: not simply our understandings of sal- vation, but our faith in Jesus as the Christ. And this issue is rightly at the center of the ecumenical agenda, for the confession "Jesus is Lord" is the confession which ultimately and rightly creates, diversifies, and unites the community of faith. The christological translation of the Methodist tradition of salvation undertaken here can therefore be seen as a contribution to the preparation of Methodism's ecumenical conversation, under standing the term to refer here, for constitutional reasons, to United Methodism, though of course the analysis is relevant to the entire Methodist spectrum.

A second preliminary question is more material in character

and can hardly be more than suggested here, for a thorough consideration of the major findings of this book would otherwise be required. What kinds of issues might be expected to emerge when Methodism's ecumenical dialogue is focused upon christology? Two kinds of issues were mentioned above: those which have to do with the reception of the apostolic faith in Methodist churches, and those which have to do, conversely, with the reception of Methodist traditions in the one, holy, catholic and apostolic church.

Taking the second range of issues first: When Methodist interests and emphases are translated into christological terms, at least two principal emphases appear, and those emphases surely belong to what Methodist tradition can expect to contribute to such a dialogue. The first is the emphasis upon "the whole Christ," meaning, as Wesley himself often said, Christ in all his offices, not only atoning for our sins, but also guiding and empowering our recovery of the image of God. "The whole Christ" served in the articulated Wesleyan discussion of salvation to emphasize the rightful place of a doctrine of sanctification within a holistic doctrine of salvation grounded at every point, including sanctification, in our justification by faith alone. And that emphasis has continued and grown in Methodism's readiness to see—if not always in its theological success at seeing—personal salvation and concern for social justice within one field of vision. In this respect, Methodism has always acknowledged, even when it has not adequately followed, Wesley's practice of construing his mission—"to spread scriptural holiness over the land"—as an evangelical mission to the poor in particular.

A second Methodist christological contribution could be the emphasis on "the present Christ." Salvation for Wesleyanism is not mainly in the past or mainly in the future, but mainly "a present thing."[4] This means, as this study makes abundantly clear, that the Christ who saves is the Christ whose cross is the present ground of a divine forgiveness which underlies everything, whom one encounters "now" in the means of grace, and whose "mind" takes form today in the renewed "affections" of the believer's heart—those affections which constitute the presence in a forgiven sinner of the progressively recovered image of God. This christological figure, not "the historical Jesus" or even "the cosmic Christ," but the Christ present to the repentant and the faithful—this presence of Christ which is indeed the point of "the whole Christ"—*this* is the christological foundation of the Methodist tradition and the main emphasis in any Methodist contribution to the ecumenical recovery of the wholeness of apostolic faith.

It should be acknowledged that the ecclesiological working out of this christological "now"—the understanding of the Body in which the whole Christ is present now—requires fresh work among Methodists. Wesleyanism did not, for the most part, articulate it, although it did practice it, in its polemic against "the solitary Christian," and in its emphasis on regular worship, regular use of the means of grace, and regular attendance upon class and society meetings where the individual's salvation was worked out, as the General Rules require, together with the body of believers. Wesley's "present Christ" implies an emphasis on the church which Wesleyan theology has yet clearly to articulate.

But to mention this ecclesiological deficit is already to have turned toward that other range of ecumenical christological issues: those which have to do with the fuller reception of the apostolic faith in the Methodist fellowship, and especially with some of the lessons which Methodism might learn from such an encounter; and as this study suggests by way of anticipation, these lessons and questions generally also have to do with the wholeness and the unity of the Christ event itself.

Two such questions can be pointed out by way of example. Both are adumbrated in this study.

One has to do with the problem of Wesley's "two-sidedness" (Lindström), which appears in many guises but is discussed in this study primarily in terms of the question: how far is the wholeness of Wesley's view of salvation—a justification and sanctification by grace through faith—threatened by a polarity, not to say a parity and even tension, between Christ and the law. Is that not at bottom a question about "the whole Christ"? about a view of salvation which can see both the moral imperative and the indicative of grace as grounded in the same incarnate Logos of God? Does it not have to do with the perception of the onto-logical grounds upon which what Wesley calls the prophetic and kingly offices cohere with the priestly office? that is, with the inseparability of what classical christology speaks of as Christ's "person," on the one hand, and on the other as the various aspects of Christ's "work"? The suggestion here is that probing this ques-tion in its christological depth in dialogue with "the Christian tradition" can help Wesleyanism correct a certain tendency to-ward moralism and thus actually strengthen its emphasis upon holiness in heart and life.

A second lesson which might be learned from a stronger grasp of the wholeness of Christ's "person" has to do with a tendency toward individualism in Wesleyan views of salvation, a tendency which can persist in an overemphasis upon the action of virtuous individuals as the key to the solution of social prob-lems. For in the christological tradition the "person" of the "personal union" of Christ—that "person" of Christ whose in-dwelling is the new life of the believer (Gal 2:20, 2 Cor 5:17)— is not simply a union of God with an individual man named "Jesus," but the incarnation of God's Word in a humanity of Jesus which also includes all "its own" (Augustine); that is, in an incarnate humanity of Jesus which has already established the relation it chooses to have with us. In Christ, God is truly Emmanuel, God *with us*. Christ's "person," not simply Christ's "work," is grace, and therefore no consideration of Christ's "per-son" can ever rightly neglect "Christ's own." The personal chris-tological center in which salvation is grounded thus already in-cludes the reality of every creature as God has chosen to be related with it, which is why our vocation to "realize" this reality is possible and urgent (Bonhoeffer).

The character of that "personal union" of Christ is thus important for theology. It provides the ontological ground for a vision not only of individual wholeness, but also of ecclesial wholeness and indeed of the wholeness of human community as such, and from such a vision Wesleyan theology could learn to speak of sanctification more comprehensively, in terms which bear witness to God's promise for church and humankind as well as the individual.

Today, we are experiencing a revolution in Christian anthropology, arising from our growing realization that what we have called "man" in our theologizing is too little. Increasingly, for Christian thinking, the basic human phenomenon is seen to be no mere individual, and certainly no mere male or female, but irreducibly co-personal and interpersonal and by nature the human person as partner in the community and complementarity of woman and man. Ontological depth is among the things that Wesleyan christology and anthropology can learn from participation in the ecumenical christological discussion: a deeper sensitivity to and perception of the reality to which the name "Jesus Christ" properly refers. That reality, classically perceived in the Chalcedonian Definition, is "personally" one in senses which transcend our contemporary understandings of personhood as individual self-consciousness. This insight is by no means foreign to Wesleyan thought, as this study shows. Indeed, Methodism historically, especially in this country, has had a special interest in the theme of "the personal." Nevertheless, it is possible that contemporary Methodist thought could strengthen its grasp of this crucial theological mystery by attending to its christological foundations, and learning through the dialogue with "the Christian tradition" to appreciate more fully what kind of personal center it is that unifies its understanding of the apostolic faith.

*Dallas, Texas*                          JOHN DESCHNER
*Spring 1985*

1. Albert C. Outler, *John Wesley* (New York: Oxford University Press, 1964), p. 10.
2. Presupposed here is the remarkably rich threefold understanding of

tradition in the United Methodist *Book of Discipline*, Part II, Sec. 3: as traditionary process, as multiple traditions, and as "the Christian tradition" —crucial distinctions which have been far too little noticed in the discussion of United Methodist standards of doctrine thus far.

3. See "Preface," Sermons; "Preface," Notes; Article of Religion V; Confession of Faith IV; and United Methodist *Book of Discipline*, Part II, Secs. 1 and 3.

4. Sermon: "The Scripture Way of Salvation," I, 1.

# Acknowledgments

MANY PEOPLE have contributed to the making of this book. Rev. and Mrs. John Deschner of Austin, Texas, my parents, and Miss Lydia Rieke of Kerrville, Texas, supplied constant encouragement as well as material assistance to make possible the period of study out of which this book grew. The National Council on Religion in Higher Education, the Institute of International Education, and the University of Basel generously provided fellowships and scholarships. To Frl. Bertha Oertli of Binningen and Frl. Pfr. Dorothee Hoch of Riehen goes the deeply felt appreciation of myself and my family for a service without which this study could not have been completed. Dean Merrimon Cuninggim of the Perkins School of Theology, as well as my colleagues of the same faculty, and Margaret L. Hartley and Allen Maxwell of the Southern Methodist University Press have been unfailingly patient and helpful in bringing this book to press. The contribution of my wife Margareta to both the occasion and the theology of this book has far outgrown my power to acknowledge; it is a joy to dedicate the book to her.

In particular, I wish to thank the theological faculty of the University of Basel, under whose instruction I learned much during the study years of 1953-56. They have accepted this book as a dissertation for the theological doctorate. It is with special pleasure that I record my gratitude to Professor Karl Barth, who guided me in this study. His open door, his wise counsel, his joy in theological work, and his constant encouragement to open my eyes and ears to Wesley played a decisive role in the preparation of this book. To all these, and many more unnamed, I am grateful.

*Dallas, Texas*                                              JOHN DESCHNER
*March 21, 1960*

# Introduction

IT IS often said that John Wesley's strength is his emphasis on practical piety. But in this Wesley shares a profound conviction of the leading Christian spirits of his age. The formative Anglican theologians of the preceding decades were deeply concerned to put the rightful emphasis on works in relation to grace. On the Continent the Protestant orthodox theologians had been moving steadily, even fatefully, along the path from the solifidianism of the Reformation to the moralism of the Enlightenment. Even German Pietism, from which Wesley received decisive impulses, was carefully cultivating the *praxis pietatis* which produced the orphanages and schools of Francke and the common life and missionary journeys of the Herrnhuters.

It may well be that the outstanding characteristic distinguishing Wesley from his contemporaries—with the possible exception of the Moravians—is the faithfulness with which he looks at practical piety from the standpoint of the cross of Christ. The direction of Wesley's development is not from grace to works, but just the reverse, from works to a transforming, sanctifying grace, and in this he contradicts his age. The young priest who steps forward in the early pages of the *Journal* is a legalist, a ritualist, and a perfectionist. The aged evangelical leader, however, lies on his deathbed and sings,

> I the chief of sinners am,
> But Jesus died for me.

The key to this development, the reason why Wesley's preaching of "scriptural holiness" converted people to the Lord, the liberating insight which made it henceforth impossible for Wesley to think of faith and works as contradictory, was Wesley's vision of Jesus Christ. Wesley's uniqueness in the England of his day lies in his fidelity to the Christological presupposition of his message.

It is the object of this volume to explore Wesley's Christological presupposition. A number of able theological studies have concentrated on the explicit themes of the Wesleyan preaching, justification and sanctification, and have attempted to exhibit the evangelical integrity of the Wesleyan view of faith and works. But even the best of these attempts have had considerable difficulty getting beyond what Harald Lindström calls Wesley's "twofold view of salvation." It is questionable whether further analysis of the problem in the same terms will yield substantially different results. But if it is true that the center of Wesley's message is his vision of Jesus Christ, then a new vantage point for viewing the problems of the Wesleyan salvation might be obtained, provided that it should prove possible to reconstruct Wesley's Christology in any substantial way. The tensions of Wesley's theology would not be removed, but they would be translated into different terms, and could be analyzed in a different context; a context, moreover, which would readily permit their comparison and correction within the ecumenical theological tradition. This procedure could also have the result of displaying the unity and interrelatedness of Wesley's view of salvation. In contemporary criticism one sometimes finds an objection to this or that feature of Wesley's thought — say, to his view of God's wrath. But the Wesleyan message hangs together; one or two elements cannot be dropped out without altering other emphases. In fact, the views of God's wrath and of the penal substitution which answers it are, as this study shows, decisive presuppositions for Wesley's peculiar emphasis on sanctification. There is a criticism to be made of Wesley's view of God's wrath. But it can best be made on Christological ground, where the consequences of altering Wesley's systematic views may be clearly seen. In choosing a Christological point of entry for this discussion, then, the intention is to be faithful to Wesley's own center, to concentrate on the point where the unity of his theology is most clear, and thereby to serve the exegesis of the Wesleyan writings and the reformulation of the Wesleyan message in the present day.

Three principal problems confront the student of Wesley's Christology. The first is: How much form shall one give to it? Wesley left no Christological treatise, and very few substantial passages on this theme. Even fewer of the passages are systematic statements, the principal exceptions being portions of the Articles of Religion, several paragraphs from his "Letter to a Roman Catholic" (Dublin, July 18, 1749), and sections of the sermons on "The Lord Our Righteousness," "The End of Christ's Coming," and "Spiritual Worship." The remaining Christological material in the *Explanatory Notes on the New Testament,* sermons, journals, letters, and tracts, while abundant, is almost entirely fragmentary. Can this material be fitted together?

Two alternative procedures suggest themselves for formulating a representative Christological statement. One could, presumably, approach this material without hypothesis, sifting it carefully, allowing it to fall into its own clusters and patterns, and, above all, doing justice at every point to the fact that the Christology is largely imbedded in or even concealed under soteriological material. This procedure would also have to allow any systematic statements to play their role in giving form to the inquiry. Such a method, if it could really be carried out without external presuppositions, would provide a highly desirable check upon the findings of this work, and, more than that, would accord Wesley the honor of searching out and emphasizing his perhaps modest Christological uniqueness.

But Wesley's Christology is not, for the most part, unique. It is part of an ecumenical stream of Christological tradition. When his systematic statements are examined, they are seen to follow classical models: the Anglican Thirty-nine Articles, the ecumenical creeds, or the doctrinal formulas of Protestant orthodoxy. Nineteenth-century Methodist systematicians continued this Protestant orthodox tradition when they sought to present a

Methodist picture of Christ. William B. Pope structures his Christology according to the divine purpose, the redemptive Trinity, the person of Christ, the mediatorial work, including the two estates and three offices, and a summary statement of the atonement. Richard Watson, working within a Chalcedonian framework, concentrates on the divinity of Christ and an atonement of penal substitution—emphases which are Wesley's own — in the language of Protestant orthodoxy. David Lerch, the contemporary Wesley scholar whose brief, incidental study of Wesley's Christology is the most careful investigation of this problem to date, also organizes his presentation according to the general scheme of Protestant orthodoxy: the person, the two states, and the three offices of Christ.

The presence of this Protestant orthodox background suggests an alternative procedure for studying Wesley's Christology, and this procedure is used in this volume. In it the Christological fragments are approached with an explicit question—with a system of co-ordinates, so to speak—and are tested for conformity to or divergence from this organizing principle. The scheme chosen is one of generalized Protestant orthodoxy, more or less common to the Lutheran, Reformed, and Anglican Christological traditions. The significant result, however, is not necessarily the degree of success in presenting Wesley's Christology according to the chosen scheme, but rather the degrees and positions of Wesley's emphasis within such a presentation. Thus, it is not especially significant that it is possible to construct a doctrine of the two natures from Wesleyan fragments; it is significant, however, to learn that when his material is made to speak to this point, Wesley betrays a decided emphasis on the divine nature and a corresponding underemphasis on the human. Strictly speaking, then, it cannot be claimed that an accurate reproduction of Wesley's Christology in either form or content is offered here. It can be said, however, that the characteristic emphases and tensions of Wesleyan Christology, when presented as a branch of Protestant orthodoxy, are represented. The appraisal has concentrated on these characteristic emphases and tensions. Theoretically, of course, another organizing scheme might have been used. The justification for our choice lies in the fact that the Wesleyan material not only answers but suggests the scheme of Protestant orthodoxy. Moreover, analogies between Wesley's Christological and soteriological emphases have been discovered, and they also tend to confirm the appropriateness of the procedure used.

The second principal problem is the need for concentrated, yet representative, source material. A study of this character requires a  large, representative body of material, but not too large, for each fragment must be analyzed intensively, from as many sides as possible. At times, useful information can come from one or two words, or a grammatical turn, or even an omission. Wesley wrote far too abundantly for this kind of intensive analysis. The thought naturally arises of concentrating on the "standard Wesley," i.e., the forty-four sermons, the *Notes on the New Testament,* and the Twenty-five Articles, while permitting other material to confirm, and occasionally expand, the basic positions taken in the standard material.

But why concentrate on the standards? For one thing, they contain the doctrine for which Wesley, himself, was prepared to take the most serious kind of responsibility. In the Model Deed of 1763, Wesley prepared a legal instrument which limited the pulpit in his preaching-houses to persons who "preach no other doctrine than is contained in Mr. Wesley's Notes on the New Testament, and four volumes of sermons."[1] The sermons are, of course, Wesley's own compositions, and revolve in characteristic fashion around the key soteriological themes of the revival. The *Notes,* on the other hand, are an abbreviation and collation of other works, together with Wesley's own alterations and additions, although in what degree, and where, no one is yet really sure. The chief source was J. A. Bengel's *Gnomon Novi Testamenti* (1742), although, to a considerably lesser degree, Wesley also used, among other unnamed sources, Phillip Doddridge's *Family Expositor* (1745), John Heylyn's *Theological Lectures at*

*Westminster Abbey, with an Interpretation of the Four Gospels* (1749), and John Guyse's *Practical Exposition of the Four Gospels* (1739). Bengel (1687-1752) was the famous Lutheran Württemberg Pietist, the pioneer biblical text-critic and leading exegete of his day; Guyse (1680-1761) was a strict Calvinist; Doddridge (1702-1751), Wesley's valued friend, was a Calvinist in all but the doctrine of predestination. Heylyn (1685-1759) was a High Church Anglican of mystical inclinations, and a personal acquaintance of Wesley's Oxford period.[2] The question naturally arises how far such a book reflects Wesley's own theology. G. A. Turner surmises that "most of the 'notes' are simply those portions of his sources which he considered most valuable rather than being his own views."[3] But the systematic student of the *Notes* cannot help being impressed by the fidelity with which the key Wesleyan emphases and doctrines are reflected there. This problem will not be solved until Wesley scholarship provides an edition of the *Notes* which enters upon questions of source criticism. The Swiss scholar David Lerch, who devotes some thirty pages to a careful study of the development of the *Notes* and the role of the sources, draws a conclusion which is confirmed by the present study:

What the comparison [of the *Notes*] with the sources shows, i.e., the independence of Wesley in the selection and reformulation of his material, is decisively confirmed by the confrontation of *Notes* with sermons. We have in Wesley's *Notes* a reliable source for his theological thinking. Other conceptions and doctrines are not to be expected here. What the *Notes* do offer is information about those Biblical motifs which had an effective share in shaping his theological thoughts.[4]

But the Wesleyan standards are to be concentrated upon for a more important reason. Not only did Wesley himself consider them central expressions of his thought; the Methodist church has accepted them as representative expressions of its message. It is generally understood that the Wesleyan standards have this ecclesiastical authority in British Methodism. It is less well known that, as Professor Albert C. Outler and others have shown, they have a similar constitutional position in American Methodism.[5] It can be demonstrated historically that the standards of doctrine referred to in the First Restrictive Rule of the United Methodist Constitution, retained unchanged since 1808 when it was first adopted, are the Articles of Religion, Wesley's standard sermons, and his *Notes on the New Testament*. These are the standards assumed when it is enjoined that neither clergy nor laity shall teach contrary to the Articles of Religion, "or to other existing and established standards of doctrine" (Paragraphs 944, 962, 969). Two important qualifications insure that the mechanical use of these standards will not stifle theological creativity in the Methodist church: (1) The main force of the disciplinary rules is negative; the standards define not so much the required content of preaching as the central tradition of doctrine which must not be contradicted. (2) The standards themselves appeal for correction on the ground of scripture (Article V, Preface to the sermons). Nevertheless, the standards are documents against which the Methodist church wishes her preaching measured. They are, indeed, sixteenth- and eighteenth-century formulations of the church's message. In making them normative for preaching, the church asks us to learn what they meant to their day, and in so doing to receive instruction, discipline, and help in formulating the gospel anew, today.

These considerations suggest a useful distinction for Wesley research. While it is one problem to investigate the theological development of the historical figure, John Wesley, it is another, equally valid problem to investigate the "standard Wesley," i.e., the doctrinal tendencies and emphases represented in the three standard documents. The first is principally a problem in the history of doctrine; the second, while it has historical aspects, is primarily a problem in symbolics. If it is done well, the latter study will not divorce itself from the former, even though it will be less concerned to account for all the historical relationships. It is useful to know, for example, that the aged Wesley made himself responsible for a curious Christological critique of Newton's law of gravitation (*infra,* pp. 79-80), if only to appreciate more fully the exegetical discipline and restraint of the standard documents.

But it is the second kind of investigation which is aimed at here. If it is methodologically necessary to limit the source material, an authoritative limiting principle lies at hand in the notion of the "standard Wesley." This does not by any means preclude material from nonstandard sources. The use of such material, however, is intended to be secondary. The main positions must be established from the standards.

Although all the important Christological references of the articles and sermons have been used in this study, the *Notes on the New Testament* have been selected for more exhaustive treatment. Three reasons underlie this heavier concentration on the *Notes.* First, the sermons have been much more thoroughly studied in Wesley research, while, apart from Lerch, no extensive, systematic, scholarly use has been made of Wesley's other standard work. Second, the *Notes* are, by far, the most fruitful source for Wesley's Christology, doubtless because the character of this book is peculiarly suited to illumine Wesley's presuppositions. Here all the biblical themes must receive their due. Moreover, Wesley allows other writers to propose themes and doctrines which Wesley himself is fully informed on, and prepared to allow and use, but not necessarily ready to preach at street corners. Third, because Wesley is a thoroughgoing Biblicist, and appeals to the Bible for support and correction, his commentary on the New Testament reveals the way in which he understands the ground to which the reader must appeal in reaching an understanding of him.

A word must be said about the use of the *Notes.* They are an extremely difficult source to use, which may partly account for their neglect. Simon, warning against misuse of the *Notes* as a doctrinal test for ordination, formulates a rule which may well guide the student of the *Notes:* "It is not enough to pick out a sentence from the *Notes* and make it a weapon for attack or defense. We have to examine the sentence, compare it with other opinions expressed in the book, and, especially, to find out whether it has a history."[6] The negative part of this rule requires little additional emphasis. Wesley's *Notes* are particularly unsuited to random proof-texting. For one thing, Wesley associates what he has to say about certain doctrines with the appropriate passages. Much of his Christology is thus found in John. He treats predestination largely in Romans 9-11, justification in the early chapters of Romans, perfection in the Johannine epistles, eschatology in Revelation, the atonement in Hebrews. The silences often indicate that Wesley has spoken on the matter elsewhere: thus the treatment of the passion in Mark is perfunctory compared with Matthew. The positive part of Simon's rule, the investigation of the note's history, while significant, has a secondary importance. It is generally useful to identify Wesley's polemical interests in the *Notes:* against the Calvinists in Romans 9-11, for example, or against the Roman Catholics in Revelation. It is also helpful to identify the relationships of the opinions expressed to the general theological-historical context, discovering, for example, the Anglican, Lutheran, Reformed, and Catholic streams which mingle in Wesley's thinking. It would also be revealing to know the exact provenance of each note, whether from this source or that, how Wesley altered it if, indeed, he did not compose it himself. Even so, the commanding datum for the interpretation of the *Notes* is the fact that both Wesley and the Methodist church have accepted responsibility for them as they stand. Historical data may illuminate their interpretation, but they cannot relieve the interpreter of the obligation to consider the whole text seriously. And that points to the primary importance of the remaining part of Simon's rule: the passage must be compared, i.e., the *Notes* must be used whole, as a book whose parts are intended to complement and interpret and even mutually correct one another. That implies that in scholarly use they must be cited liberally as befits their fragmentary character. This may explain the unusually heavy citation employed in this volume, although, even so, a relatively modest amount of the available material has been used.

*In citing the* Notes, *reference is made herein simply to the scripture passages to which they apply.* In the very rare case where the scripture passage itself is intended, the context will make it clear. Sermons are cited by number, section, and paragraph. Since there is no standard numbering of all Wesley's sermons, Sugden's numbering has been followed for the first fifty-three, and that of Jackson's third London edition (1829-31) for numbers 54-141. To permit the use of other editions, a complete list of sermons, as numbered in this book, is given in Appendix I. The Articles of Religion are, of course, readily available in any Methodist *Discipline;* they are here frequently referred to as "the Twenty-five Articles," although Wesley is not responsible, of course, for Article XXIII, "Of the Rulers of the United States of America." Other works have been cited from Jackson's third London edition by volume and page number. Since doctrinal formulation is essential to the method of this work, a comprehensive summary will be found in the conclusion.

The third principal problem confronting the student of Wesley's Christology is the two-sidedness of Wesley's thinking. We have referred to Wesley's "twofold view of salvation." The twofoldness of faith and works does not disappear when translated into the twofoldness of the priestly and the prophetic-kingly work of Christ, although the character of Wesley's solution to the problem is perhaps clarified. This twofoldness is the basic problem of this book, and is treated at length where necessary. Here it should perhaps be said that the attempt to find the ground where Wesley's thinking is unified requires, at the appropriate point, and as a hypothesis for further investigation, a provisional decision about the ultimate direction of that thinking. The decision here made, that Wesley ultimately stands on the ground of justification by faith and the priestly work of Christ, is the one the writer judges to be most appropriate to the facts, and most fruitful for interpretation. Nevertheless, the study and its conclusions are best understood not as a demonstration, but as a question directed to the reader: Is Wesley's Christ, so interpreted, the Christ of the Methodist standards?

It should perhaps be stated that the reader will not find here any thoroughgoing attempt to make Wesley speak the language of contemporary theology. The internal problems of his Christology are such that he must first be understood in his own language before the attempt at translation can be fruitful. This procedure by no means implies that contemporary Methodist preaching and theology should return to the language of Wesley, although it can be asked whether we today have learned to speak at every point with Wesley's precision, especially about the Christian life. Nevertheless, the task of understanding Wesley cannot be considered finished until we have learned to speak not only Wesley's, but the Bible's message about the life of obedient faith to men who live in the presence of depth psychology, the new physics, political revolution, Biblical criticism, and the new world of theological, philosophical, and practical understanding which these forces have created since Wesley's time.

1. E. H. Sugden, *Wesley's Standard Sermons* (London, 1951), i, 13.

2. David Lerch, *Heil und Heiligung bei John Wesley* (Zürich, 1941), pp. 8-13, 167-80, gives further information about Wesley's named and unnamed sources.

3. G. A. Turner, *The More Excellent Way* (Winona Lake, 1952), p. 211.

4. Lerch, *Heil und Heiligung*, p. 24 (translated).

5. A. C. Outler, "The Methodist Standards of Doctrine" (mimeographed essay, Perkins School of Theology, Southern Methodist University, Dallas, 1958). His line of argument is largely followed here, as it is also in *The Book of Discipline* of the United Methodist Church, Part II.

6. Cited in Lerch, *Heil und Heiligung*, p. 2.

# CHAPTER ONE

# The Person of Christ

JOHN WESLEY shares the Protestant distrust of abstract Christology. This does not mean that he has no Christology; it means that he has an eye for what is useful for plain people, and a respect for the mysteries of faith. The happy man is the one who simply confesses and believes (Rev 20:2). How these mysteries operate is no concern of faith. In regard to the "manner" of the incarnation he can say: "I know nothing about it; I believe nothing about it: it is no more the object of my faith, than it is of my understanding" (S. 55, 14). But concerning the "fact," he had a different language: "That Jesus is the Christ; that He is the Son of God; that He came in the flesh, is one undivided truth: and he that denies any part of this in effect denies the whole" (I Jn 2:22). Wesley's willingness to think and let think does not extend to the "facts" of the Trinity, of the divinity of Christ, of the atonement: "I do not know how any one can be a Christian believer . . . till God the Holy Ghost witnesses that God the Father has accepted him through the merits of God the Son: and, having this witness, he honours the Son, and the blessed Spirit, 'even as he honours the Father'" (S. 55, 17).

However, in spite of his wish to set the "manner" of this doctrine aside, Wesley has an elaborated Christology. Moreover, it accompanies his soteriology in such a way that the Christology faithfully reflects the soteriology, and vice versa. It is true that Wesley's theology is not a settled system of doctrine, as Calvin's or Schleiermacher's theologies are. It is rather the effort of an energetic mind to organize for popular use the principal elements of a message. The peculiarity of this theology is that the essential message, which is rooted in Wesley's conversion, speaks through a preconversion theological structure and language. The result, it is not too much to say, is a continuing theological conversion, in which the living, justifying, and sanctifying Christ struggles to break out of and transform the somewhat intellectualistic and moralistic theological categories of Wesley's youth. But it testifies to the genuineness of Wesley's conversion that its stresses and tensions do reach into the deepest of his theological presuppositions, into his understanding of Christ. These tensions are most evident in Wesley's teaching about the work of Christ; but it is necessary to begin with his view of Christ's person, for there lie the deepest presuppositions of the "fact" which is the cornerstone of his gospel.

## 1. THE TWO NATURES

### a. Christ in Two Natures

"Real God, as real man," "perfect, as God and man," "the Son of God, and the Son of Man ... the one [title] taken from His divine, and the other from His human, nature" (Phil 2:6, Heb 2:10, Lk 22:70): an abundance of such formulas makes it clear that the Wesleyan Christology and its problems will unfold themselves within the Chalcedonian framework. Whatever may subsequently come to light concerning an emphasis on the divine nature, with its attendant problems for the personal union, it is well to begin by emphasizing that Wesley considers his Christology to be that of the Anglican Thirty-nine Articles, and therefore of the ecumenical creeds. The crucial passage from the Anglican second article is taken over verbatim into the second of his own Twenty-five Articles: "two whole and perfect natures, that is to say, the Godhead and Manhood, were joined together in one person, never to be divided; whereof is one Christ, very God and very Man."

### b. The Divine Nature

There is no hesitation, there is rather a tendency in the *Notes*, to call Jesus simply "God" (Col 1:17, Rev 1:4, Jn 12:41).

The Wesleyan Jesus not only allows, He claims the divine name, and especially the "I am," of Exodus 3:14 (Jn 8:24, 27, 28, 58). Correspondingly, one of Wesley's frequent names for Jesus is 'O 'ΩN, The One Who Is, of Romans 9:5, which Wesley reads as a Christological statement (S. 16, intro., 9; S. 49, i, 1).[1] But Wesley is too thoroughgoing a Trinitarian not to qualify this tendency. To honor the Son is to honor the Father, and indeed, the Trinity, for "the whole Godhead, but more eminently, God the Father—was in Christ" (II Cor 5:19, Jn 5:23). One title, one glory, belong to all three (I Cor 2:8).

Christ is divine by virtue of an eternal generation of the Father, through which the Son has absolute, independent life in Himself (Jn 7:29, 5:26, Heb 1:5).[2] He is the Word, the eternal Wisdom, whom the Father begot or spoke from eternity (Jn 1:1). This correlation of Christ's divinity and eternity is also found in a series of statements which stress Christ's everlasting-ness, His being both beginning and end (Rev 1:17, 21:6, 22:13). Wesley's point here is directly related to salvation: this eternity of Christ is not empty duration; it is filled with Christ's fulness, with His endless life, which is the life shared with the church through regeneration and sanctification (Heb 7:16, Col 2:10). The eternal generation is also important as a ground for Christ's pre-eminence as the source of man's salvation (Col 1:8). It distinguishes Him categorically from all creatures, including angels (Jn 1:1, Col 1:15, Jn 5:18, Heb 1:7), and underlines the absolute sense in which Christ is called "God" (Jn 1:1). The Son is not only equal to, He is one with the Father, and therefore to be honored as the Father (Jn 5:23, Phil 2:6). "He has all the natural, essential attributes of his Father, ... the entire Divine Nature" (*Compend of Natural Philosophy*, v, 215). His unity with the Father is, first of all, a unity of divine "essence," "nature," "substance," or "glory" (Lk 10:22, I Jn 5:8, Jn 14:10, 17:10, Phil 2:6, Col 2:9; S. 62, ii, 1; S. 77, i, 1; S. 117, 8). But it is also a unity of "perfections" or "attributes," those particularly mentioned being omniscience, omnipresence, and omnipotence (Jn 17:10; S. 77,

i, 1; Mk 13:32, Jn 3:13, Mt 28:18); and, finally, it is a unity of
"operations," or acting, or works (Jn 17:10, 14:10; S. 77, i, 1).[3]
There is only one other reality to which Wesley can assign similar
— sometimes very similar — predicates, and that is the moral law
(S. 29, ii, 3; S. 19, intro., 1; Ro 7:12). This juxtaposition will be
studied in Chapter IV. Wesley's main point here is again a practical one: because Christ is related to the Father "in a singular
and incommunicable manner," it is through Him alone that men
find their knowledge of and relation to God (Jn 20:17).

Although Wesley's emphasis falls on the unity of Father and
Son, there is a teaching about the distinctness of the two persons,
but always, emphatically, within their unity of essence (Jn 1:1,
8:16, 19). In this distinctness would lie the ground for the doctrine of Trinitarian appropriations which is reflected throughout
Wesley's theology. The most frequent and characteristic set of
appropriations is the familiar one of creation to the Father,
redemption to the Son, and sanctification to the Holy Spirit
(Rev 16:13). But any emphasis on this distinctness of persons
is uncharacteristic of Wesley. He stresses at every opportunity the
deity of the Son. Christ is to be worshipped (I Th 3:11, 5:27,
I Cor 1:2), and because He is worthy of worship, "therefore
Christ is God" (Rev 20:6).[4]

Two peculiarities, perhaps not unrelated, may be noted in
Wesley's doctrine of Christ's divinity. The first is the very heavy
emphasis on the divinity throughout the Wesleyan writings.
It is not uncharacteristic for Wesley to define the authority of
the one who preaches the Sermon on the Mount as "something
more than human; more than can agree with any created
being! It speaks the Creator of all! A God, a God appears! Yes,
'O 'ΩN, the Being of beings, JEHOVAH, the self-existent, the
Supreme, the God who is over all, blessed forever!" (S. 16,
intro., 9.) A second peculiarity is a tendency in some statements
to speak of Christ's divinity as a substance or abstract quality,
which can be seen, judged, measured, and, when deserved,
ascribed to Jesus. More than once Wesley speaks of "rays" of

majesty and glory irradiating Jesus' body (Mt 17:2, Mk 9:15, Jn 1:14, 14:11, Mt 17:27). One of the principal problems of this study will be to analyze possible explanations for both the emphasis on the divinity and the way of conceiving it.

## c. The Necessity for the Incarnation

Why did God become man? Wesley wrote on this theme mainly because he was pressed to answer the Calvinist doctrine of predestination. He called his answer Arminian, although it is doubtful whether Arminius was the significant source of his ideas. It is worth analyzing Wesley's answer for itself, for it has charactertistic accents all its own. In general, Wesley's answer is this: Christ came in the flesh because God decreed it from all eternity. However, God decreed it in order to remedy the fall, which He could foresee, since all time is simultaneously present to Him. The presupposition of this decree appears to be man's freedom-to choose or reject salvation. God's sovereignty is demonstrated in choosing this way of restoring His fallen creation. And yet, the logic of this consistent infralapsarian position is disturbed when Wesley, moved by his concern for sanctification, also asserts that it was God's eternal counsel to allow the fall and send the Son in order to make His good creation better.

The starting point for understanding this teaching more clearly must be Wesley's understanding of God's attributes of love and justice. God's love is "His darling, His reigning attribute, the attribute which sheds an amiable glory on all His other perfections" (I Jn 4:8). Alongside this attribute, however, is God's justice, "even that vindictive justice whose essential character and principal office is, to punish sin, and which must be preserved inviolate" (Ro 3:25-26). The relation of these two attributes will be seen to be one of the crucial questions for Wesley's theology.

When man sins, two necessities arise. The first is that God's fallen creation must be restored to its original goodness, for creation is powerless to restore itself (I Tim 2:5; S. 38, ii, 3; Ro 8:3). It is certain that the Creator cannot despise the work of

His own hands, and the "remedy" can come from Him alone (S. 57, ii, 8). Therefore it was "needful" for the Son of God to take man's nature (S. 59, i, 1). But there is a second necessity as well: logically, the fall raises a question about the harmony of God's attributes. According to Romans 3:26, the fall creates a situation in which God's justice, which must punish the sinner, and God's mercy, which wants to restore the creature, require the punishment of Christ in order to be harmonized. This tendency to consider God's justice and mercy separately will be studied more closely in relation to justification. Here it can be noted that on this presupposition, there is a necessity for the incarnation in God, Himself. Both necessities arise, however, because of man's free choice of sin.

Against this background, Wesley asserts that the Son came in the flesh because God decreed or decided it from all eternity. More precisely, and with an Arminian accent, God decided from all eternity that the Son should become man in order that every man should be offered the choice of believing in Him or not, and, as a result of this choice, eternal life or eternal damnation. In this eternal decision, both necessities for the incarnation are answered: the possibility of restored creation is provided in the offer to all men of salvation by faith, and God's justice and love are harmonized in the penal substitution of Christ on the cross for man's sin.

Some of the main characteristics of this eternal decree may be noted here. It is God's "evangelical" or "gracious" decree that believers should be saved (Col 2:14, Eph 2:14), "ordained before the foundation of the world" (S. 66, i, 1; II Tim 1:9). Nevertheless, it is not to be thought of as the cause of any particular man's salvation or damnation; if the Bible sometimes speaks of predestination, it means not "a chain of causes and effects," but "the method in which God works, the order in which the several branches of salvation constantly follow each other" (S. 58, 4). The decree offers man the choice of salvation, and it is this possibility which is grounded in God's will from eternity;

the cause, therefore, why all men are not saved is "that they will not be saved" (S. 128, 22). This offer of salvation is universal: God wilfully excludes no man (Jn 17:2). Wesley was frequently attacked for teaching a "conditional salvation," but he accepted the term and vigorously defended it, habitually appealing to Mark 16:16 as scriptural ground. If God's sovereignty is questioned when so much is made to depend on man's freedom, Wesley replies that God shows his sovereignty more in choosing this kind of decree than in dealing with the contingencies which determine the eternal states of men, where "it is clear, that not sovereignty alone, but justice, mercy, and truth hold the reins" (W. X, 235; Ro 9:21, Mk 3:13).

This highly paradoxical conception, an eternal decree which presupposes the fall of man, is possible on the ground of God's foresight, which, in turn, presupposes that all events in time are eternally present to God. God does not make His eternal decision about a man who is capable of sin, nor does He decide after man sins. Rather, He sees from all eternity what man in the fall freely and actually does, and His remedy can, therefore, be provided from before the foundation of the world.

Because of its importance here and elsewhere, Wesley's doctrine of time deserves some attention. Wesley tends to dissolve time when looking at man's history from God's point of view.

All time, or rather all eternity, (for time is only that small fragment of eternity which is allotted to the children of men,) being present to Him at once, He does not know one thing before another, or one thing after another; but sees all things in one point of view, from everlasting to everlasting. (S. 58, 5; Ro 11:2.)

Although Wesley uses the resultant concept of "foreknowledge" in the polemic against the Calvinists as the key to his own doctrine of predestination, he can elsewhere question whether it is properly called "fore-knowledge."

Strictly speaking, there is no foreknowledge, no more than afterknowledge with God: but all things are known to Him as present from eternity to eternity. [The text's speaking of foreknowledge] is therefore no other than an instance of the divine condescension to our low capacities. (I Pet 1:2; S. 58, 15.)

Wesley can even ask, with regard to God's decree, "What need of a moment's consultation in Him who sees all things at one view?" (Ro 8:28.) Does this mean that talk of a "decree" is only a metaphorical, "popular representation" of God's "infallible knowledge and unchangeable wisdom," as Wesley himself can say in his most extended discussion of the matter (Ro 8:28)? It must be allowed that Wesley could here be stretching his own point against the Calvinists. In other contexts he can speak with great decisiveness about "the unalterable decree," "His free, fixed, unalterable purpose," "the eternal, unchangeable will of God" (Eph 1:11, 1:5, Jn 6:40); in other words, of God's decision and not only of God's "unchangeable wisdom." Indeed, although all time is eternally present to God, man's time is nonetheless real to God, who uses it for His own purposes (Heb. 9:26). Ultimately, Wesley confesses that God's ways are higher than man's and that God decrees, works, and knows in a manner impossible for us to conceive (S. 58, 15). Two conclusions must be reached: man's free decisions are eternally foreknown by God, but there is, nonetheless, an eternal decreeing, i.e., a real decision in God, concerning the creature's ultimate destiny.[5]

Does this divine decree have any positive significance for Wesley's theology, or is it simply an anti-Calvinist polemical device? It is important that Wesley, although opposing the Calvinists, does not reject the concept of God's decree out of hand; he affirms it, in another form. Moreover, Wesley takes the trouble to relate the decree to several of his main emphases: not simply to justification by faith, but also to regeneration and sanctification. Nor is he content with the simple notion that God devised salvation after the fall. Although the conditional character of salvation is not given up, salvation by faith, the fundamental proposition of the Wesleyan message, is anchored in the ultimate theological ground, the eternal will of God.[6]

The content of salvation is eternal life, and there are a number of statements which ground this life also in God's eternal decision. "God decrees, from everlasting to everlasting, that all who believe ... shall be saved from all inward and outward sin, into all inward and outward holiness" (S. 58, 7). Having chosen the Son from all eternity to be the foundation of the church (I Pet 2:4), God promised Him eternal life as our Head before the world began (Tit 1:2). To the Son, whom God appointed heir before He made the worlds (Heb 1:2, 4, Ro 4:13), God has, "by an unchangeable decree," given all who believe, love, and obey to become joint-heirs of the glorious inheritance (Jn 10:27-29, Eph 1:11, 5). Indeed, it was to effect this justifying, regenerating, and sanctifying decree that the Son was "commissioned" by the Father (Jn 10:18).[7] In short, here is an attempt to ground in the eternal decree of God the heart of Wesley's theology, i.e., the eternal life inherited in regeneration, and the recovery of the lost inheritance with Christ in sanctification. Salvation remains conditional, but it is salvation with an eternally-grounded content.

The nearer Wesley's thought moves toward the theme of sanctification, however, the more God's decree threatens to break out of its polemical, infralapsarian mold. When concerned with the Calvinists and justification, Wesley stresses God's foreknowledge of man's free choice to sin. But when Wesley thinks of the fall in the context of sanctification, a supralapsarian motif can suddenly appear: God not only foresees the fall and provides a remedy; God decrees, foresees, and permits the creation, fall and incarnation in order to effect His overriding purpose, that man should be made holier and happier than Adam before the fall! Man's freedom is no longer the fulcrum of the doctrine: man's freedom here serves God's supreme purpose of increasing holiness. God foresaw the fall, but knew that "it was best upon the whole not to prevent it," because "abundantly more good than evil would accrue to the posterity of Adam by his fall" (S. 59, intro., 3). "Mankind in general have gained ... a capacity of

attaining more holiness and happiness on earth, than . . . would
have been possible . . . if Adam had not fallen" (S. 59, i, 1;
Ro 5:20).[8] This is more than a remedial decree. God's whole
dealing with man here acquires a progressive character. God
plans the world from the beginning for the purpose of increasing
happiness and holiness in man. Creation, fall, and incarnation
are all subordinated to the furtherance of this eternal counsel
(S. 59, i, 16). To the extent that this supralapsarian motif is
emphasized, a third necessity for the incarnation is suggested:
i.e., God's eternal decision to create an increasingly holy creation.

And yet, it must be noted that although creation, fall, and
incarnation can be considered parts of God's plan for the world,
this plan is not irresistible, and a man's disbelief can still prevent
its consummation in himself. Adam's sin can serve God's
ultimate plan; it is questionable whether any other man's sin
can. The conditional character of the decree remains, even, and
especially, in its positive formulation; and at this point, at least,
Wesley's claim to be an Arminian is justified. Christ is sent to be
"a savor of death" to unbelievers, and "a savor of life" to believers
(Lk 2:34-35, Jn 5:34, 17:12).

In general, Wesley does not see the problem of God's decree
in relation to election and predestination simply in terms of the
seventeenth-century debate. His key interest, even here, is sanctification, and this leads him to a formulation which has a formal
correspondence to both the infralapsarian and supralapsarian
positions in the earlier discussion.

It may be observed, finally, that Wesley places no particular
emphasis on the comfort or consolation to be derived from this
decree, a note which is prominent in Calvin, Luther, and the
Thirty-nine Articles. Comfort and consolation are not built on
so conditional a foundation: for them the Wesleyan turns to his
doctrine of assurance, i.e., the inner witness of the Holy Spirit,
which must be seen in this context as that Methodist doctrine
which functionally corresponds to Calvinism's doctrine of
predestination.

## d. The Human Nature

Rattenbury reports that the English hymnbook committee of 1932 could find only two of Charles Wesley's more than six thousand hymns to illustrate the earthly life of Christ, and one of these was an allegory on the healing of the sick.[9] This fact may serve as a signal for one of the problems of Wesleyan Christology: the lack of emphasis on the human nature of Jesus Christ.[10]

Although Wesley does not discuss when the human nature begins, it is consistent with his doctrine of the eternal decree and his view of time to say, with his own Article II, that "the Son . . . took man's nature in the womb of the blessed Virgin." It is a human nature ("impersonal" in the orthodox sense), and not an independent man's existence, which is there assumed by the Son of God. Article II speaks of Christ's "God*head*" and "man*hood.*" The Son takes the initiative to unite Himself to man's nature (Jn 1:14), which Wesley can regard as a body prepared for Christ to sacrifice (Heb 10:5), or even as a "veil" through which rays of indwelling deity dart at the transfiguration.

Nevertheless, Christ's manhood is, in principle, complete. The "flesh" of John 1:14 signifies not simply the body, but "the whole man." He is "a real man, like other men," even "a common man, without any peculiar excellence or comeliness" (Phil 2:7-8, Heb 2:17, 11). As a man He marvels, although as God nothing is strange to Him; as a man He is neither omniscient nor omnipresent, though as God He is both (Mk 6:6, 13:32). He becomes weary (Jn 4:6). He grows in bodily strength, and the powers of His mind daily improve; He increases in wisdom "as to His human nature" (Lk 2:40, 2:52). The grace of God rests upon Him, "even as man" (Lk 2:40). This earnest reader of Irenaeus can remark, "Our Lord passed through and sanctified every stage of human life. Old age only did not become him" (Lk 2:43, Eph 1:10).

Nevertheless, it is just when this assertion of a whole manhood is taken seriously that certain omissions are noticeable, and perhaps significant. There is a tendency to limit Christ's human

emotions: at Lazarus' funeral "the affections of Jesus were not
properly passions, but voluntary emotions which were wholly
in His own power"; He wept "out of sympathy with those who
were in tears all around Him, as well as from a deep sense of
the misery sin had brought upon human nature" (Jn 11:33-35).
He is not capable of having any evil thoughts (S. 35, ii, 21). In
the Thirty-nine Articles, Article II reads: ". . . took man's nature
in the womb of the blessed Virgin, of her substance." Wesley
deletes "of her substance."[11] Even more curious is Wesley's
repeated explanation for Jesus' escape from angry crowds: He
simply becomes invisible (Jn 8:59, Lk 4:30)! It must be admitted
that Wesley's reserve about Christ's human nature stands in
sharp contrast to his emphasis upon the divine.

Christ's sinlessness—and in this respect Wesley like orthodoxy
in general teaches His unlikeness to man's fallen nature—is
important for Wesley's doctrine, both as a norm for sanctification
and as a presupposition for the atonement. He is the only one
born of woman who knew no sin (S. 62, ii, 5; Ro 8:3, Heb 7:26,
II Cor 5:21). In contrast to the seventeenth-century theologians,
Wesley places no great emphasis on Christ's not inheriting Adam's
sin and guilt, possibly because he emphasizes the fact that God
was Christ's father in His human nature (Eph 1:3). Christ's
sinlessness is characteristically related to Wesley's teaching about
perfectible perfection: as Christ, though pure, increased in favor
with God, so a man, no matter how sanctified, always has room
for increase in holiness (Lk 2:52).[12] It must not be thought,
however, that Christ assumes only a perfect human nature:
He also assumes man's imperfect nature, bearing as it does
the consequences of sin and tendencies to temptation. It is only
sin, itself, which He does not assume. With this human nature
He becomes man's high priest (Heb 2:17, 14, 13). If, in addition,
He bears man's sins upon the cross, it is because the Father
lays them upon Him (Mt 26:37).

But again, although he speaks of Christ's identification with
man's "miserable nature" and "innocent infirmities" (Jn 1:14),

Wesley is eager to remind his reader of Christ's dignity. Especially in the passion story, Wesley takes pains to point out that Christ's suffering is different from the suffering of other men. He feels the sin of His crucifiers more than the wounds they give Him, and "seems to forget His own anguish out of a concern for their own salvation" (Lk 23:34). He weeps in Gethsemane because of the dishonor sin had done to so holy a God, although when Hebrews, three verses later, refers to Jesus as "the Son," Wesley comments: "This is interposed, lest any should be offended at all these instances of human weakness" (Heb 5:7-8). This tendency comes to a climax when Wesley stresses the voluntary character of Jesus' death:

He died . . . in a way peculiar to Himself. He alone, of all men that ever were, could have continued alive, even in the greatest tortures, as long as He pleased, or have retired from the body whenever he had thought fit. And how does it illustrate that love which He manifested in His death! inasmuch as He did not use His power to quit His body as soon as it was fastened to the cross, leaving only an insensible corpse to the cruelty of His murderers; but continued His abode in it, with a steady resolution, as long as it was proper. He then retired from it, with a majesty and dignity never known or to be known in any other death; dying, if one may so express it, like the Prince of Life (Mt. 27:50).

It must be remembered that in the Wesleyan atonement Christ performs a penal substitution. Moreover, in the study of Christ's priestly work it will be seen that Wesley insists we are forgiven in Christ, but not holy in Christ (S. 49, ii, 20). And here, Wesley shows a clear tendency to reinterpret references to human weakness in the passion. In the context of these points, is there really any theological necessity for Wesley to emphasize the point that Christ fully bears man's nature as well as man's punishment on the cross?

In passing, it may be noted that right alongside Wesley's reserve about Christ's humanity there appears a kind of anticipation of the nineteenth century's biographical interest in Jesus.

Especially in the gospels, Wesley comments freely on Christ's appearance, age, tempers, attitudes, His courage and intrepidity, and on His wise strategy in carrying through His ministry.[13]

Wesley has something to say about Christ's glorified humanity. There was a bodily ascension: God "exalted Him in His human nature" (Eph 1:20, Lk 24:51). And Wesley seems to connect this thought with the continuation in the present of Christ's mediatorial office. There are explicit references to Christ's ascended glorified humanity in relation to each of the three mediatorial offices: prophet, priest, and king.[14] But once again the Wesleyan reserve about the human nature manifests itself: although Christ did truly rise from the dead, believers are warned against the excesses which can arise from "knowing Christ after the flesh."[15]

Against that background, what can be said about the function of Christ's human nature in Wesley's theology? Two key Wesleyan themes are related to the human nature: Christ, the Second Adam, or the penal substitute; and Christ, the image of the Father, or the norm for sanctification. Christ, the Second Adam, "a second general Parent and Representative of the whole human race," is the key figure of the Wesleyan doctrines of atonement and justification (S. 5, i, 7; Ro 5:14, 19, I Cor 15:47). Equally important for Wesley's doctrine of sanctification is Christ as the express image of the Father's person, "a copy of His divine righteousness, so far as it can be imparted to a human spirit" (Heb 1:3, II Cor 4:4, Col 1:15; S. 49, i, 2). But there is nothing in Wesley's persistent qualification of Christ's human nature which seriously threatens either the Second Adam theme or the *imago* theme. What Wesley needs for his Second Adam concept is precisely a representation of human nature in principle. And he obviously considers the *imago* theme strengthened rather than weakened by the emphasis on an ideal human nature. Only if there were a strong doctrine of imputed righteousness, and especially of becoming holy in Christ, would there be a serious threat in Wesley's qualification, and to this kind of imputation doctrine Wesley answers a deliberate "No."

It is too much to say that Wesley's is a docetic Christology. There is a clear teaching about the human nature, and he intends it to fall within Chalcedonian limits. But the accent lies elsewhere. Wesley's translation of I John 4:2 exactly characterizes this absence of accent. The Authorized Version (here supported by the Greek text and the Revised Standard Version) reads: "Every spirit that confesseth that Jesus Christ is come in the flesh is of God." Wesley translates: "Every spirit which confesseth Jesus Christ, who is come in the flesh, is of God." The human nature appears in a relative clause.

## 2. THE PERSONAL UNION

As might be expected, the unequal distribution of emphasis between the two natures has consequences for Wesley's doctrine of the union of the two natures in one person. In all which will be said here, however, normative place must be given to Wesley's claim to follow the ecumenical tradition. His decisive formulation is contained in his own Article II, transcribed verbatim from its Anglican predecessor: "two whole and perfect natures ... were joined together in one person, never to be divided."

### a. The Assumption of Human Nature by the Son

There is no hint in Wesley that the personal union is a bringing together of two natures to create a new person. The person is presupposed: He is the Second Person of the Trinity. He, with His divine nature, condescended to unite Himself, not with a man, but with a human nature (Jn 8:16, 1:14, Heb 9:5). "Christ, the Second Person, had a being, before he was born of a virgin" (*Compend of Natural Philosophy*, v, 215). On this basic point, Wesley follows classical doctrine.

Behind this undertaking, as a whole, stands the entire Trinity. "The work of redemption is the work of the whole Trinity.

Neither is the Second Person alone concerned in the condescension that was needful to complete it" (Heb 9:14). As will be seen, this Trinitarian background becomes explicit in Wesley's teaching about the role of the Holy Spirit in the virgin birth.

During the incarnation, the Son also remains present in heaven. Wesley lacks the modern critical understanding about John 3:13, and, commenting on the generally deleted phrase, "who is in heaven," says: "Therefore He is omnipresent; else He could not be in heaven and on earth at once." But this does not signify for him a pre-existent humanity for Christ. Such a doctrine—he has encountered it in Watts, and regards it as "exceeding dangerous, yea, mischievous"—compromises Christ's co-equality and co-eternality with the Father (S. 62, ii, 2).

## b. The Virgin Birth

There is no Christmas sermon among Wesley's published works, and although there are many references to the virgin birth, the significance of this event for Wesley is not entirely clear, beyond its being the moment when the assumption of the human nature occurs and Christ's mediatorial ministry, in the widest sense, begins. Two other meanings of the event are mentioned, but not exploited: He is thus made under the law, although Wesley can also indicate the circumcision as the moment when this happens (Gal 4:4, Lk 2:21); and He inherits, through His mother, "the right of the kingdom of David" (Jn 19:25).

The event takes place in the fulness of time, "just in the middle age of the world" (Jn 1:11; S. 62, ii, 4; Gal 4:4). In the doctrine of the conception by the Holy Spirit, the point is that Christ's human nature also comes from God (Jn 8:13, Lk 1:35, 32). Mary's humility in this act is an example for our faith (Lk 1:38). Joseph, "His supposed father," is there so that, in "the wisdom of God, ... to prevent reproach, He might have a reputed father according to the flesh" (Lk 1:27).

Concerning Mary, Wesley has a curious double attitude.

On the one hand, the Catholic tradition of her perpetual virginity is upheld with vigor (W. X, 81; Mt 1:25).[16] On the other hand, Wesley sharply repudiates any adoration of the virgin, and indeed seems concerned to place her in the ranks of ordinary believers for whom backsliding is an ever-threatening possibility (Lk 1:28, 11:28, 1:47). The clear implication is therefore that Mary is also a redeemed sinner, and the virgin birth cannot be the means of Christ's preservation from original sin. In the light of this attitude toward Mary, why does Wesley insist on the virgin birth, and emphasize Mary's perpetual virginity? It could simply be Wesley's way of emphasizing the divine origin of both natures. Again, his caution about the humanity of the Lord, in this case its association with human procreation, might be considered a contributing motive.

In this connection, the critical question about the personal union will have to be: is Mary the mother of Jesus Christ in both natures? At this point, where Nestorianism foundered, Wesley lacks precise indications. His Article II does not explicitly address the point, and most of his other statements put the emphasis on Christ's divine sonship in both natures. Luke 1:47 speaks of "the Son of the Highest" being born of Mary, but the same note calls her "His mother after the flesh."[17]

This lack of precision with respect to Mary as mother of Christ in both natures, taken together with the reserve about the human nature, may be permitted to suggest a question: granted that Wesley's is a Chalcedonian Christology, does he, within these limits, also make a reservation or qualification with respect to the personal union? There is no need to make a Nestorian of Wesley for this question to have interest and point for this study.

### c. The Reality of the Personal Union

Before going further, it is worth asking the question about the completeness of the personal union more thoroughly, for the unity of Wesley's theology, and of the doctrine of salvation in particular, largely depends on the answer.

There can be no question about the existence of the personal union. The entire foregoing discussion has presupposed it. Twice, at least, the term "God-man," the θεάνθρωπος of classical Christology, occurs in the *Notes* (Ac 10:36, Heb 2:9). The personal union, as such, is at least once explicitly confessed (Eph 1:3), and repeatedly and transparently presupposed (Col 1:19, 2:9, 10, Jn 2:19, Heb 8:2, 4:14, I Cor 11:3). The question concerns not the existence but the character of the personal union.

Nevertheless, there is a group of statements where the two natures seem to be separable from one another in the incarnate Lord, a given act in some cases being attributed to only one of the natures. When He marvels, it is as man, for as God nothing is strange to Him (Mk 6:6). When Jesus says that He does not know the time of the day of judgment, Wesley attributes this saying to His human nature: "as God He knows all the circumstances of it" (Mk 13:32; S. 35, i, 6). And here Wesley cannot mean simply that the divine Son who remains in heaven knows, for there are other occasions when the incarnate Lord is omniscient (Mk 14:13, 27, Jn 4:1). Here also must be mentioned those puzzling moments when Jesus' human nature seems to evaporate, as when he becomes invisible before the resurrection (Jn 8:59, Lk 4:30).

The conclusion must be drawn that there are occasions in Wesley when the personal union is strained, if, indeed, there is not occasionally a separation of natures. But why? Where in Wesley does this strain on the personal union have its roots? Pope, on this same ground, has taken pains to make a correction: "All the [mediatorial] functions of the Christ must be attributed to neither of His natures distinctively, but to His one person."[18] The answer must lie in Wesley's concern to emphasize the divinity of Christ, and in his reserve about associating human weakness too closely with the divine Lord. Somewhere in the background of Wesley's thought there must lie an attitude toward human nature,

as such, which forbids him from taking with final seriousness
the idea that the incarnation means an affirmation of human
nature, not simply subjection to it. Or, remembering the "rays"
of divinity, is it that he has some concept of "divinity" or "holiness" which cannot be brought too close to his concept of human
nature—an idea which, at least in part, he brings to rather than
learns from the New Testament, and which clouds his vision of
how Jesus Christ, the God-man, redefines "divinity" in the lowness
of the man from Nazareth? Or has Wesley's concern for practical holiness required an idealization of Christ's human nature
which is more a sanction for works, law, and a pattern for sanctification than the ground for an offer of mercy, forgiveness, and
firm justification for sinners? That offer of forgiveness is, of
course, met with on every hand in Wesley, and this can be a
warning that these questions deal with tendencies rather than
with doctrines. Nonetheless, as will be seen, even in justification
there is a curious lack of finality which, related to an underemphasis on Christ's active obedience, may be traced right back
to the underemphasis on the human nature and the looseness of
its participation in the mediatorial act of the one person, Jesus
Christ. Again, when the Christ of Wesley's last judgment can
judge men in the light of His own perfect *imago dei*, and admin-
ister a judgment of wrath to some "without any mixture of mercy,
without hope" (Rev 14:10), does not this tendency to separate
wrath and mercy in the final justification have its ground in the
underemphasis of Christ's identification with human weakness,
and the corresponding looseness in the personal union? Wesley
ultimately takes his stand with a penal substitution on the cross,
and that means, here, that he insists on the personal union. But
it may be asked whether the strained personal union does not
reflect a tension within Wesley himself between an evangelical
and a moralistic way of preaching sanctification.

### 3. THE COMMUNICATION OF PROPERTIES

On the basis of the union of two distinct natures, classical

Christology developed a systematic doctrine of the manner in which the properties, graces, and work of each nature are mutually shared with the total person, or, as the case may be, with the other nature.[19] Is it legitimate to impose on Wesley a discussion of this doctrinal technicality? There is in the *Notes* only one explicit reference to the doctrine (Jn 3:13), and it concerns a passage which textual criticism has since shown probably does not belong to the original text. However, Methodist theology and Wesley scholarship have by no means been silent about the doctrine.[20] It is also true that whatever Wesley's explicit attention to the doctrine, he, like any man who speaks about Jesus Christ, makes on every page the kind of assertions which this doctrine tries to clarify. Because of the claims which have been made about Wesley's reference to and use of the doctrine, this Christological problem must be investigated here, although, in view of the paucity of explicit data, considerable care must be used in drawing conclusions.

The investigation can begin with a few of the abundant examples where Wesley presupposes a doctrine of shared attributes or properties *(communicatio idiomatum)*. In some instances, attributes of the divine nature are communicated to the divine-human person. In the incident where Jesus curses the fig tree, Wesley defends the action on the grounds that Jesus is "the Creator and Proprietor of all things" (Mk 11:22). Here the divine name, "Creator and Proprietor of all things," can be given to Jesus Christ because it is presupposed that the divine properties of the Son of God have been shared with the person of the God-man, Jesus Christ (cf. Mt 10:5, Jn 8:28). Examples of the communication of human properties to the divine-human person are only a little less frequent in Wesley. More than once he speaks of "the blood of the Son of God," thus presupposing that the human properties of the man Jesus have been shared with the person of the God-man, Jesus Christ (II Cor 5:19, Ac 20:28).[21] A third example may indicate more clearly the soteriological significance of this doctrine. In John 6:57 Wesley comments that Jesus Christ lives by the Father, being one with Him, while the Christian lives by Christ, being one with Him. Here Jesus Christ's union with the Father, which originally applies to the divine nature, is ascribed to the divine-human person who speaks the words. Therefore, through his believing union with the divine-human person, the Christian's union with God is effected. In all these examples Wesley uses the doctrine of communicated properties in an orthodox way.

But there are other instances where a doctrine of communications appears to be lacking. If the pre-resurrected Jesus sometimes becomes invisible, then there is a communication of a divine attribute directly to the other nature, rather than to the total person. It is conceivable that the reality, "Jesus the Christ," would be invisible, except as one, by grace, sees it with eyes of faith. But is it right to say that the visible reality of the man, Jesus, can be switched off and on, so to speak, by virtue of the personal union? Again, there is the problematic statement about the Son of God being without father, as to His human nature, without mother as to His divine (Heb 7:3). A thoroughgoing doctrine of communicated properties would have guarded Wesley against mis-exegesis here. The concrete of thè divine nature, "the Son of God," is here clearly used to refer to the divine-human person, and He cannot be said to be without a mother. But Wesley's zeal for typology leads him in this instance to overlook the communication of human properties to the divine-human Son of God.

Against this background the single instance where Wesley refers to the doctrine may be examined. In John 3:13, Christ speaks with Nicodemus about the spiritual mystery of the new birth which is known only to Him who has ascended into heaven. Wesley comments:

*For no one hath gone up to heaven, but he that came down from heaven, who is in heaven* — Therefore He is omnipresent; else He could not be in heaven and on earth at once. This is a plain instance of what is usually termed the communication of properties between the divine and human nature: whereby what is proper to the divine nature is spoken concerning the human; and what is proper to the human is, as here, spoken of the divine.

It is assumed that the pronoun, "He," refers to the divine-human person, although Wesley has notes where Jesus Christ apparently does something in only one of His natures (Mk 6:6). It is also assumed that the "instance" referred to means an occasion where scripture speaks of something which is always true, although there is evidence that Wesley could sometimes mean an instance where an actual communication of properties took place (Mk 6:6 and 13:32 compared with Mk 14:13, 27, Jn 4:1). The most significant point in Wesley's definition is then the sharing between natures, rather than between nature and person, a point which is characteristic of the Lutheran position. The similarity, however, is more in form than in substance. Both Wesley and the Lutherans are more interested in the natures than, as the Reformed, in the person. But in Wesley's case the accent falls on the divine nature, whereas for the Lutherans it lies, though not in the modern liberal sense, on the human. A more significant difference arises when Wesley refers to the communication as something "spoken." The Lutherans insisted on an actual transference of properties between natures.[22] It was the Reformed who tended to speak of a verbal, though true, communication or predication, whereby each nature retains its own properties.[23] Where Wesley distances himself from the Reformed is in making it a predication from one nature to the other, rather than to the person.[24] In so far as this note, with its scanty evidence, can be taken as indicative, Wesley has points of affinity with both sides of the Lutheran-Reformed debate.[25]

It can certainly not be said that Wesley's indications give anything more than a hint of the direction of his thinking about a doctrine which he used without making a systematic clarification. Nevertheless, this hint is not inconsistent with Wesley's Christological emphases. The emphasis on the two natures in this doctrine goes along with his preponderant interest in the divine nature. The underemphasis on the total person in this doctrine has a certain correspondence with the fact that strains appear in Wesley's Christology at the point of the personal union. As far as it goes, Wesley's use and teaching of the doctrine of communicated properties confirms previous findings about his Christology.

Even more caution must be exercised in treating Wesley's use of the other aspects of the doctrine: the sharing of graces, and the sharing of work. There is no explicit Wesleyan reference to the doctrine of sharing of graces (*communicatio gratiarum*). A study of how Wesley deals with the underlying theological problems would lie largely in the realm of speculation. In general, Wesley seems to side with the Reformed, as contrasted with the Lutherans and their *genus majestaticum*.[26] Is it possible that for Wesley the problem of Christ's humanity, which is the focus of this doctrine, is not very central? If so, his seeming affinity with the Reformed must not be taken too seriously. Wesley's reserve about the *genus majestaticum* could root simply in his preoccupation with the divine nature. The Reformed resistance to the *genus majestaticum* was rather on the grounds that emphasizing the total person, rather than the natures, helps theology to remember that the humanity of Christ is and remains human.

Wesley nowhere mentions the sharing of work (the *communicatio operationum,* or *apotelesmaticum*), and, apart from an occasional note, shows no special concern to emphasize that the peculiar contribution of each nature is always present in the work of Christ (Jn 14:19, I Pet 3:18).

Is it right to say, with Lerch, that the doctrine of shared properties, and in particular the *communicatio idiomatum,* is the key to Wesley's Christological position? Certainly not, if the criterion is Wesley's explicit attention to it, although some doctrine of communications must be crucial for every Christology which takes the two natures seriously. The conclusion of this study,

however, must be made in the light of Wesley's wider teaching
about the two natures and the personal union. In that context,
it can be said: When the doctrine of communications is made
the key, then Wesley's Christology points away from his legalistic
youth to his evangelical maturity, for it is the bridge by which
his tendency to consider Christ as a divine sanction for the moral
law keeps contact with the Christ crucified "for me" of his
evangelical conversion. Because this *was* Wesley's direction,
Lerch is essentially right in his claim about the *communicatio
idiomatum:* it is the Christological key for an evangelical reading
of Wesley.

## 4. COMMENT

In Wesley's Christology, and especially in the doctrine of the
person of Christ, one is dealing with a great Wesleyan presupposition. Indeed, the Wesleyan Christology might not inappropriately
be titled, "The Presupposed Christ." This is clear even from the
materials with which the author of this book has had to work:
hundreds of short, almost incidental allusions, with virtually no
help from carefully worked out systematic statements, or even
sermons. It must be asserted, however, and with no qualification,
that Wesley does make this presupposition! Without it, his ministry and his theology would have been impossible. It is artificial
to judge the importance of a Christology by the amount of explicit
attention it receives. Many parts of Christology, the doctrine of
communicated properties, for example, are certainly not to be
preached, but are rather the attempt critically to understand and
correct what is preached. Nevertheless, once all that has been
granted, a further question can be asked: Is it well for a
Christology to remain so completely within the sphere of presupposition? Could the Wesleyan message be strengthened if the
preaching focused more explicitly on Christ? Although much
Christology is not to be preached, it is also true that the New
Testament preaches salvation by preaching Christ. The author's
conviction is that an explicit examination of Wesley's great pre-

supposition can lead to clarification and even correction of preaching in the present-day Wesleyan tradition.

A related question may also be put: How is Christology presupposed in Wesley? Salvation is obviously the center of Wesley's interest. Is Christ the source from which Wesley's understanding of salvation derives its character, or is the Christology somehow finally shaped by the soteriology? It has been suggested that Wesley's ideas of divinity and holiness lie at the root of some of the tensions and strains in his Christological doctrine. If that is even in some measure true, it becomes a matter of first importance to learn whether this idea of holiness is being learned from Jesus Christ's revelation of what holiness is in human terms, or whether any part of it is being learned from another source and applied to the understanding of Jesus Christ, so to speak, from the outside.

The aim of this book need not be concealed here: to show that Wesley's Christology really is the presupposition, not the appendix, to his theology, and that Wesley wants to learn the content of holiness from Jesus Christ. But that demonstration will require a thorough examination of the work of Christ, and more particularly of the crucial high-priestly office.

1. Many modern scholars punctuate the verse so as to make it, on the contrary, an ascription of praise to God. Cf. Sugden, *Wesley's Standard Sermons*, ii, 426, and J. Lawson, *Selections from John Wesley's Notes on the New Testament* (London, 1955), p. 42.

2. Against the background of Christ's eternal generation, Wesley shows some concern about explaining the New Testament's application of Psalm 2:7 ("this day have I begotten thee") to the resurrection. Once he interprets it to mean that the resurrection "declares" Christ's divine Sonship (Ac 13:33). Again, he appeals to his doctrine of time: "I have begotten thee from eternity, which, by its unalterable permanency of duration, is one continued day" (Heb 1:5).

3. Implied, but never specifically mentioned, is a doctrine of *perichoresis*, whereby the persons of the Trinity wholly interpenetrate one another (Mt 6:13, Jn 10:38, 5:19). The Augustinian rule, *opera trinitatis ad extra sunt indivisa*, the works of the Trinity are externally indivisible, is transparently assumed in such a note as John 14:10.

4. Wesley takes a position toward several of the classical Christo-

logical heresies. The Arian heresy, which "totally destroys the unity of the Godhead," is one of the eschatological calamities prefigured in the Book of Revelation (S. 117, 5; Rev 8:10-11, Tit 2:13). Any who speak of Christ as inferior to the Father must heed Paul's warning about knowing Christ after the flesh (S. 117, 5). The abundance of references to the Arian heresy probably indicates Wesley's awareness that it attacks his main emphasis: the divinity of Christ (cf. Jn 10:30; S. 55, 5; S. 49, ii, 14; W. X, 358-59). The rejection of Sabellianism is clear, though not so elaborate (Jn 10:30). The Socinians are censured more heavily: because they seek to exalt Christ by praising His humanity, they are less desirable, even, than the Arians (I Jn 2:28; S. 117, 4-5).

5. It is of interest that the work of Christ is likewise eternal, yet temporally anchored. He is the same from everlasting to everlasting (Heb 13:8, Rev. 1:8), and His reconciling work is present in the Old as well as the New Testament (S. 29, i, 4; S. 6, i, 7), although this work has a historical ground in the moment of the cross: "Suffering once He atoned for all the sins which had been committed from the beginning of the world" (Heb 9:26). Does this make Christ an eternal principle, and the incarnation unnecessary? No, it is one atonement, historically anchored in time, present in other dispensations. Wesley, editing Brevint's treatise on the sacrament, allows Augustine's formula to stand: Christ's flesh was offered in three manners, in "prefiguring sacrifices," in the "real deed" on the cross, and in a "commemorative sacrament" after the ascension (quoted in J. E. Rattenbury, *The Eucharistic Hymns of John and Charles Wesley* [London, 1948], p. 187). It is doubtful whether Wesley ever explicitly connected his understanding of God's time and Christ's time. One is tempted to suggest that the Christ-time reveals the content of that mysterious God-time which seems paradoxically to be timeless, and yet to contain a real decision or decree. But it must be admitted that to say this would give Christ a different role in the divine plan of salvation than that of a "remedy."

6. Although Wesley never explicitly says so, is it not implied, if faith is a possibility eternally decreed by God, that the object of faith, i.e., the atonement, is also eternally present? In this case, the conflict in God's attributes caused by the fall would also be eternally reconciled. That does not remove this thorny problem from Wesley's theology, but it is an important qualification of it.

7. Wesley, however, rejects the Calvinist idea of a pact between Father and Son, whereby the Son agrees to undertake his mediatorial

commission, and the Father agrees to give the Son the elect (W. X, 381, 324-25). W. B. Pope, *A Compendium of Christian Theology* (London, 1880), ii, 202, supports Wesley's position.

8. The notion is also found in Richard Baxter. Cf. P. E. More and F. L. Cross, *Anglicanism* (London, 1935), p. 326.

9. J. E. Rattenbury, *The Evangelical Doctrines of Charles Wesley's Hymns* (London, 1954), p. 162.

10. The problem has received considerable incidental comment. Rattenbury (*Evangelical Doctrines*, p. 156) notes that the problem of Charles Wesley's Christology is what he meant by the Lord's humanity. Lawson (*Selections*, pp. 46-47) questions the soundness of Wesley's attempt to limit Jesus' passionate emotions. Lerch (*Heil und Heiligung*, pp. 74-75) admits the danger of a weakening of Jesus' humanity, and connects it with Wesley's underemphasis of *Heilsgeschichte*, and his fight against Deism. Theophil Spörri, *Das Wesentliche methodistischer Theologie* (Zürich, 1954), p. 27, following Schempp, notes that "the concrete picture of Jesus which we see in the evangelists, plays, in general, no role in the preaching." Martin Schmidt, *John Wesleys Bekehrung* (Bremen, 1937), p. 33, claims that the earthly life of Jesus has a high significance for Wesley, but the context for this claim is a comparison with the infinitely more abstract William Law; Lerch (*Heil und Heiligung*, p. 74), moreover, explicitly disagrees with Schmidt here.

11. H. Wheeler, *History and Exposition of the Twenty-five Articles of Religion of the Methodist Episcopal Church* (New York, 1908), p. 16, conjectures that Wesley found the phrase superfluous in the light of the following statement about "two whole and perfect natures." On the other hand, it is the only deletion Wesley troubled to make in this article; Wesley frequently made theologically significant deletions (Appendix III); and this deletion corresponds to the lack of emphasis on Christ's humanity elsewhere. If the phrase is permitted to stand in Galatians 4:4, it can signify that this is a matter of emphasis, not principle, for Wesley.

12. It is surprising to find Wesley omitting from his Twenty-five Articles the Anglican article "Of Christ Alone without Sin." Wheeler thinks that though Wesley agrees with it, it obscures his doctrine of perfection. But it has just been shown how Wesley uses it to strengthen his doctrine of perfection. One still wishes to know why Wesley omits, rather than abbreviates, a doctrine so important for his understanding of both justification and sanctification.

13. The Messianic secret is explained as Christ's attempt to avoid

the appearance of vainglory, to prevent the press of people, and to avoid antagonizing the scribes and pharisees, in addition to the explanation that the time for its revelation had not come (Mk 5:43, Jn 4:26, Lk 6:39). He hesitates to flatter John the Baptist; He heals a blind man in such a way as "to make the miracle more taken notice of" (Jn 9:7). Jesus looked older than He really was (Jn 8:57). He suffers heroically (Mt 26:50). Wesley explains how sweat could appear as drops of blood in Gethsemane (Lk 22:44), and marvels, with his layman's medical knowledge, at the blood and water on the cross (Jn 19:34).

14. With the kingly office: He "went to heaven to receive His sovereign power as man, even all authority in heaven and earth" (Lk 19:12). With the prophetic office: the exalted Lord who gives John the Book of Revelation is "according to His holy, glorified humanity, . . . the great Prophet of the Church" (Rev 1:1). With the priestly office in heaven: John sees the exalted Christ "with the prints of the wounds which He once received" (Rev 5:6).

15. It seems that the Herrnhuters, with their erotic imagery for the love of Jesus, made a profoundly negative impression on Wesley. He carefully edits out of his brother's hymns any "fondling" expressions, and devotes an entire sermon to explaining his concern: "We no more know Him as a man. . . . We no more think of Him as a man, or love Him under that character. . . . He is 'God over all, blessed for ever'" (S. 117, 8 and 2-3). His comment, or lack of comment, on Luke 24:39, I John 1:1, and John 20:28 could reflect the same concern. Against this background, it is possibly significant, Wheeler (*The Twenty-five Articles,* p. 18) notwithstanding, that where the Anglican Article on "The Resurrection of Christ" says that He "took again His body, with flesh, bones and all things appertaining to the perfection of man's nature," Wesley deletes the words, "with flesh, bones." But it must be noted that these statements do not constitute a denial of Christ's exalted humanity; rather they reveal a certain reserve, corresponding to Wesley's nervousness, if one may call it that, about Christ's human nature in general.

16. Wesley insists, sometimes obviously at variance with the New Testament text, that Christ's "brothers" were in reality His cousins or kinsmen (Mt 12:46, 13:55, Jn 7:3, 19:25, Gal 1:19, but cf. Jas 1:1). Lawson (*Selections,* p. 49) criticizes Wesley here.

17. Hebrews 7:3 says that Christ is without father, as to His human nature, without mother, as to His divine. But this note must be used with great care, for Wesley is obviously governed here by a com-

plicated typology concerning Melchizedek. Moreover, Wesley elsewhere contradicts himself, in so far as he teaches that God is also father of Jesus Christ in His human nature (Jn 8:13, Lk 1:35, 32, Eph 1:3).

18. Pope, *Compendium*, ii, 203. Cf. Calvin's rule: "Let us, therefore, regard it as the key of true interpretation, that those things which refer to the office of Mediator are not spoken of the divine or human nature simply" (*Institutes*, II, xiv, 3).

19. Reformed theology of the seventeenth century spoke of a threefold sharing: (1) a *communicatio idiomatum*, the sharing of attributes or properties from each nature with the person; (2) a *communicatio gratiarum*, the sharing of the human nature in the graces of the person; and (3) a *communicatio operationum*, the sharing of each nature in the work of the mediatorial person. Lutheran dogmatics titled the whole doctrine the *communicatio idiomatum*, and spoke of a *genus idiomaticum*, a *genus majestaticum*, and a *genus apotelesmaticum*. The first and third of the Lutheran terms correspond to the respective Reformed definitions, but the second involves the "true and real" sharing of all properties of the divine nature to the assumed human nature. Great controversy raged over the second point. The Reformed charged that the direct communication of properties from the divine to the human nature meant a confusing of the infinite and the finite and a resulting deification of the human nature, which must remain eternally human. The Lutherans replied that with the Reformed insistence on communication only to the person goes a dangerous abstraction of the incarnation, dictated essentially by the philosophical principle that the finite is not capable of the infinite. The whole debate grew out of the sacramental controversy, whether Christ is spiritually or substantially present in the elements. The Lutheran doctrine of the real presence required a doctrine of the ubiquity of Christ's human nature, of which the *genus majestaticum* was the Christological presupposition. Cf. concerning the Reformed, H. Heppe, *Reformed Dogmatics* (translated: London, 1950), pp. 434-47; concerning the Lutherans and the controversy, cf. H. Schmid, *The Doctrinal Theology of the Evangelical Lutheran Church* (translated: Philadelphia, 1875), pp. 312-16, 329-34.

20. Pope makes use of the doctrine (*Compendium*, ii, 118-22, 202-3). But more striking, in view of the slender attention it receives as a doctrine in Wesley, is the attention it has received at the hands of Wesley scholars. F. Hildebrandt, *From Luther to Wesley* (London, 1951), p. 40, finds in the Wesleyan picture of Christ's flesh and blood at God's right hand an "exact correspondence to the Lutheran doctrine

of the *communicatio idiomatum*." Lawson turns to the principle of "the communication of properties" (Wesley's phrase) to explain the seeming inconsistencies in Wesley's observations about Christ's knowing or doing one thing as man, another as God (*Selections*, pp. 47, 44). More striking is Lerch's claim that the *communicatio idiomatum* is "the key" to Wesley's Christological position (*Heil und Heiligung*, p. 76).

21. Properly to understand this communication, use must be made of the classical distinction between the concrete and the abstract of each nature. The names of either nature, "Son of God" or "Son of Man," are the concretes. The "divinity" or "humanity" are the abstracts. Classical Christology allows the communication of a property of one nature to the concrete of the other, used as a designation for the entire person. Thus, the expression, "the blood of the Son of God," is in order. Improper would be the communication of a property of one nature to the abstract of the other, e.g., "the blood of the divinity." Wesley does not make this mistake. Cf. Schmid, *Doctrinal Theology*, pp. 323-24, note 13.

22. Hollaz, in defining the *genus majestaticum*, says: "The Son of God truly and really communicates the *idiomata* of His own divine nature to the assumed human nature, and in consequence of the personal union, for common possession, use, and designation" (cited in Schmid, *Doctrinal Theology*, p. 315). It should be noted that the Lutherans also spoke of properties of either nature as being "ascribed," but to the entire person of Christ, and under the heading of the *genus idiomaticum* (Schmid, *Doctrinal Theology*, p. 314). Only if Wesley's notes about Jesus becoming invisible (Jn 8:59, Lk 4:30) are true examples of Wesley's application of the doctrine, can it be said that he really agrees with the Lutherans.

23. Heppe, *Reformed Dogmatics*, p. 441.

24. Wesley draws a puzzling conclusion in this note: something proper to the human nature is spoken concerning the divine. Since he is trying to prove the omnipresence of Jesus, he could be expected to assert the reverse: something proper to the divine nature is spoken concerning the human. Has Wesley's intention been inverted, in either the writing or the transmission of this note?

25. It is interesting to note, by way of testing this finding, that Wesley, with the Reformed, teaches a spiritual presence in the sacrament. It is probably significant that Hildebrandt, who finds in Wesley a Lutheran doctrine of communicated properties, criticizes Wesley for lack of a satisfactory sacramental doctrine of the real presence (*From*

*Luther to Wesley*, p. 149). At this touchstone of the Lutheran-Reformed controversy, Wesley will not give solid satisfaction to either side.

26. The classical texts, Luke 2:40 and 52, clearly show Wesley teaching a Spirit-imparted growth in Christ's human powers and gifts, and even an increase in God's favor based on an increase in Jesus' perfect holiness. The gift of the Spirit is necessary to fit Jesus for His official ministry (Mt 3:16, Jn 3:34, Lk 4:18, I Pet 4:14). Jesus has faith (Heb 2:17), and is given grace (Jn 1:14). In contradiction to Lutheran teaching that "the impartation of the divine attributes to the human nature occurs at the very moment in which the Logos unites itself with the human nature" (Schmid, *Doctrinal Theology*, p. 314), Wesley teaches that in Gethsemane "His human nature needed the support of Omnipotence; and for this He sent up *strong crying and tears*" (Heb 5:7). There is, moreover, no tendency in Wesley to say that the humanity of Jesus, as such, is to be worshipped. Indeed, "We no more think of Him as a man, or love Him under that character" (S. 117, 2).

# CHAPTER TWO

# The States of Christ

## 1. CHRIST'S HISTORY

THE DOCTRINE of Christ's states, i.e., of His pre-existent glory, of His humiliation in the incarnation and death, and of His exaltation in the resurrection and ascension, presents Christology as a kind of history. It focuses attention on a series of stages through which the eternal Son passed on His way to find and save the creature. This perspective, much preferred by contemporary theology, is not emphasized by Wesley, for whom the decisive *Heilsgeschichte*, "history of redemption," is the internalized order of salvation. Yet even with him there is an irrepressible movement in his doctrine of Christ. Though Wesley never systematized it, the outlines of a doctrine of Christ's glory, humiliation, and exaltation are clearly there.[1]

### a. The Renunciation of Glory and Its Reward

The key word for Wesley's understanding of Christ's humiliation and exaltation is "glory." In one sense, this glory reaches from everlasting to everlasting (Heb 1:2). In another sense, it is this glory which is veiled, renounced, of which He empties Himself in His humiliation (Phil 2:7). Wesley can variously define what Christ renounces: sometimes it is His "incommunicable nature," or "the fulness and supreme height of the Godhead" (Phil 2:6). But glory, which is "the nature of God revealed in its brightness" (Heb 1:3), seems to be the summary of all.

In order that He might purge our sins, "it was necessary He should for a time divest Himself of His glory" (Heb 1:3). And in commenting on this "divesting," Wesley manages to use all three terms of controversy: veiling, renouncing, and emptying. The key passage is Philippians 2:7:

*He emptied Himself* — Of that divine fullness, which He received again at His exaltation. Though He remained *full* (John i.14), yet He appeared as if He had been *empty;* for He veiled His fullness from the sight of men and angels. Yea, He not only veiled, but in some sense, renounced, the glory which He had before the world began. *Taking*—And by that very act emptying Himself. *The form of a servant* . . .

The choice of term here reflects one's understanding of how the two natures are present in the one incarnate Christ. If "veiling," at one extreme, indicates a complete, though hidden, maintaining of the divine glory in the incarnate Christ; and "renouncing" marks the middle position, where "in some sense" Christ suffers a real humiliation of His glory; while, at the other extreme, "emptying" is understood to mean the liquidation of the co-presence of the divine nature in the incarnate Christ; then Wesley's position is to be found somewhere between "renouncing" and "veiling."[2]

There is in Wesley the traditional double meaning in Christ's humiliation: in the incarnation He humbles Himself to become like man, and on the cross He humbles Himself further to bear man's sin and punishment. At the last supper the Wesleyan Christ declares: "I take no state upon Me, but sit . . . on a level with the lowest of you" (Lk 22:27). But He humbled Himself "to a still greater depth" in becoming obedient unto the death of the cross (Phil 2:8).[3]

There is a consistent contrast in Wesley's *Notes* between Christ's active humiliation and His passive exaltation. Although the moment of His exaltation is fixed from eternity, Christ must first suffer (Jn 12:23, Mk 5:43), and that suffering, like the whole humiliation, is a "voluntary humiliation" (Phil 2:9, Eph 4:10). But in sharp contrast, God exalts Him (Phil 2:9, Eph 4:10, 2:1).

Closely associated with God's active role in Christ's exaltation is the thought of Christ's reward. God recompenses His humiliation, and Christ is now glorified and honored "as a reward for His having suffered death" (Phil 2:9, Heb 2:9, Eph 1:20-23). As will be shown later in greater detail, the content of this reward is Christ's dominion over church and world.

Finally, the glory of Christ's exaltation is no other than the glory which He had from eternity, now "evidently seen." It is a glory which "no angel was capable of; but the Son alone, who likewise enjoyed it long before" (Heb 1:3).

## b. The Stages of Christ's History

Wesley gives no definitive statement of how he understands the particular stages or moments in Christ's history. He does, at least once, remark that the states "admit of various degrees" (Rev 5:7), and he produces a number of differing listings in varying contexts. The following construction and analysis is based upon a representative selection of these listings.[4]

Traditional Protestantism had reached virtual consensus here. Lutheran orthodoxy spoke of Christ's humiliation as including His conception, nativity, circumcision, education, visible intercourse in the world, suffering, death, and burial. His exaltation included His descent into the lower world, His resurrection, ascension, and session at the right hand of the Father. Reformed orthodoxy spoke in similar terms, with the exception that it assigned the descent into hell to the humiliation rather than the exaltation.[5]

There is nothing in Wesley's listings to suggest that he would have disagreed fundamentally with either the Lutherans or the Reformed. His omission of the descent into hell makes it even more difficult to assign him to either one of the two traditions. Perhaps a special place among the moments in Christ's history should be made for Wesley's emphasis on the transfiguration. As will be shown, it involves a suspension of Christ's humiliation, and must be treated as some kind of pre-resurrection exaltation. More important is Wesley's tendency to extend

the list of stages to include Christ's effusion of the Spirit at
Pentecost, His inward manifestation in believers, thus destroying the works of the devil, and, finally, the second coming and
last judgment. These points are usually subsumed under the
session at God's right hand, but Wesley wants to make them
explicit. It may be noted that they all refer to Christ's continuing or future history, as contrasted with what has happened
once for all.[6] It is of interest to note that the word which Wesley
often uses to describe what has happened to Christ in each of
these stages is: "He was manifested" (S. 62, ii, 1-7). It is an
appropriate word for those moments in Christ's history which
Wesley emphasizes, for the emphasis is relatively more there
on who Christ is than on what He does.

In the light of this data and analysis, Wesley's understanding of the stages of Christ's humiliation and exaltation will be
presented as follows:

*Humiliation:* birth, circumcision, baptism, ministry, passion
and death. To this a discussion of Wesley's thought about the
descent into hell will be appended, without considering it to be
a stage in Christ's history.

*Exaltation:* transfiguration, resurrection, ascension, session.
The treatment of the session will be expanded to include the
effusion of the Spirit, Christ's manifestation in believers, and
His coming in judgment.

## 2. The Humiliation of Christ

1. *Birth:* Wesley teaches that Christ suffered humiliation in
bearing not only our punishment, but also our flesh. Here a
question arises: Is it the assumption of human nature, as such,
or the assumption of our sinful perversion of it, which humiliates
Christ? If the human as well as the divine nature of Christ is
fathered by God, and if Christ remains incarnate in His state of
exaltation to all eternity, then the incarnation, as such, is not
necessarily or unqualifiedly a humiliation. On this point Wesley
is not entirely clear.[7] In the note on Philippians 2:7 Christ's humil-

iation is identified with three things: His appearing in the form of a creature, His appearing in the form of fallen creatures, and His suffering their punishment. The possibility that incarnation as such signifies humiliation is also present in Hebrews 10:20, where Wesley, by analogy with his note on John 1:14, can mean that Christ's (not necessarily corrupt) flesh, as such, is the "veil" of his humiliation. This reading is strengthened by the notes on Revelation 1:7 and Philippians 2:11, where there is doubt whether the incarnation was a form of existence "worthy of the Son of God." There are further hints of humiliation associated with His birth (Mt 2:23, Lk 2:14, Gal 4:4). On the other hand, Wesley teaches that Christ's human nature (His wounds) belongs to His exalted office as intercessor before the Father, and the note on John 1:14, speaking of "condescension" rather than "humiliation," emphasizes that Christ's glory was revealed in the incarnation.[8]

Wesley does not clarify this ambiguity. But while it never comes to the explicit statement that the incarnation, as such, is humiliation, there is here much the same tendency which was observed in Wesley's doctrine of Christ's person: human nature is the negative, not the positive, pole of his Christology.

2. *Circumcision:* Wesley states three meanings of Christ's circumcision: "that He might visibly be 'made under the law,' by a sacred rite which obliged Him to keep the whole law; and also that He might be owned to be the seed of Abraham, and might put an honor on the solemn dedication of children to God" (Lk 2:21). The question whether Christ's obligation to keep the law plays a significant role in the atonement is discussed in the chapter on the priestly work.

3. *Baptism:* The principal significance of Christ's baptism is the anointing with the Holy Spirit, and thus the inauguration of Christ's official public ministry (Ac 10:38, Mt 3:16). Again, Wesley can emphasize that on this occasion the Trinity testified that the Son was the Christ (1 Jn 5:8, Jn 5:33, 37, Mt 3:17). A third emphasis, made with an eye on the Moravians, who hesi-

tated to use the means of grace, is that Christ, who had no sin
to wash away, submitted to baptism in order that He might
fully perform every part of the law of God (Mt 3:15-17).

4. *Ministry:* Christ's ministry is for Wesley "the actions and
words by which Jesus proved He was the Christ" (Intro. to Mt).
The theme of humiliation is not especially emphasized, although
there are occasions, as when Jesus washed His disciples' feet,
when "though conscious of His own greatness, [He] thus humbled
Himself" (Jn 13:3).

5. *Passion and Death:* Christ's passion was a "grappling with
the powers of darkness," a "feeling the weight of the wrath o
God" while persecuted and distracted by "a mighty host of devils'
(Lk 22:44). God Himself let loose the powers of darkness upon
Him, withdrew the "comfortable discoveries of His presence," and
"filled His soul with a terrible sense of the wrath due to the sins
which He was bearing" (Mt 27:46, Mk 15:34). Thus God took
away that enmity to Himself "which could not otherwise be
removed than by the blood of the Son of God" (II Cor 5:19).
For "we with our sinful flesh were devoted to death. But God
sending His own Son, in the likeness of that flesh, though pure
from sin, *condemned* that *sin* which was *in* our *flesh;* gave sentence, that sin should be destroyed, and the believer wholly
delivered from it" (Ro 8:3). Though He died with "majesty and
dignity," "like the Prince of Life," it was nevertheless not only
to share the disgrace, but to suffer the punishment due to the
meanest and vilest among men, "the greatest instance both of
humiliation and obedience" (Mt 27:50, Phil 2:7-8). Even here,
Wesley notes that the conversion of the thief "was designed to
put a peculiar glory on our Saviour in His lowest state" (Lk
23:40). And it was necessary for Him to go through this suffering
and death in order to enter into His glory, "which could be done
in no other way" (Lk 24:26). The enormous significance which
Wesley sees in this event is fully discussed in Chapter VI.

6. *Descent into Hell?* Wesley's resistance to this doctrine is
well known and documented. He omitted reference to it from

his Twenty-five Articles, and the American Methodist Conference of 1786 followed his lead and deleted the article from the Apostles Creed as used in Sunday services.[9]

In handling the classical texts, Wesley uniformly opposes the doctrine. I Peter 3:19-21 is referred solely to the time of Noah, Christ's Spirit there preaching to unholy men before the flood through the ministry of Noah. Ephesians 4:9 interprets the descent into the "lower parts of the earth" to refer to the womb or the grave. And the note on Acts 2:27 makes the flat statement: "It doth not appear that ever our Lord went into hell."

What could lie behind this departure from the doctrine of his church? Wheeler may be right in saying that the practical Wesley considered the doctrine too controversial—there had been a violent controversy about it in Elizabeth's reign—and the fact and interpretations of the descent too controverted to make dogmatic formulation wise. Could there also be a theological reason: that Wesley was loath to teach anything suggesting a second chance for those who resisted repentance in this life? The saints who die before Christ will indeed be reconciled by Christ's blood (Col 1:20). But Wesley regards every man's final state as determined at the moment of death (Heb 9:27). The perfecting which Wesley occasionally allows to be possible in paradise can be assumed to apply only to the saints.

If not in hell, then, where was Christ's soul between Good Friday and Easter? It is very likely that Wesley held the view that it departed into paradise.

In Luke 23:43 Christ tells the thief on the cross that he shall be with Him that same day in paradise, "the place where the souls of the righteous remain from death till the resurrection." In Acts 2:27 Wesley says, Christ's "soul, when it was separated from the body, did not go thither" (i.e., to hell), "but to paradise." In a very early sermon (S. 141, ii, from 1736), we hear how Christ's "divine life" after His death, "in a state of separation, comforted the soul, but did not raise it above the intermediate region of paradise." Finally, the "Letter to a Roman Catholic," written in

1749, eleven years after the revival started, and only five years before the *Notes,* confesses that "His soul went to the place of separate spirits," Wesley's definition of paradise (W. X, 82).

It does not appear, however, that the departure of Christ's soul into paradise plays any significant role for Wesley, apart from its being a blessed rest for Christ until the resurrection. Wesley does say that Christ will "remember" the thief in paradise, but no significance is drawn from this statement. In Colossians 1:20 Christ's blood also reconciles to God "those who are now in paradise, the saints who died before Christ came," but there is no reference to a necessity that Christ's soul had to go there in order to accomplish this.

If this is a true reading of Wesley's position, it may throw some light on his Reformed tendencies, although his doctrine is not that of the Reformed.[10] Wesley teaches not a descent into hell, but a departure into paradise. His teaching that Christ's soul is séparated while His body remains in the tomb—which is an emphasis missing from the simple statement of the Anglican Article III, "He went down into hell"—has a formal similarity to the Reformed position, and in this respect indicates that Wesley's lack of sympathy for the Lutheran *genus majestaticum* was consistent. But the Reformed intention — that in this separation Christ underwent His deepest humiliation for our sakes—is quite foreign to Wesley's position, where the separation has, properly speaking, no significance for his theology. The departure into paradise belongs to neither Christ's humiliation nor His exaltation, and as such must be considered a problematic parenthesis in Wesley's understanding of Christ's history.[11]

### 3. The Exaltation of Christ

1. *Transfiguration:* It must be claimed that the transfiguration represents for Wesley a suspension of Christ's humiliation, a momentary "specimen of His glory at the last day" (II Pet 1:16), and as such a moment in His exaltation. Wesley plainly says, "He no longer bore the form of a servant" (Mt 17:2). And

he explicitly relates this thought to the doctrine of Christ's states:

*And was transfigured* — The Greek word seems to refer to "the form of God," and "the form of a servant," mentioned by St. Paul (Phil. ii, 6-7); and may intimate that the divine rays, which the indwelling God let out on this occasion, made the glorious change from one of these forms to the other (Mk 9:2).

The significance of this event for the disciples and us is its confirmation of our faith in Christ as the great prophet and lawgiver (Mk 9:7, Mt 17:3). Only passing reference is made to the coming sacrifice (Mk 9:12). The emphasis falls rather on the relation between Moses and Christ, Sinai and the Mount of Transfiguration. The luminous cloud, which accompanied Israel in the wilderness, and departed at the death of Moses, "now appeared again, in honour of our Lord, as the Great Prophet of the Church, who was prefigured by Moses" (Mk 9:7, Mt 17:5, II Pet 1:16-18). Here it can be seen that Christ's divine glory functions, in part at least, as divine sanction for the law.

2. *Resurrection:* Wesley's normative statement, in his Article III, confesses that "Christ did truly rise again from the dead, and took again his body, with all things appertaining to the perfection of man's nature." Though he omits the Anglican article's reference to flesh and bones, the *Notes* bear out that it was, indeed, a bodily resurrection. The flesh of the resurrected Christ bears the print of the nails (Lk 24:40), and Christ eats before His disciples, "not that He had any need of food, but to give them still further evidence" (Lk 24:43).

Jesus is raised up by God the Father, although it is also claimed that in contrast to our immortality, Christ's alone is "underived, independent" (Ro 4:24, I Tim 6:16). It is a resurrection of Christ's human nature only; He remained the Living One in His divine nature (Jn 14:19). Nevertheless, the divine nature "was not manifested in its full evidence till after the resurrection" (Ro 1:3). Wesley probably means by this that only in the resurrection was Christ decisively proved to be the Son of God (Ro 1:4, Mk 8:30). It is of interest that he associates with the resurrection certain changes in Christ's title: the titles "Jesus" and "Son of Man" belong primarily to the pre-resurrection, the titles "Christ," "Son of God," "Lord" to the post-resurrection Christ (Lk 24:6-7, I Pet 1:3, Mk 16:19, Ac 2:36). However, this seems to be a matter of Christ's designation, not His reality, for there is explicit warning that "His being the Son of God did not arise merely from His resurrection" (Heb 5:8).

The significance of the resurrection for Wesley may be briefly catalogued as follows:

a. The scriptural promises were thereby fulfilled (Ac 2:24, 13:34).

b. Various things were "proved." Christ was thereby proved to be a divine teacher, since His resurrection proved the certainty of a general resurrection which He expressly taught (I Cor 15:20). God attested the sufficiency of our atonement "by raising up our great Surety from the grave" (I Cor 15:17). Further, the resurrection is the "proof of His future coming to judgment" (I Th 1:10), for God "raising Jesus demonstrated hereby, that He was to be the glorious Judge of all" (Ac 17:31). Finally, the resurrection is "the grand proof" that He was the Christ (Mt 16:20).

c. The resurrection was a victory. Satan and sin had been conquered in the cross, and now, lastly, death was conquered in the resurrection (I Cor 15:26), although Matthew 27:52-53 implies that death had already been conquered on Good Friday.

d. The kingdom of God "did not properly commence till His resurrection" (Lk 22:16), nor did Christ inherit the Davidic kingdom, promised to endure forever, before He died (Ac 2:31).

e. After His exaltation (which must here mean the resurrection), "the glory He had from eternity began to be evidently seen" (Heb 1:3). The exalted humanity helps to manifest the image of the Father (Col 1:15).

f. The resurrection has some role in justification. Christ died to expiate our sin, and rose again for our justification (Jn 10:17). Christ's resurrection is not only a pledge of our resurrection, but part of its "purchase-price" (I Pet 1:3). Subjectively, His resurrection justifies us by empowering us to receive the atonement by faith (Ro 4:25).

g. Not only Christ's essential fulness, but also the event of the resurrection belongs to the foundation of our new birth. Christ's rising, in itself, is a kind of new birth of the Son of God (Ac 13:33). And His rising has a close connection with our rising from spiritual death, for as He lives, so shall we live with Him (I Pet 1:3, I Cor 15:20). Therefore, in baptism, when we are ingrafted into Christ and made conformable to His death, we are given the promise also of the power of His resurrection working in us (Ro 6:3-5).

h. The resurrection thus underlies our sanctification as well as our justification (Col 2:13). From it "flows all the life, spiritual and eternal, of all His brethren" (Col 1:19).

i. For these reasons, Wesley regards the resurrection as "the principal motive of faith." Those who stumble at this reject all the rest (Ac 17:32). The resurrection from the dead "is both the fountain and the object of our faith; and the preaching of the apostles was the consequence of Christ's resurrection" (Ro 1:4, 8:34).

3. *Ascension:* In his *Notes,* as well as in his Article III, Wesley teaches the orthodox doctrine that Christ ascended into heaven with his human nature (Heb 7:26, Eph 1:20). It is emphasized that the ascension is a literal, local transference of His body from earth into a spatial heaven (Lk 24:51). In this Wesley's position is similar to that of the Reformed theologians.[12] Wesley is quite ready to identify this heaven further as "the glory which He had before the world began," or as "the immediate presence and right hand of the Father" (S. 62, ii, 6; S. 141, ii). The power which effects the ascension is the right hand of God, i.e., "the mighty power of God" (Ac 2:33).

The ascension signifies at least four things for Wesley, when considered in its strict sense as Christ's transference into heaven, rather than His subsequent work in heaven:

a. Christ must enter heaven in His human nature in order to perform there His priestly work of intercession (Heb 4:14, 7:26).

b. In ascending, Christ took our "real, spiritual life" away from the world and hid it with God: henceforth "our citizenship, our thoughts, our affections are already in heaven" (Col 3:3, Phil 3:20). The thought that our sanctification consists in our participation in this hidden life, however, is not developed. Wesley s polemics make it clear that he considered this understanding of sanctification too close to the Moravian quietism. Rather, a kind of imitation of Christ's ascension is suggested: as Christ, being risen, immediately went to heaven, so we are to seek holiness immediately, and not rest content with regeneration (Col 3:1).

c. The Church's constitution begins on the day when Christ ascends: this is the beginning of the Acts of the Apostles (Ac 1:2; "Preface" to *Notes*, 13; Eph 4:10).

d. The ascension marks a moment in Christ's victory. "At His ascension, 'angels, and principalities, and powers were subjected to Him'" (Rev 5:7).

4. *Session:* When Wesley speaks of Christ's sitting on God's right hand, he means Christ's participation in the mighty power of God. God, Himself, has so exalted Him, and there, in contrast to other priests, who stand in a humble posture, Christ sits down (Ac 2:33, Heb 10:11-12, 1:3, Ac 7:56). In this session, Christ receives the "recompense" for His sufferings: His human nature now receives its participation in "a quiet, everlasting possession of all possible blessedness, majesty, and glory," and, in particular, the authority to rule the cosmos and the church (Eph 1:20-22).

It has already been indicated that the session is a very important doctrine for Wesley. Its significance for him can be summarized under four headings, the first of which is the comprehensive one, while the three following comprise special emphases which Wesley wishes to make.

a. Christ rules the cosmos and the church. Christ rules the

cosmos because God "hath invested Him with uncontrollable
authority over all demons in hell, all angels in heaven, and all
the princes and potentates on earth, not only in this world, but
also in that which is to come" (Eph 1:21). He has likewise been
given to rule over the church as its head: "A head both of guidance and government, and likewise of life and influence, to the
whole and every member of it. All these stand in the nearest union
with Him, and have as continual and effectual a communication
of activity, growth, and strength from Him, as the natural body
from its head" (Eph 1:22). For this church the great high priest
makes continual intercession (Ro 8:34).

b. Christ pours out the Holy Spirit. Wesley considers the
effusion of the Holy Spirit to be integral to his doctrine of the
exalted Christ.[13] Christ ascends to the Father in order to send
the promised Holy Spirit (Jn 14:12, Lk 24:49). Having ascended,
He pours out His Spirit, and "not on the day of Pentecost only"
(Ac 2:17). The Holy Spirit is sent for Christ's sake, in His place,
as His agent (Jn 14:26), as an advocate, instructor, or encourager,
who "reveals, testifies, and defends the truth as it is in Jesus"
(Jn 14:16-17). Pentecost — which along with "the Pentecost of
Sinai in the Old Testament" was one of the "two grand manifestations of God"—"was an earnest that the whole world should in
due time praise God in their various tongues" (Ac 2:1, 4).

c. Christ rules victoriously in believers. Because Christ rules
church and world, and has poured out His Spirit onto the church
and every member of it, therefore Wesley can also emphasize as
part of Christ's exaltation, His inward manifestation in believers,
by which the works of the devil are effectually destroyed (S. 62,
ii, 7). This victory of Christ "in me" will be further explicated
in relation to sanctification and Christ's kingly work.

d. Christ will gloriously come again in judgment. In his
third article, Wesley, following his Anglican model, closely connects the session and the coming again in judgment. Because He
had emptied Himself, therefore God exalted Him and ordained
Him to try the children of men (S. 48, ii, 1). Only now does He

come to men in a manner worthy of the Son of God (Rev 1:7). Now "the Lord shall manifest His glory, in taking vengeance of His adversaries" (Ac 2:20), and the blessed "shall be openly acknowledged as God's own property, and His glorious nature shall most visibly shine forth in them" (S. 48, iii, 5).

## 4. COMMENT

Obviously, the accent here is on the exaltation of Christ. It is no accident that progressively more space is required to present the stages of the exaltation: Wesley has more to say about them. More of his explicit theology is grounded here. A sentence from Wesley's introduction to Hebrews in the *Notes* is revealing about his possible motives: "The scope of [this epistle] is, to confirm their faith in Christ; and this [Paul] does by demonstrating His glory." That does not mean that Wesley considers the humiliation to be unimportant: every stage in it is, in some sense, significant for his thought. But it is a humiliation which moves from the position of a "renouncing" toward the position of a "veiling," with the constant implication that Christ's glory remains, in principle, untouched. One cannot avoid the impression of a certain uneasiness in Wesley about the humiliation as a whole. He is relieved to say concerning the exalted Christ of the Book of Revelation, "See how great He is, who appeared 'like the Son of Man'!" (Rev 2:18.) As a matter of fact, Wesley seems to sense a problem here, and on all too rare occasions can remark: "Was it a mean attitude wherein our Lord then appeared? mean even to contempt? I grant it; I glory in it: it is for the comfort of my soul, for the honour of His humility, and for the utter confusion of all worldly pomp and grandeur" (Mt 21:5, Lk 24:26). But the characteristic emphasis is otherwise. Earlier, a decided emphasis on the divine as contrasted with the human nature in Christ was observed. Now a related tendency can be noted: when Christ is viewed in terms of His history, there is a tremendous energy in the movement from the humiliation toward the exaltation. Nowhere is the "teleological" character of Wesley's theology clearer.

Upon close analysis, Christ's history, as Wesley sees it, consists of several interwoven themes. The prevailing theme of the
birth, baptism, ministry, and of the entire exaltation (especially
the transfiguration), is in some sense *manifestation*, or unveiling
of the glory and majesty of Jesus Christ. Alongside this theme
appears—primarily in the passion and death, but also in the birth
and circumcision, and to a certain extent also in the resurrection,
ascension, and session—the contrasted theme of Christ's *substitution* for us, with the emphasis on His bearing our punishment.
But there is yet a third theme discernible—in the passion
and death, with its elements of victory, but especially in the resurrection, ascension, and session—namely, Christ's *dominion*. How
are these themes related? A partial, not entirely satisfactory
answer lies in the concept of reward. Christ's dominion is a
"recompense" for His suffering on our behalf. But there is no
clear indication, as yet, of the relation between the manifestation
theme and the other two, except that, formally speaking, they
belong to the same history. This question must be treated more
fully in the analysis of the closely related themes of Christ's
prophetic, priestly, and kingly work.

How necessary or important is this doctrine of Christ's states
for Wesley's theology? The answer must probe deeper than the
obvious one that Wesley never felt it necessary to write a systematic Christological treatise. It has just been noted that there are
several leading Christological motifs for Wesley: manifestation,
substitution, dominion. The great merit of the doctrine of Christ's
states is that it presents this entire work of Christ, together with
the teaching about His person, in the unity of His history. The
gospel story is one history, and Wesley needs this unity under
all the tensions and strains of his theology. It is significant that
not one of the stages in Christ's humiliation and exaltation could
be omitted without serious damage to Wesley's theological interests, i.e., to his particular viewpoints on justification and
sanctification.

But there may be an even more immediate correspondence

between Christ's history and ours in Wesley's thinking. Christ is born of God; we are made children of God by the Holy Spirit. Christ inherits as the Son; we also, in being born again, become joint heirs with Him. Christ suffers and is glorified; our sanctification is a path of suffering and glory. Christ is given the Holy Spirit as a fountain of joy (Heb 1:9); we likewise receive the Holy Spirit. It is doubtful whether Wesley anywhere develops this correspondence between Christ's history and our order of salvation, as a whole, but parallels of specific moments are not lacking. Wesley hints that the desert of Christ's temptation may have been the wilderness of Israel's wanderings, implying a recapitulation of Israel's history in that of Christ (Lk 4:1). Christ's passion words, "Ye shall not see me: and again, a little while, and ye shall see me," are also applied by Wesley to the inner experience of the believer; his sense of mourning will be followed by the assurance of the Holy Spirit (S. 16, ii, 5). The detailed working out of this correspondence lies beyond the limits of this volume. If it could be done, a much more profound *imitatio Christi* would be found in Wesley than the somewhat legalistic one customarily assigned to his early period.

1. Wesley's sensitivity or insensitivity to the history of redemption deserves a thorough study of its own. Lerch (*Heil und Heiligung*, p. 75) says that for Wesley *Heilsgeschichte* is in the background. It is probably more accurate to say that Wesley's understanding of *Heilsgeschichte* is considerably at variance with our own. The important historical scheme for Wesley is, without doubt, the internalized *Heilsgeschichte* of the order of salvation. But that does not exhaust the matter. There is also an objective *Heilsgeschichte*, especially in relation to the giving of the law, to the various covenants and dispensations, and to the events of the last days. Wesley's exposition of the Book of Revelation presents us with an embarrassment of riches: a *Heilsgeschichte* worked out in detail until 1836! That Wesley follows Bengel here does not necessarily mean that it is un-Wesleyan teaching. In this connection, the interested reader may wish to examine the following passages: Mt 1:16; 8:29; 10:5; 11:9, 11, 13; 12:27; 16:3, 14; 17:10; 26:18; Mk 1:15; 5:43; 8:30; 9:1, 12; Lk 1:13; 2:38; 3:23; 9:51; 19:12ff.; 20:9f.; 21:24; 22:53; Jn 1:23; 2:4; 5:4; 7:30; 11:9, 49;

12:23; 17:1; Ac 3:17, 21, 24; 15:16; Ro 5:6; 13:11; I Cor 10:11; Eph 1:10; 2:5, 7; I Tim 2:6; 4:1; II Tim 3:1; Tit 1:3; Heb 9:26; and the entire book of Revelation. Related sections of this volume are: in Chapter I, "The Necessity for the Incarnation"; the entire Chapter II; in Chapter III, "The Son's Work in Creation"; in Chapter IV, "Christ's Fulfilment of Old Testament Prophecy," "The History of the Law," and "Christ's Prophetic Relation to the Law"; in Chapter V, "Christ's Victory," and "The Kingdom." The doctrine of Christ's passive obedience (Chapter VI) should probably be considered the anchor for the whole. In the context of Wesley's doctrine of time (*supra*, pp. 20-21), this material may suggest more sensitivity to the problems of *Heilsgeschichte* than Wesley has yet been given credit for.

2. Each of these terms has been the slogan of a theological school:

a. *"Emptying"*: The nineteenth-century advocates of this term, seeking some way to maintain contact with Chalcedonian orthodoxy while preoccupied with the historical Jesus, found the concept *Kenosis*, "emptying," the key for speculation about how the divine nature was voluntarily set aside when Christ became a man, and then gradually recovered as Christ moved toward the consummation of His career. Wesley, though he makes frequent use of the word "emptying," does not mean this. There is no liquidation of Christ's fulness or glory, but rather an emphasis on the co-presence of divine attributes in the incarnate Christ.

b. *"Veiling"*: The Lutheran Tübingen theologians of the seventeenth century, against the subsequent better judgment of their church, used the term "veiling" to indicate that in His state of humiliation Christ simply concealed from human eyes His continuing exercise of the dominion which belongs to the Logos. Wesley also knows of a continuing omnipresence and omniscience in the incarnate Christ, and has some preference for the idea of a "veiling," the veil being Christ's flesh (I Jn 3:2, Heb 10:20). But Wesley's motive is not, like that of the Tübingers, to explain the sacramental ubiquity of Christ's human nature. Wesley's motive is to establish the norm of sanctification: Christ as the revealed image of the Father's holiness.

Wesley makes explicit connection between Christ's holiness, which He came to reveal to us, and His glory, in a pregnant formula: "Holiness is covered glory, and glory is uncovered holiness" (Rev 4:8). This formula presupposes an understanding of the humiliation where glory somehow remains present. There are moments in the earthly ministry where that glory becomes visible for Wesley, e.g., at the transfiguration, or in the miracles. But the motive for this veiling is revelation! Christ's invisible glory is veiled in his visible holiness. It is not renounced in principle, but is continually being translated into terms which we can bear.

c. *"Renouncing":* This was the slogan of the Lutheran Giessen theologians whose view eventually prevailed over that of the Tübingers in the seventeenth century. And although Wesley's tendency is toward "veiling," he explicitly says, in the key passage: "He not only veiled, but in some sense, renounced, the glory . . . and by that very act emptied Himself . . ." (Phil 2:7). The precise function of the term "emptying" is now clear: it indicates that the renunciation was a real one. Something was given up as well as covered. The manner of the renunciation is not discussed. It does not go so far as a total liquidation of His glory, but farther than "veiling" it does go. In "veiling" the glory remains there in principle: in "renunciation" some part of it, at least, is in principle given up.

3. Lerch suggests (*Heil und Heiligung,* p. 78) that the contrast of Creator-creature characterizes Wesley's entire understanding of the humiliation of Christ. This contrast is indeed prominent in Wesley's key note on Philippians 2:7, and Wesley does have a tendency to see the incarnation, as such (i.e., the identification with the creature), as humiliation. Nevertheless, Wesley's emphasis on Christ's humiliation in bearing our punishment makes this a doubtful characterization of Wesley's entire doctrine.

4. There are several Wesleyan lists of both states:

". . . the acts of Christ—His conception, birth, childhood, baptism, preaching, passion, resurrection, ascension" (Lk 1:3).

He was manifested as the only-begotten Son "before and at the foundation of the world," He was manifested to Adam and the patriarchs; He was made of woman; He was manifested to Israel through His preaching, miracles, and sinless life; He was crucified; He was further manifested in the resurrection, the ascension, and the pouring-out of the Holy Spirit at Pentecost; finally, there is the inward manifestation of Himself to His followers, effectually destroying the works of the devil (summarized from S. 62, ii, 1-7).

He was the Son of God; He was made man, i.e., conceived and born; He "suffered inexpressible pains both of body and soul, and at last death, even the death of the cross"; He was buried; "His soul went to the place of separate spirits"; He rose from the dead; He ascended; He remains in the midst of the throne of God; He will come to judge every man according to his works (summarized from "Letter to a Roman Catholic," W. X, 81-82).

"... the life, death, resurrection, and intercession of Christ" (W. XI, 486; cf. Ac 2:11, I Cor. 1:24).

Several notes, in addition, list only the degrees of the exaltation: "... the glory of His resurrection, ascension, exaltation, and the effusion of His Spirit; the glory of the last judgment, and of His eternal kingdom; and also the glories of His grace in the hearts and lives of Christians" (I Pet 1:11, cf. Rev 5:7, I Tim 3:16).

5. For Lutheran orthodoxy, see Schmid, *Doctrinal Theology*, pp. 378-81; for Reformed, see Heppe, *Reformed Dogmatics*, pp. 488-509.

6. Is there a correspondence here to Wesley's order of salvation, where, though justification is the starting point, the emphasis is on the continuing growth in grace and hope of perfection?

7. On this question see Heppe, *Reformed Dogmatics*, p. 488, and Schmid, *Doctrinal Theology*, pp. 377 f.

8. Pope (*Compendium*, ii, 141-42) struggles with the same problem when he uses "condescension" in his doctrine of an incarnation before Christ's conception, and applies the term "humiliation" only to "His literal assumption of the flesh in the miraculous conception that added the element of self-abasement."

9. Wheeler, *The Twenty-five Articles*, pp. 16-18.

10. The Lutherans had insisted on a literal descent of the whole Christ, so much so that Christ's return to bodily life is presupposed. For this reason, together with the fact that the purpose of the descent is "to exhibit Himself as the conqueror of death to the evil spirits and to damned men," the Lutherans also reckoned the descent into the lower world as the first step of Christ's exaltation (Schmid, *Doctrinal Theology*, p. 379). The Reformed, insisting on the local limitation of Christ's body to the tomb for three days, said that the descent "is not to be thought of as a spatial event" but "like all human souls which separate from their bodies, even Christ's soul had to descend into Hades, because His whole divine-human person was punished with real death." For the Reformed, then, the descent is the depth of Christ's humiliation, the reality of His human death, and figuratively, the "pang which Christ suffered in His soul, when He felt the punitive judgment of God, and especially the abyss of humiliation which met the Redeemer, by the Father's abandonment of His whole divine-human person for a time to the power of death" (Heppe, *Reformed Dogmatics*, p. 491).

11. It is of interest that Pope (*Compendium*, ii, 166-69) distances himself from Wesley both in teaching a descent and in handling it, like the Lutherans, as the beginning of Christ's exaltation.

12. The Lutherans had a doctrine of the ubiquity of Christ's human nature which made them hesitate to speak of the ascension as a local and physical passing-over to a circumscribed and physical locality (Schmid, *Doctrinal Theology*, p. 402). Pope *(Compendium,* ii, 180), like Wesley, teaches a local withdrawal, and, as may be expected, opposes the Lutheran formulation of the doctrine of Christ's real presence in the sacrament (iii, 333).

13. Pope *(Compendium,* ii, 181), who is of the same opinion, gives the formula: "The sequel of the Ascension is the Session at the right hand of God in heaven; with its attestation on earth, the Pentecostal descent of the Holy Spirit, the Promise of the New Covenant."

CHAPTER THREE

# *The Work of Christ*

WESLEY, upon occasion, makes a distinction between Christ's mediatorial and non-mediatorial activity, meaning by the latter His sharing in the creative and providential work of the Father (I Cor 15:24, 8:6). In the one He acts as incarnate Lord, in the other as the eternal Second Person of the Trinity. Even though a question can very well be raised about how consistently Wesley can or does maintain this distinction systematically, it may, nevertheless, serve provisionally in organizing this presentation of Christ's work.

1. CHRIST'S NON-MEDIATORIAL WORK IN CREATION AND PROVIDENCE

The major question, of course, is whether the attempt to call creation and providence non-mediatoral work implies that they are not works of grace. Wesley does, in several notes, lend support to the schematic separation of creation and grace (Jn 13:7, I Cor 8:6). Once he says that grace could not reign before the fall (Ro 5:21). However, more substantial statements explicitly ground creation in grace (Rev 4:11, Eph 3:9). "It was free grace that 'formed man of the dust of the ground, and breathed into him a living soul,' and stamped on that soul the image of God, and 'put all things under his feet'" (S. 1, intro., 1). It is probable that full clarity on this point is not possible, since Wesley never gave it his systematic attention. However, it must be said, at the outset, that the distinction between mediatorial and non-mediatorial work does not necessarily signify that Wesley makes a systematic distinction between the spheres of grace and creation. Indeed, the heavy emphasis on Christ's role in both creation and providence may be taken as an indication of the underlying doctrine of grace.

## a. The Son's Work in Creation

Wesley probably regarded creation as a work of the entire Trinity (I Jn 1:1, Jn 17:3). Frequently, he makes the traditional appropriation of creation to the Father (Rev 16:13, Mt 6:9, Ja 1:18). Nevertheless, the New Testament's teaching about the Son's role in creation finds a ready, even enthusiastic interpreter in Wesley. The Christ of Hebrews is the eternal Son, "the Creator Himself" (Heb 1:7, 10, 2). The entire visible and invisible creation is ascribed to Him (Col 1:16). Yet more striking, because not required by the text, are Wesley's reference to Jesus, at the cursing of the fig tree, as "the Creator and Proprietor of all things" (Mk 11:22), and his assertion that it was the Son of God who pronounced the creation words, "Let there be light" (S. 62, ii, 1). This Word-motif is taken up in John 1:1 where the Son is the Word "by whom the Father speaking maketh all things." Indeed, in a somewhat modern accent, it is the almighty Word of God "which bounds the duration of all things: so that it cannot be either longer or shorter" (II Pet 3:5). Wesley explicitly warns that this Christological understanding of creation is a mystery visible only to faith (Heb 11:3). But as a man of faith, Wesley goes even farther in his speculations: the Son is "the foundation of life to every living thing, as well as of being to all that is"; He is "essential life," as well as "the light of men, the fountain of wisdom, holiness, and happiness to man in his original state" (Jn 1:4). "He sustains all things in being ... He is the cement, as well as support, of the universe" (Col 1:17).[1]

Wesley does not provide any substantial explanation for this role of the Son in creation. There are references implying that the Son is the instrument of the Father's creative work: He is the Word "by whom the Father speaking maketh all things" (Jn 1:1, Heb 1:3).[2] It is probably best to leave the problem of the relation of the Son's and the Father's creative work unexplained as Wesley does in one note where, in parallel sentences, the creative work is ascribed first to the Father and then to the Son, without any attempt at elucidation (I Cor 8:6).

## b. The Son's Work in Providence

The general point, that Wesley can regard Christ as the supporter, governor, and preserver of all things, must be considered established by the foregoing section. Wesley's interest with regard to providence focuses upon the degree and character of God's providential care for all mankind. It is the Christological background of this problem which will be investigated here.

Wesley subsumes general and particular providence under a threefold circle of divine providence (S. 77, i, 8-9), and his tendency is to regard all providence as particular (S. 32, 28). God's providential care presides over three concentric circles of men. From outermost to innermost, they are: all men; the visible church, or all who claim to be Christians; and the invisible church, or all "real Christians." Moreover, God presides in such a way that He has "additional regard" and "nearer attention" for the inner circles, the innermost of which, it is interesting to note, is defined by sanctification.

This teaching is echoed in the *Notes*. The outer circle is clearly presupposed in the comment that all men receive temporal blessings at God's hand, though "spiritual blessings they will not receive" (Mt 5:45). It is the innermost circle of real Christians whom the inseparable love of God will save as well as protect (Ro 8:39). In I Timothy 4:10 Wesley teaches that God preserves all men and is willing to save all, but that He is "in a more eminent manner the everlasting Saviour of all that believe." In one important passage, Wesley teaches that those who have reached the innermost circle understand that all their blessings, temporal, spiritual, and eternal, depend on Christ's intercession, which is one branch of His priestly office (W. XI, 396).

It cannot be ignored that in this teaching Christ's mediatorial work has some relation to the degree of God's providential care. How far does this mediatorial work reach? Is Christ's

mediatorial intercession the ground for the providential care of
all men, or only for those in the inner circle, the invisible church?

Although Wesley offers no explicit answer to this question,
there are elements which can be developed into an answer,
consistent with his intention. Wesley takes particular care to
point out that God's providential care and guidance of Christ,
Himself, while on earth, is a special instance of particular
providence (Lk 4:17, Jn 11:9-10). This providential government,
indeed, underlies Christ's crucifixion and entire reconciling act
(Ro 3:26, Eph 1:10). But this means that the innermost circle
of divine providence also includes God's providential administration of the atonement, which, as Wesley constantly emphasizes, is
an event objectively applying not to a limited elect, but to all
men. There is thus a direct line from divine governance of creation
to the offer of salvation to all. Contrariwise, the atonement is an
attracting power at the heart of the circles of God's providence.
God's providential work gravitates toward salvation; its intention
is to move men toward the inner circle, that they may grow in
grace there. This means that the primary reason for God's providential care of all men is that they may have the opportunity
to move toward the innermost circle of God's care. General
providence serves this particular providence. And in this light
it is certainly in order to observe that the "innermost" Christians
are not asked simply to congratulate themselves on their good
fortune, but to participate in the ministry of their Head for the
"outermost," caring for, suffering for, and loving all men
(Col 1:24). No one has emphasized more urgently than Wesley
that God's love leads to love of brother. He also emphasizes,
as will be shown, that Christians are made holy in order to
bear witness.

It remains true for Wesley that God's providential care of
the outer circle is not so direct as that of the innermost, but
the reason is that God does not intend for men to remain in the
outer circle. Wesley does not mean that nonbelievers enjoy
less of God's preserving care than believers. All enjoy His

preserving care (I Tim 4:10). Wesley means that nonbelievers do not permit themselves to enjoy God's saving grace, and it is simply not possible for Wesley to think of this spiritual blessing apart from God's temporal blessing (Mt 5:45).

Once again, this is an interpretation and development of Wesleyan presuppositions, although it aims to be faithful to Wesley's intention and conclusions. If it is correct, then it must be clear that there is no hard and fast line between God's creative or providential work, on the one hand, and the mediatorial work of grace on the other. There is no contradiction in Christ, as long as He is fully the preserver of the outer circle, and the distinction between His care for them and His "nearer attention" for the inner circle is the distinction between temporal and spiritual blessings. The key point is that one Christ underlies both temporal and spiritual blessings, and accounts for the possibility that temporal blessings are intended to lead to spiritual blessings. God's gracious decree to make a holy creation dominates Christ's work in creation, providence, and redemption. One grace underlies all three.

## 2. Christ's Mediatorial Work of Grace

The remainder of this study is devoted to Wesley's doctrine of Christ's mediatorial work in its threefold prophetic, kingly, and priestly aspect. Before beginning a detailed examination of that work, however, it is necessary to provide a general orientation, and to that the remainder of this chapter is devoted.

### a. Man's Need of Salvation[3]

Man's *status integritatis* is explained by Wesley, traditionally enough, in two terms: the threefold image of God, and man's original righteousness. Explicating the threefold image, Wesley teaches a "natural image," which means that man is a spiritual being, endued with understanding, freedom of will, and various affections; a "political image," wherein man, having dominion over creation, is like his Creator; and a "moral image," which

is righteousness and holiness (S. 39, i, 1; I Cor 11:7). Man's
original righteousness is his perfect obedience to the perfect
moral law engraved on his heart in creation by the finger of
God (S. 29, i, 3; S. 5, i, 1-3). In the study of Christ's prophetic
work this law will be investigated in detail. Here it may be
pointed out as significant that the fall nevertheless takes place
in disobedience not to this engraved moral law, but to the one
positive law, "superadded" to it (S. 5, i, 3). At the critical point,
God's will is known not by nature, but by revelation.

The fall roots in the malice of the devil (S. 62, i, 8; Jn 8:44,
I Jn 3:8, I Cor 15:26). He deceived Eve so that she disbelieved
God, was tempted to self-will, and finally committed "outward
sin" (S. 62, i, 9). The Wesleyan analysis of sin will therefore
speak of the being, the power, and the guilt of sin, to which
corresponds the threefold character of the sinner: a sinful nature,
sinful tempers, and sinful actions (Tit 2:14, Ro 3:23).

The consequences of the fall followed immediately. God's
sentence allowed the "threat" to be carried out: man died, spiritually, because his soul was separated from God without whom
it could have no life; as a consequence he died bodily in becoming
corruptible and mortal (S. 5, i, 5).[4] Moreover, death, entering
by one man, passed upon all, because this one man, Adam,
was the federal head or representative of mankind (Ro 5:12, 16;
W. IX, 332).[5] Adam's sin is imputed to all mankind as original
sin, or, as Wesley repeatedly called it, "entire depravity" (S. 6,
ii, 5; Jas 4:12, Ro 6:6). It must be noted, nevertheless, that
Wesley doubted whether any man dies eternally merely for the
sake of original sin (W. IX, 315; W. X. 223). Damnable sin has
the character of deliberate personal choice (S. 8, ii, 11). Adam's
guilt, as well as his sin, is imputed to us (W. IX, 307, 317; Col
2:14). Moreover, the whole creation suffers in bondage when
man, its lord, rebels against God (W. IX, 318; Ro 8:19-22;
S. 60; S. 64).[6]

The *status corruptionis* may correspondingly be summarized
in the almost complete loss of the threefold image of God, and

in the curse of the law on the depraved sinner. The natural and political images are partly lost; the moral image is wholly lost (S. 57, ii, 6; S. 39, i, 2, 4). Wesley, when he emphasizes human depravity, is thinking of the loss of the more important moral image. Upon occasion he can also speak of an "indelible nobleness, which we ought to reverence both in ourselves and others," remaining in man after the "likeness" (surely the moral image) of God is lost (Jas 3:9). Since man is now morally a depraved sinner, however, the moral law, which defined his original righteousness, becomes the curse of God against him (Gal 3:13, 4:4, 5:18). And since the law drives inbred sin to become exceedingly sinful, the law is for the man of unfaith an impossible way of justification (Ro 7:13, 10:4, 5, 6:14, Heb 7:19).

But the decisive element in man's predicament remains to be mentioned: it is that man's sin is primarily an offense against God Himself. Not the victorious devil, not the damaged image of God in man, not the unfulfilled law and man's lost righteousness, not the world in bondage, but the wrath of God lies at the center of the situation to which Christ's mediatorial work is addressed. This concept will be examined more thoroughly in the chapter on Christ's priestly work.

In summary it can be said that for Wesley there are two principal consequences of the fall, two reasons why man needs the atonement: from God's side, the just wrath of God puts alienated man under sentence of death; from man's side, death, the substantial loss of the image of God, is suffered, together with the curse of the law. The atonement of Christ, addressed to these two situations, will result in the Wesleyan doctrines of justification and sanctification.

## b. The Mediator and His One Task

God decided from all eternity to send the Son into the world in order to save men from their fallen condition. This was the single task for which Christ became incarnate. The relevant statements from the Twenty-five Articles (Arts. II, XX) underline the priestly sacrifice as the center of this mediatorial work, and these statements must be taken as normative for Wesley's understanding of Christ's work. It is noticeable, however, that when Wesley makes his own formulation, the motif of restoration is also in the foreground (S. 62, iii, 5, 6; S. 141, ii). But it is not faithful to Wesley to play one of these motifs off against the other. It is true that salvation includes both justification and sanctification, and in this "twofold view of salvation" lie both the strength and the problem of Wesley's doctrine of Christ's mediatorial work. But the crucial point is that Wesley regards this total salvation whole, and its accomplishment as the one task for which Christ became man.

Wesley defines "Mediator" all too briefly as someone who, being both God and man, stands between God and man to transact the whole affair of our salvation by giving Himself (I Tim 2:5; Art. VI). This Mediator is sent into the world. He comes as bearer of a "commission," as an "apostle" of the Father (Jn 10:18, 14:31, 20:21, Heb 3:1).

The Mediator Himself is essentially one with God, and Wesley has a tendency to emphasize this equality precisely where he speaks of Christ's being sent into the world (I Jn 4:2, Mt 1:23). Why? In Romans 1:7 a reason of capital importance is given: "It is one and the same peace, and one and the same grace, which is from God and from Jesus Christ." Wesley wants to emphasize that it is ultimately one grace which meets man in creation and redemption. Underneath all the two-sidedness of the Wesleyan reconciliation, the law and gospel, God's vengeance and mercy, Wesley intends us to see one grace, grounded in the essential Trinitarian equality of Father and Mediator. Nonetheless, in His mediatorial office, Christ is subordinate to the Father (I Cor 3:23, 11:3, Jn 8:49), although Wesley is quick to add that one must not therefore infer that they are not of the same divine nature (I Cor 11:3).

It is probable that for Wesley the mediatorial office actually begins with the incarnation, although it is officially inaugurated with Christ's baptism. He refuses to permit either Revelation 13:8 or I Peter 1:20 to speak of Christ's sacrifice before the foundation of the world, although in view of Wesley's doctrine of time, it is at least conceivable that this sacrifice was eternally present before the eyes of God.[7] Wesley's stress, however, falls upon the official inauguration of the mediatorial office in Christ's baptism. Here Christ was anointed with the Holy Spirit (Lk 4:18) in such a way that He was set apart for and assumed the three official functions in Israel: prophet, priest, and king (Mt 1:16). This event publicly established Christ's identity with the long-awaited Messiah of the Old Testament (Mt 1:1, Jn 1:1). The "foundation" of the mediatorial office is, however, the blood of Christ shed on the cross. Herein lies the "virtue" or, in Wesley's more usual word, the "merit" of Christ's mediatorial work (Heb 12:24).[8]

There is at least one statement which suggests that Christ's mediatorial task comes to an end: Christ is "Mediator till the end of the world, ... God to all eternity" (W. X, 82). However, this is by no means certain. It will be seen that in some sense each of the three mediatorial offices, but more particularly the priestly one, continues to all eternity.

In general, in so far as it can be maintained that the cross lies at the center of all Christ's mediatorial work, Wesley's view of the mediatorial ministry is essentially one. Moreover, unity here can be of utmost importance for unifying Wesley's theology as a whole, as he himself suggests when, wishing to emphasize sanctification, he simply speaks of the "complete Saviour" (Phil 3:10, I Jn 5:7). Against this background, the doctrine of the three offices must always be understood as a way of making plain how remarkably rich is the one salvation which is promised in Jesus Christ.

## c. The Three Offices

The division of Christ's one mediatorial office into a threefold prophetic, priestly, and kingly work has a prominent place in

Wesley's thinking. This scheme will, accordingly, provide the framework for the remainder of this volume.[9] In order, however, to justify this choice, and to ground the important decision implied in it, it is well to pause with the doctrine of the three-fold office itself, and study how Wesley understood this division.

In Appendix II will be found a careful examination of six explicit references to the doctrine as a whole—there are many more references to one or the other of the offices—in the *Notes*, as well as to three references from other sources as a check upon the inferences drawn from the *Notes*. In the light of this material, the following summary statement of Wesley's understanding of Christ's mediatorial office can be given.

1. *The theological context* of the three offices is Christ's one mediatorial work undertaken as a fulfilment of Old Testament prophecy. There is some indication of the Trinitarian background of the doctrine, for the offices officially begin with Christ's anointment with the Holy Spirit at baptism, and there is some indication that the offices of the exalted Christ, and especially the prophetic and kingly offices, are executed through the Holy Spirit.

2. *The order of the offices* may offer some clue as to their significance for Wesley's thinking.[10] When Wesley merely identifies the doctrine, he uses the traditional order of prophet, priest, and king. But when he considers the matter, he tends to begin with the priestly office, even though his interest in using this doctrine may be to emphasize sanctification. It may be said that Wesley's understanding begins with the priestly work and moves in the direction of the prophetic and kingly work, although it must be left an open question whether it does not also end in the priestly work in view of the twofold justification which will yet be encountered.

3. *The content* of the three offices may be identified in a general way from a careful comparison of the statements. There are clearly two principal elements in the *priestly* office: the *atonement*, whereby Christ is the sacrifice for sin, reconciling

men to God by His blood, and the priestly *intercession,* whereby the living Christ bears His wounds to heaven and there intercedes for transgressors before the throne of grace. In the *prophetic* office the leading idea is certainly that of the *teacher,* Himself the wisdom of God, teaching or revealing to men the whole will of God, enlightening men's minds with His ever-present Word and Spirit, and guiding believers into all truth. In short, Christ as prophet is the teacher of both the *law* and the *gospel.* In the *kingly* office, the leading elements seem to be the *victory* of Christ, whereby he subdues all things to Himself, and Christ's *dominion,* or His ruling of all things in power and perfect strength. But the point of this office for Wesley is that Christ reigns in such a way as progressively to conquer sin in the believer, and thus He restores the damaged image of God and brings in everlasting righteousness.[11]

4. Wesley's tendency upon occasion to divide the three offices into two parts requires closer analysis of *the inner relation of the three offices.* When he warns against preaching the priestly office only, Wesley implicitly identifies the priestly office with justification and the other two with sanctification (S. 31, i, 6). He can also say that the priestly office concerns our state with respect to God, and the prophetic and kingly offices our state with respect to ourselves (Mt 1:16). This cryptic indication must mean that the priestly office justifies, or restores the broken relation to God, while the prophetic and kingly offices sanctify, or restore the damaged image of God which is true human nature. There is, in addition, the significant fact that a bridge was found precisely between the priestly and kingly offices: because Christ was slain, He is worthy to preside over the end events; because He was humiliated, He is rewarded with dominion over church and world. In the light of these indications, Wesley's statement in Matthew 11:28-29, that the threefold office accomplishes a twofold work, justification and sanctification, can be underlined. And that means that in so far as there is a problem of a "twofold salvation" in Wesley, that problem will

be reflected Christologically in the relation of the priestly office to the other two offices.

5. *Wesley's intention* in the prominent use of this doctrine seems clear: by it he emphasizes the "complete Christ" of his sanctification doctrine. It is important, however, that he does not simply emphasize the prophetic and kingly offices, but rather the unity of all three offices, the "whole Christ." Is this not also indirect evidence that Wesley's native ground, as a mature leader, was the justification by faith alone which he learned in his conversion, and the priestly office of Christ which he came to associate with it? Because he stands here, he can look toward sanctification. The Wesleyan Christ is not interested in sanctification alone, but in "restoring those to the image of God, whom He had first reinstated to His favour" (S. 31, i, 6).

6. *The subjective accent* in Wesley's account of the three offices is unavoidable: Christ does this work for us, in us. This is already clear from the identification of the offices with justification and sanctification. It is also indicated by their correspondence with Wesley's analysis of man's inner need and sin. Nevertheless, in spite of this accenting, Wesley is able to include elements of a historical, cosmic character in his understanding of Christ's work.

7. *The perspective of the exalted state* characterizes Wesley's view of Christ's work. Not once does Wesley take an unqualified historical view of the order of the three offices.[12] Always he considers them from the perspective of the exalted Christ, although there are hints of some historical reference, especially in connection with the priestly office and the beginning of the kingly work. To this flattening out of the historical process must be related the tendency to consider the offices eternal, and also the wholesome indication that all three offices are involved in the last judgment. It is curiously at the last judgment that the three offices are clearly related by Wesley to history and the whole creation. This many-sided view of Christ's exaltation may be a warning against one-dimensional, too-individualistic

interpretations of what Wesley means when he speaks of sanctification.

In summary, it must be admitted that this doctrine has considerable importance for the structure of Wesley's Christology. Although its use does not bulk large in Wesley's writings, compared with some other doctrines, neither does formal Christology bulk large. When it is compared with other elements of Wesley's Christology, however, its importance can be seen. Wesley is not merely content here to affirm his agreement with classical doctrine. He needs and uses the doctrine of the three offices, and indeed for his leading theological interests. When he wishes to talk about the work of Christ, this is his habitual formula. For these reasons, this doctrine will be used as the formal organizing scheme for the remainder of this work.

### 3. COMMENT

A word may be said about the significance of the order of the three offices in the remainder of our discussion. The problem in reading Wesley, as has been repeatedly pointed out, is how to get behind his two-sidedness. He has a moralistic side, which had great influence in shaping the form and categories of his theology. He has an evangelical side, stemming from his conversion, which, it is here asserted, labors to convert his theology, but with only a partial transformation of its form. Yet this evangelical side rules the intention of his theology. The result is the two-sidedness which has been found again and again in this study: in Wesley's view of God's justice and mercy, in the infra- and supra-lapsarian decree, in the manifestation-dominion theme and the substitution theme. The two-sidedness will also come near dominating Wesley's "twofold view of salvation." But the effort to understand Wesley cannot be allowed to rest at this point: it must search for the ground from which his effectiveness as an evangelist and evangelical leader grew. It is certain that no evangelical revival of the scope, depth, and permanence of Wesley's could have been built on an antinomy.

The answer to this problem can, of course, rightly be given only at the end of this discussion. However, at this point a provisional decision, affecting the final result, is already called for, in order to make any headway with the material which lies ahead. The right procedure does not seem to be to develop both sides of Wesley parallel until the end, and then face the gigantic decision for one or the other, and the search for some relation between them. Such a procedure would be by no means free of a debatable initial presupposition. Rather, at this mid-point, such hints as there are must be pressed for their meaning, and a decision must be made about the best way to come to a unified understanding of Wesley. Wesley must then resolutely be interpreted in that light until the end, when the decisive question must be put: is this Wesley, or not?

Among the hints available at this mid-point are the following: (a) The mediatorial office as a whole has its "foundation" in the cross. (b) Wesley prefers to start with the priestly office and move from there to the prophetic and kingly offices. (c) Wesley considers the three offices to be a unity, and it is, moreover, seriously to be questioned whether the unity of the three offices ever proves possible except on the ground of the priestly office.[13] In fact, it could be argued that systematic two-sidedness is the necessary result of trying to make one of the other offices fundamental. (d) As will be shown, Wesley's doctrine of justification by faith appears at both ends of his doctrine of sanctification. (e) There is, finally, the historical fact that, whatever the long steps of preparation, it was the conversion discovery of justification by faith which led immediately to Wesley's share in the revival. His revival preaching, of which the standard sermons are a powerful witness, repeatedly ground salvation in faith in the merits of Christ.

In face of this problem, in light of these hints, and wishing to read Wesley in the best sense he allows, we shall at this point make a provisional decision: to consider it Wesley's intention that the priestly office is fundamental to the other two, and to consider the other two in large measure as aspects of this. However, the better to express this centrality and unity, the priestly office will be presented last, as the climax and summary of Wesley's doctrine of salvation, while the prophetic and kingly offices will be presented first, as indispensable components of this larger, unified view. Therefore, in faithfulness to Wesley, the order we shall use will be: prophet, king, and priest.

This decision does not mean that justification is more important than sanctification. Both are important and central for Wesley. The intention here is to get underneath the all too frequent false antithesis or parallelism of justification and sanctification in Wesley study, and to say that with respect to both the priestly work is fundamental, and the prophetic and kingly work indispensable. The merit of approaching the problem from the angle of Christology is that the unity of the work of salvation is already given in the unity of the mediatorial work in the person of the Mediator.

Finally, it must be noted that the relative priority of the priestly work is not a static and final matter in Wesley. Rather, because he stands on the ground of the priestly work, a continual conversion of his two-sidedness takes place. One does not eliminate Wesley's two-sidedness by this manner of presentation. One can perhaps show that this two-sidedness is not the ultimate intention or result of the Wesleyan theology.

1. In one remarkable sermon, "On Spiritual Worship," published only three years before his death, Wesley deals with Christ's role in creation and providence with a speculative freedom unmatched elsewhere. He begins by ascribing to the eternal Christ "the incommunicable name, JEHOVAH" (S. 77, i, 1). This Son is "the only cause, the sole creator of all things" (i, 2). He is "also the supporter of all things that He hath made," upholding "all created things . . . by the same powerful word, which brought them out of nothing. . . . Were He to withdraw His hand for a moment, the creation would fall into nothing" (i, 3). He points out "what perhaps has not been sufficiently observed," that Christ "is the true author of all the *motion* that is in the universe" (italics Wesley's). There follows a discussion on inert

matter which owes all its motion, "Sir Isaac" notwithstanding, to the "ethereal" or "electric fire" attached to every particle of it, and which is "the first material mover; the main spring whereby the Creator and preserver of all things" (in this context, the Son) "is pleased to move the universe" (i, 5-6). Without transition, there is a short paragraph on Christ as the Redeemer of all men (i, 7). The section closes with three paragraphs on Christ as the governor of a threefold circle of Divine Providence (i, 8-9), and on the Son as "the End of all things." "All things are of Him, as the Creator; through Him, as the Sustainer and Preserver; and to Him, as the ultimate end of all" (i, 10). "In all these senses," says Wesley at the close of the entire section, "Jesus Christ is the true God" (ii).

This material must be used with care, although there is nothing in it unrepresentative of Wesley's fragmentary utterances elsewhere. It can best be taken as an example of Wesley's tendency toward high Christological predicates. It shows how, with his emphasis on Christ's exaltation, he can subsume all Trinitarian appropriations under his Christology. And it is not without interest for the problem of nature and grace that the mediatorial work appears in this series, without distinction, without transition.

2. This is one of the places where the division of mediatorial and non-mediatorial work breaks down. The implicit subordination of Son to Father here in the non-mediatorial work of creation, and presumably therefore in their eternal inner-Trinitarian relations, creates a problem for Wesleyan Christology, unless Wesley somehow views Christ's role in creation as part of His mediatorial work.

3. The brevity of this discussion is explained by the relative abundance of good studies of Wesley's doctrines of man, sin, and the fall. Mention may be made of Harald Lindström, *Wesley and Sanctification* (London), pp. 19-54, who offers the best study of the matter; Lerch *(Heil und Heiligung,* pp. 25-68); William R. Cannon, *The Theology of John Wesley* (New York, Nashville, 1946), pp. 176-200; and the primary material collected in Robert W. Burtner and Robert E. Chiles, *A Compend of Wesley's Theology* (New York, Nashville, 1954), pp. 109-35. For related discussions in this study, see *infra,* pp. 118-21, 150-52.

4. It is of interest that Wesley could ground knowledge of man's spiritual death Christologically: if Christ died for all, then all are dead, "for had any man been otherwise, Christ had not needed to have died for Him" (II Cor 5:14).

5. Wesley can also ground Adam's representativeness Christologi-

cally. Since Christ was the representative of all mankind in the cross, and since Adam was a type or figure of Christ, "therefore, [Adam] was also, in some sense, our representative" (W. IX, 332).

6. This bondage is not only the natural result of man's misrule: it is also God's curse put upon creation for Adam's sake (S. 57, i, 4; Ro 8:20). Moreover, the devil seizes power over creation by sin and death (Jn 12:31).

7. Classical Protestantism discussed this as the question of the *logos incarnandus*, i.e., of a "mediatorship [of Christ] already exercised before His manifestation in the flesh," whereby "in the Father's eyes the sacrifice of Christ had been prepared from eternity" (Heppe, *Reformed Dogmatics*, p. 452). Heppe cites Polan's explanation: "Before the assumption of the human nature Christ was Mediator according to both natures, because at that time He was Mediator as being *incarnandus* (about to become flesh), just as He is now our Mediator as being *incarnatus* (become flesh). In addition the two natures were regarded as being united in the knowledge and predestination and acceptance of God, since with Him things done and to be done, present and future are in the same place."

Wesley offers no explicit support for this doctrine; indeed, he seems to deny it, as might be expected from his polemic against its crucial presuppositions of predestination and a pact between Father and Son. Wesley refuses to permit Revelation 13:8 to speak of "the Lamb who was slain from the foundation of the world" (Authorized Version). His note implies that the proper translation would be: ". . . whose name is not written from the foundation of the world in the book of life of the Lamb who was slain." Wesley appeals to Revelation 17:8 in support of this reading, which is, of course, a possible reading of the Greek, and is used in recent translations (Revised Standard Version). He omits any comment on I Peter 1:20, with its reference to the Lamb who was foreordained before the foundation of the world, except that he translates "foreknows" for the Authorized Version's "foreordained." He also rejects Watts's "ingenious dream" of the preexistent humanity of Christ, on the grounds that it qualifies the Godhead of the Son (S. 62, ii, 2). It must therefore be claimed that Wesley's doctrine of the Mediator applies explicitly to the *logos incarnatus*.

There are, however, several instances, mostly in connection with the regiving of the law after the fall, where Christ, Himself, and not simply a "type" of Christ, is present in the Old Testament, doing His reconciling work (see Chapter IV). It must also be remembered that Wesley's doctrine of time allows the fall to be present before

God's eyes from all eternity. Does that not allow Christ's mediatorial work also to be present before God eternally? How else is God's eternal decree to send Christ in the flesh for man's salvation to be explained? In the light of such questions, and the earlier study of God's decree as grounded in Christ's atonement, must not the possibility be held open that, once Wesley has finished his antinomian polemic, he remains open in principle to the possibility of an eternally present *logos incarnatus,* if not a *logos incarnandus?*

8. There may be an echo in Hebrews 5:9 of the orthodox distinction between the merit, by which Christ acquired salvation for men by His blood, and the efficacy, by which He confers and conserves the salvation acquired. Cf. Heidegger XIX, 25, cited in Heppe (*Reformed Dogmatics,* p. 451).

9. Lerch (*Heil und Heiligung,* p. 79) also finds that for Wesley "the work of Christ [is] conceived in terms of the threefold office, Prophet, Priest, King."

10. In discussing Wesley, Professor Karl Barth suggested that the writer consider which of the offices is the starting point for understanding the others. It is not an unimportant question for Wesley's theology. Wesley can be read as a legalist or enthusiast if the prophetic or kingly offices are made fundamental to the entire work of Christ. He can be read in a decidedly more evangelical light if the priestly office becomes the starting point for understanding the others.

It is observable that in the seven instances where Wesley uses the traditional order, prophet, priest, king, he is, in effect, quoting a formula by which he identifies the doctrine. In one of these cases, where he does develop the content of the office (the "Letter to a Roman Catholic"), he is writing a personal credal statement; i.e., it is a situation where the formula-like order would naturally recommend itself.

There is one case where Wesley follows the order of priest, king, and prophet (Rev 5:6), but it must be noted that the order here is determined by the order of symbols in the text.

In the two remaining cases, the order is priest, prophet, and king, and it is significant that in both cases Wesley is giving a somewhat freer, fuller, and more personal statement of the doctrine. In Matthew 1:16 this order is the more striking, for Wesley has just identified the offices in their usual order, and he then proceeds to discuss the priesthood first, obviously because alienation from God is the starting point for his own thinking about salvation. In the remaining instance

(S. 31, i, 6) the motive is again clear: the priestly office is here identified with justification, and Wesley's point is that we are not "wholly to confine ourselves to this," clearly implying that we start here.

11. A special question must be asked about Wesley's single explicit remark that Christ the King is giver of laws. Ought this to be taken as his authoritative statement about the relation of the law to the three offices?

The law will have to be dealt with in some sense under each of the three offices. Nevertheless, in spite of Wesley's explicit indication, the giving of the law will here be considered principally under the heading of the prophetic office, for the following reasons: (1) For Wesley, the kingly office does not begin in some important sense until after the resurrection. (2) But the law plays a crucial part in his thought from the beginning. To assign the law to the kingly office alone would distort the impressive continuity of the law in Wesley's thinking. (3) This omnipresence of the law is reflected in the prominence of the law in the order of salvation, not only in sanctification but also in justification. Wesley's doctrine of the three uses of the law will not permit it to be identified only with that office which he relates principally to sanctification. For these reasons it is here considered that Wesley's paragraph (S. 31, i, 6) was written to emphasize the third use of the law, i.e., its relation to sanctification. Wesley can describe sanctification, upon occasion, as Christ, through the Holy Spirit, re-inscribing the law on man's heart. That is very likely what Wesley means by identifying Christ the King as the giver of laws. This study will accordingly follow the majority of Wesley's indications and relate the giving of the law to the prophetic office which is primarily concerned with the revelation of "the whole will of God." That in no way minimizes the importance of the law for both Christ's priesthood and kingship.

12. Pope (*Compendium*, ii, 206-7), on the contrary, strongly emphasizes the temporal sequence: prophet until the passion, priest on the cross, king after resurrection.

13. It is no accident that the doctrine of the three offices, which has been widely used only since the Reformation, grew historically out of the doctrine of Christ's priestly work, the prophetic and kingly offices elaborating indispensable aspects of that one work. See Schmid (*Doctrinal Theology*, pp. 337-38, and especially the note).

# CHAPTER FOUR

# The Prophetic Work of Christ

THERE ARE few points where Wesley offers less formal guidance than in understanding his conception of Christ's prophetic or revealing work. This fact does not at all indicate that revelation is unimportant for him. Quite the contrary, it seems more likely that Wesley never satisfactorily formulated, even for himself, the largeness of this theme for his thinking. The following inquiry will therefore follow the simplest possible outline, studying Christ as prophet, and then analyzing this ministry, according to one of Wesley's few systematic indications, in its double character as an evangelical and legal prophecy (Heb 12:25).

## 1. THE MINISTRY OF CHRIST THE PROPHET

Prophecy means, for Wesley, in addition to its common meaning of "foretelling," primarily "that whereby heavenly mysteries are declared to men" (Ro 12:6). In this primary sense, Christ is a prophet (Heb 1:1-2, Mk 9:7, Rev 1:1, Phil 3:8, Heb 3:1, Lk 4:24, Ac 7:37, 3:22, Jn 17:3).[1]

Christ's prophetic work is grounded in His relation to the Father. No one has ever seen God. Only in and by "the Son of His love," has God ever, "at any time," revealed Himself to His creatures (S. 62, ii, 1). And this exclusiveness of revelation through Christ is, in turn, grounded in Wesley's understanding that this "highest unity" between Father and Son implies the "most intimate knowledge" of Father by Son (Jn 1:18, 10:30, 8:13, I Jn 1:1).[2] This Christ-centered revelation in some sense also underlies Wesley's much-emphasized doctrine of the witness of the Spirit: because the Spirit participates in the Trinity, the testimony which He bears in our hearts, when we believe, is also testimony to the authority of the Son (I Jn 5:9-11). The emphasis is thus put on the mediatorial subordination of the Son as the revealer of the otherwise unknowable God, and on the Trinitarian unity of Father, Son, and Holy Spirit to explain how only the Son knows and can reveal God in His fulness (Heb 3:1, Jn 8:19).

Christ's prophetic ministry is publicly inaugurated by His baptism, when He is anointed with the Holy Spirit for His office, in correspondence to the anointing of prophets in the Old Testament (Mt 1:16, Lk 4:18). Christ's official "solemn, stated preaching" begins at a definite time, and yet it is addressed not only to His first-century hearers, but to the whole race, including all generations to come (Mt 4:17, Mk 1:15, Tit 1:3; S. 16, intro., 4). Likewise, His preaching is not simply a series of isolated utterances, but "one discourse, with one even tenor, from the time I first spake to you" (Jn 8:25). Certain revelations were given after His ascension, as His prophetic office continues in heaven (Rev 1:5, I Jn 5:8). However, these revelations are strictly in conformity with the scriptural revelation about Christ; in principle, apart from Christ, "no other revelation is to be expected" (Heb 1:1-2).

It is possible to discern three phases in Christ's prophetic ministry: before, in, and after His death. Before His death the earthly ministry consists of both words and deeds, of teaching in synagogues and preaching, but also of healings and miracles (Mk 8:38; S. 16, intro., 1). There is no point of doctrine which has not been taught in public (Jn 18:20), although Wesley is careful to note that the use of parables is intended not only to impress the humble and serious, but "by an awful mixture of justice and mercy" to hide the truth from the proud and careless (Mt 13:3). The climax of His itinerant ministry comes in His deliverance of the Sermon on the Mount. Here He speaks as He never did otherwise, in that He lays down in one sermon "the whole plan of His religion," "a general view of the whole," to which nothing in the Bible compares, except possibly "that short sketch of holiness" delivered on Sinai (S. 16, intro., 7).

Wesley also emphasizes Christ's prophetic ministry in His death, for the cross confirms the truth of what He teaches, and is itself a revelation of who Christ is (Jn 8:28, Heb 10:20). The passion plays a particular role in declaring the truth to the "princes of the Gentiles" in a ministry otherwise devoted primarily to the Jews (Jn 18:37). In the Methodist revival this point was stressed: Christ's blood is for the sinner "a speaking blood" (S. 16, i, 12).

After Christ's death, the resurrection is "the grand proof" of Christ's Messiahship (Mt 16:20, I Cor 15:6). By it the Spirit publicly declared Christ to be the Son of God, and the testimony of the three disciples about the transfiguration was thus made credible and confirmed (I Tim 3:16, Mt 17:9). "Brighter evidence" was given after the resurrection in Christ's eating food before the disciples, but chiefly at Pentecost (Mk 8:30, Lk 24:43, Jn 14:20). That indication points to Christ's prophetic ministry after the ascension, which must be studied later in connection with the continuance of this ministry through the church.

The message of this ministry, in a word, is "the gospel of the kingdom," "the whole will of God," including both gospel and law (Mt 4:23, Rev 1:5, Heb 12:25). To the elaboration of this assertion, the following two sections are devoted.

## 2. THE EVANGELICAL PROPHECY

Because Christ's prophetic ministry is heard in both the Old Testament and the church, it is appropriate to study both Christ's fulfilment of Old Testament prophecy, and His continuing, living Word in the church and in the believer.

### a. Christ's Fulfilment of Old Testament Prophecy

The continuity of Old and New Testaments is a presupposition of considerable importance for Wesley, for it is the formal ground of the continuity of law and gospel, of Israel and the church. The Christological expression of this continuity is impressive. In a later context the continuity will be seen in terms of Christ as the sanctifying temple to which both the old and the new dispensations point. In the present context, at least three ways may be discerned in which Christ is related to Old Testament prophecy.

First of all, Christ, Himself, is simply present and speaking in the Old Testament. The angel of Moses' burning bush is the Son of God, Himself (Ac 7:30). He it was who "thundered out of heaven" on Mount Sinai (S. 16, intro., 8).

Secondly, Christ speaks through His messengers in the Old Testament. He sent the prophets (Mt 23:34, Rev 22:6). David speaks in His name (Ac 13:35, Heb 10:7-8). Christ preached to mankind before the flood through Noah (I Pet 3:20). Moses everywhere wrote of Christ (Jn 5:46). Whoever, then, believes the prophets believes Christ (Ac 26:27).

But Wesley usually relates Christ to the Old Testament in a third way, through "types." Types are facts, persons, ceremonies, things which, in a measure, embody Christ's significance, and in a sense speak for Christ in the Old Testament, yet remain signs which press for "an answer" in Jesus Christ Himself (Heb 13:12).[3] In Hebrews 8:5 Wesley explains in some detail how these "patterns" and "shadows" lead our minds "to something nobler than themselves." The ability to understand and explain them is reckoned by Wesley among the extraordinary gifts of the Spirit (I Cor 12:8, 14:6).

But the light of Old Testament prophecy, taken in its entirety, is as lamplight before the daylight of the New. Light it is, and not to be despised, for it shone where there was no "light nor window." But it points toward the coming "full light of the gospel," and its "morning star, Jesus Christ" (II Pet 1:19). The Old Testament prophets, themselves, are not fully aware of the meaning of what they say. They search, like miners digging after precious ore (I Pet 1:10), for the One who will say: "*Today is this scripture fulfilled in your ears*—By what you hear

Me speak" (Lk 4:21, Mt 11:13, 2:17). Then, when the veil
is removed by faith, men can see how "all the types and
prophecies of the law are fully accomplished in Him" (II Cor
3:16, Heb 5:4, 7:11, 9:23, Lk 22:16). Moses had prophesied the
coming of another prophet, and the apostolic church testified
that in Christ this prophet had come (Jn 5:46, Ac 7:37).

For Wesley, two points are ultimately important in Christ's
fulfilment of Old Testament prophecy. First, continuity: the
new prophet was like the old one, a true "answer" to the Old
Testament type. Second, uniqueness: the new prophet was nevertheless "infinitely superior," the light of the sun swallowing up
the light of the lamp (Ac 3:22).

## b. Christ's Continuing, Living, and Transforming Word in the Church and the Believer

The same Christ who spoke in and through the Old Testament, who came as "the great Prophet" in the fulness of time,
now continues His prophetic ministry, after His ascension, in
and through His church, "by His ministers and His Spirit"
(Eph 2:17). Christ's speaking has constituted the church
(Jn 10:27-29). Now Christ also sustains the faith of all believers
through His Word (Eph 2:20, Ac 20:32). He stands in the
center of His church, "as the precentor of the choir," and "sets
forth the praise of God ... by His Word and His Spirit," and
He will continue to do so throughout all generations (Heb 2:12,
Eph 3:10). Apostles and ministers are the human conveyors of
this living Word (Heb 1:2, Jn 4:37, Ac 20:32), but Christ's
Spirit is the active power in it, the teacher, the "greater witness"
(Ac 5:32, Jn 14:26). It should be noted, however, that this
Spirit can occasionally also speak through some, like Socrates,
who are outside the church (Ac 4:19).

Christ's Word, which is the vital concept, is not to be distinguished from God's Word (Jn 5:38, Col 3:16). In the church,
Christ's Word is a word spoken by a human tongue, but the
power is God's, and the words are given, approved, and blessed

by Christ (II Cor 2:17). As such, it becomes a preaching so actual that in it Christ crucified is set forth among men (Gal 3:1). Christ's Word cannot fail or be hindered in its course (II Tim 2:9, 13). It conveys "either life or death to the hearers" (Heb 4:12). Received in faith, it is full of divine virtue, and the power of God for present and eternal salvation; it brings forth fruit, and is a sword against the devil (I Pet 1:23; W. XIV, 253; II Th 3:1, Eph 6:17). Rejected, i.e., unmixed with faith, the Word becomes a judgment and increases the damnation of those who hear it (Heb 4:2, Mk 6:5, Mt 3:12, Rev 2:12; S. 16, intro., 2).

But Christ's preached Word is to be tested by the written Word of God, and if preaching is not according to this, the spirit which actuates it is not from God (I Jn 4:1). The scriptures contain the Word of God first directed to the patriarchs and written down in the time of Moses, together with the inspired writing of the prophets and apostles, and the preaching of the Son of God; the holy scripture so formed is the Word of God which remains forever ("Preface," *Notes,* 10). Its human authors were "purely passive," setting down what was "dictated" to them by Christ and the Holy Spirit (II Pet 1:20-21, Jn 19:24, Rev 2:1; "Preface," *Standard Sermons,* 5). Sometimes the authors had "a particular revelation"; at other times "they [wrote] from the divine light which abode with them, the standing treasure of the Spirit of God" (I Cor 7:25). The result of this process is "a most solid and precious system of divine truth ... one entire body, wherein is no defect," and wherein all future controversies are both foreseen and determined ("Preface," *Notes,* 10; Jn 10:35, Gal 3:8). Nevertheless, "as God has made men the immediate instruments of all those revelations, so evangelical faith must be partly founded on human testimony"; God has condescended to use human language, as well as "natural ideas and conceptions" as instruments of His revelation (*Compend of Natural Philosophy,* v, 207-8). On this ground, Wesley finds it possible and necessary to exercise his considerable common sense in interpreting scripture.[4] In short, Wesley's doctrine of the written

Word of God presupposes the Trinity as author and revealer; it has literalistic tendencies; but it arrives at an authoritative norm for preaching, thinking, and acting which must be wisely interpreted to the best of our human ability. Although he goes far toward literalism, the Wesley of the *Notes* cannot be claimed as an uncritical proponent of a static, verbal theory of scriptural inspiration and authority.[5]

Not only the outward preaching of Christ, but also the inward application by His Spirit belongs to Christ's prophetic office (Jn 9:5). Christ, Himself, teaches men inwardly by His Spirit (Eph 4:21)—who acts for Christ's sake, in His "room," and as His agent (Jn 14:26)—and by this "inward manifestation" of Himself enables men to believe in Him (S. 62, ii, 7). The Spirit, for His part, reveals, testifies, and defends the truth as it is in Jesus (Jn 14:17, Gal 1:16), and gives men—in a Methodist phrase —"the witness in themselves" that Christ's words are "the wisdom and power of God" (Jn 10:4).[6] Further, the teaching of Christ, through the illumination of the Spirit, takes away the veil which hides from us, as it did from the Emmaus disciples, the meaning of scripture (Lk 24:45). Natural man, i.e., man without the Spirit, has no way of receiving the things of the Spirit (I Cor 2:14, Mt 11:27). But those whose eyes have been enlightened by the Spirit of wisdom and revelation know a most "powerful kind of demonstration . . . which works on the conscience with the most convincing light, and the most persuasive evidence" (I Cor 2:4, Eph 1:17-18), but in which there is "no rhapsody, no incoherency" (Mt 5:9). The revelation of this Spirit is "always the same, always consistent with itself" (I Jn 2:27). Taught by this prophet, illuminated by this Spirit, believers come to understand scripture as "the grand instrument" of God's dealings with us (Jn 15:3).

The human role in revelation must be seen against this background of Christ's prophetic work through the Holy Spirit. There is, first of all, a limit to human knowledge of God. None can know God's mind "before or any further than He has

revealed it" (Ro 11:34). This revelation as contained in preaching
and scripture must not be understood in "the bare, carnal, literal
meaning," which profits nothing, but in "the spiritual meaning
... by which God giveth life" (Jn 6:63-64). Furthermore, if
Wesley could also sometimes think of revelation as direct
guidance from God, he nevertheless warns that such revelations
are extremely rare outside the Bible, and ought to be disciplined
by "consulting the oracles of God" (S. 32, 21-22). But mortal
man can never know perfectly any of God's works; it is
enough to love and obey now, and to know hereafter (Jn 13:7,
I Cor 13:10-11).

The human role in revelation is conceived entirely as a
receiving by faith (Jn 17:8). The knowledge which Jesus gives
is never given simply to gratify curiosity, but to be loved and
obeyed (Jn 9:3). Without love of God and neighbor, and the
corresponding love of truth, there can be no knowledge (I Cor
8:2, Jn 18:37). And without willingness to obey, we will not be
given, nor can we understand, Christ's teaching (Jn 8:43, 14:23,
Mt 13:13). In fact, it is by ingrafting into Christ, with all
that this implies of faith, love, and obedience, that Christ is
made unto us wisdom (I Cor 1:30, Jas 1:21). Then the Word
nourishes believers, and they grow "in faith, love, holiness,
unto the full stature of Christ" (I Pet 2:2). And this light is
not for believers alone: God enlightens the Christian that the
Christian may give light all around (S. 19, ii, 5).

The role of human reason, properly qualified, receives a
high valuation from Wesley. Reason is an instrument for appre-
hending, judging, and discoursing (Journal, June 15, 1741),
and religion is not designed to destroy, but to exalt and improve
this natural faculty (I Cor 14:20, Ac 17:11, 27:31). He flatly
declares, "To renounce reason is to renounce religion" (Letters
V, 364). But—and here is Wesley's qualification—our ability
to use this faculty properly was lost in the fall when the devil
veiled the eye of our understanding (S. 9, i, 1; II Cor 4:4).
Natural man is "wholly ignorant" of God (Tit 3:3; S. 9, i, 2),

and this is the root of all wickedness and misery (II Th 1:8).[7] It is true that Wesley can speak of a certain knowledge of God's existence which is available to fallen human reason (S. 38, ii, 3; Ac 17:34). But even "the light of nature" Wesley believes "to flow from preventing grace" (*Compend of Natural Philosophy* v, 211), and the *Notes* make explicit the Christological ground of this natural knowledge (Ro 1:19, Jn 1:9). Nevertheless, this "unsanctified learning" actually only makes the sinner's bonds stronger (Ac 22:3). The restoration of reason to its proper use begins when Christ the prophet takes away the veil and both opens and enlightens the eyes of the understanding (Phil 3:8, II Cor 3:14; S. 62, iii, 1). Engrafted into Christ, the believer becomes through Him a "partaker" of the truth (I Cor 1:30, Jn 1:14). Now reason, assisted by the Holy Ghost, is free to serve the gospel. It enables us to understand scripture, to understand God's dispensations, to comprehend the order of salvation, and, in a word, to know the mind that was in Christ (S. 70, i, 6).[8]

Revelation in Christ provides the foundation for "true and solid doctrines" (I Cor 3:10, 12). Wesley conducts a polemic against making salvation dependent upon "opinions," by which he means particular explications of fundamental truths. With regard to such "opinions" he gives his famous rule to "think and let think" (S. 55, 1-2; Tit 3:10). But Wesley is by no means prepared to dispense with fundamental doctrine. The doctrines of the Trinity, of Christ's deity, of Christ's atonement are to be held, whatever opinions we may have about how to explain them (*Compend of Natural Philosophy* v, 209). Doctrines such as these are to be preached (Heb 5:12, I Cor 3:2, II Tim 3:16), and, when necessary, "controversial divinity" must not be neglected, for "we cannot build without it" (Ro 14:19).

### 3. THE LEGAL PROPHECY

The Wesleyan Christ is repeatedly called "the great Lawgiver" (Mt 5:22, 7:29, Mk 2:28, I Tim 1:9, Heb 10:29). Christ preaches not only the gospel but the law ( S. 20, iii, 1; S. 31, i, 1), and this preaching belongs to His prophetic work (S. 16, intro., 2).

Few themes in Wesley's theology are as thoroughly thought out as his doctrine of the law. At few points does his Christology appear so consistently and transparently. But, also, there are few points where the problem of Wesley's theology is so evident. The following analysis is based primarily on Wesley's four sermons on the law (Ss. 29, 30, 31, 20), for in them Wesley presents something like a systematic treatise.[9]

## a. What Is the Law?

Wesley, following the Thirty-nine Articles and the Reformers, also makes the distinction between the ceremonial and the moral law. The ceremonial law plays a relatively minor role for him. When he speaks of "the law," he means the moral law (S. 29, intro., 2-3; ii, 1-2; S. 30, intro., 3). Wesley makes frequent use of this distinction when interpreting Paul on the law. He tends to attribute the more negative statements to the ceremonial law alone, which was abolished in Christ (e.g., Gal 2:4, 14; 3:19, Ac 15:11, 25).[10]

It is perhaps useful to give a summary definition of the Wesleyan moral law at this point, although the detailed documentation for it will be given in the following section. The moral law is the immutable rule of right and wrong (S. 29, iii, 8). It is based on the order (i.e., on the nature and relations) of creation. This order is righteous because willed and created by God. The moral law is a copy of the divine character, and was originally written on the heart of man as his image of God. This correspondingly free and intelligent creature knew the law through his conscience. After the fall, it was codified in the decalogue. Christ subsequently revealed its inner demand to have been and to be love.

In practice, Wesley has a strong tendency to derive his laws from scripture. The principal sources are the decalogue and the Sermon on the Mount, especially the Beatitudes. He also makes prominent use of Christ's double command, the golden rule, and the ethical instruction of the epistles (S. 31, i, 5; S. 13, ii, 3; S. 20, iv, 7; Mk 12:31). Wesley distinguishes between the external and internal demands of the law. The internal demand is emphasized, and there is some tendency to associate the external demand with the decalogue and the internal demand with the Sermon on the Mount (S. 20, iv, 11). The external demand is more than once summarized in three propositions: do no harm; do good; use the means of grace (S. 20, iv, 11; "General Rules").

From this basic understanding of the moral law, and depending heavily on scriptural texts, Wesley derives numerous concrete rules for Christian living, which, taken together, have a certain puritanical color. The "General Rules" of the Methodist societies summarize some of the more important rules. The Methodist must not swear, become drunk, hold slaves, smuggle, take unlawful interest. He must care for the hungry and sick, instruct and reprove all men, and use all the means of grace. But Wesley does not hesitate to include in the moral law such additional propositions as: eat only what is needful and cheapest; do nothing merely to gratify curiosity; allow no superfluity or finery or fashionable elegance in furniture or apparel; regard only cleanliness, necessity, or at the most very moderate convenience; allow no idle talk (S. 30, iii, 4, 5, 6). Use of curled hair, gold, and costly raiment is expressly forbidden to Christian women, and in this respect, "no art of man can reconcile with the Christian profession the wilful violation of an express command" (I Tim 2:9, I Pet 3:3).

Notwithstanding the foregoing definitions, it must be remembered that for Wesley the law is ultimately not definable in words, but only in living obedience. Lerch's words are entirely just to Wesley: "Written words do not teach us what the law is. That is mediated to us in a living way, and indeed only in Christ, who is the end of the law."[11]

## b. The Giving of the Law

So fundamental is the law to Wesley's thought that virtually the whole *Heilsgeschichte* can be understood as the giving of the law. It stretches from the act of creation to the consummating final judgment, and is profoundly related to man's fall and salvation. The history of the giving of the law can be outlined in five principal stages.

1. *The giving of the law in creation:* The foundation of the law is the uncreated mind of God which exists from all eternity. The moral law is "a copy," "a transcript" of this (S. 29, ii, 4, 6; iii, 3; iv, 9). Wesley's enthusiasm for this thought led him to speak of the moral law as "the fairest offspring of the everlasting Father," and at least once quite deliberately to assign to the moral law the Christological predicates of Hebrews 1:3: "the outbeaming of His glory, the express image of His person" (S. 29, ii, 6, 3; Ro 7:12).

The law was originally given when the "original ideas of truth and good," which were lodged in the mind of God, were "drawn forth and clothed with such a vehicle as to appear even to human understanding" (S. 29, ii, 4). This event was the creation, and God's original determination of the nature and "fitness" (or essential relations) of all things in creation is the moral law (S. 29, iii, 8, 5, 9; ii, 5; S. 20, i, 2, 4; S. 16, intro., 2).[12] However, as the nature and relations of things are willed and created by God, the ultimate ground of the moral law is God's will (S. 29, iii, 6-9). Wesley must be understood against this background when he asserts that the moral law is "supreme, unchangeable reason . . . unalterable rectitude" (S. 29, ii, 5; S. 20, i, 2, 4). He can also express the thought of the law's ultimate ground in terms of love. "Love existed from all eternity, in God, the great ocean of love." When God created His children He made love the law of their existence (S. 31, ii, 3, 6). Is the eternal law of creation identical with the eternal law of love? Wesley doubtless means that the law of love is the hidden center of the law of creation. But this relation needs further investigation, since Wesley tends to use the two formulations with different parts of his order of salvation.

God first of all gave this law to the angels, not for any restraint of evil, but to provide an opportunity for a continual increase in their happiness, "seeing every instance of obedience to that law would both add to the perfection of their nature, and entitle them to a higher reward" (S. 29, i, 1-2; S. 31, ii, 3). The giving of the law is here seen to be ultimately grounded in God's eternal supralapsarian decision to create a creation of increasing holiness.

The same moral law was engraved upon man's heart in creation, so that it would never be far off or hard to understand (S. 29, i, 3; S. 20, i, 2; S. 5, i, 1-3). Again, Wesley can express the same thought in terms of love filling man's heart in paradise (S. 31, ii, 5). But Wesley remarks that in addition to this law of man's being, "against which, perhaps, he could not sin directly," there was one "superadded" positive law: "Thou shalt not eat of the fruit . . ." As has been shown, the Wesleyan fall occurs in relation to this revealed law, and not in relation to the moral law engraved upon man's being (S. 5, i, 3).

With Adam, on the basis of the moral law, God established a covenant of works, i.e., God accepted Adam on the condition of Adam's perfect, universal obedience to the law. But this covenant applied only to Adam, and only before the fall (S. 30, ii, 3; S. 5, i, 2; S. 6, i, 1-6, 11-14).[13]

One insufficiently noticed aspect of the moral law requires special mention: it has its effect, it is fulfilled, either by obedience, or by bearing its punishment. This distinction will underlie Wesley's penal substitution theory of atonement (Mt 5:18; S. 30, iii, 2; W. X, 324).[14]

2. *The partial re-inscription of the law on man's heart after the fall:* Later, Wesley will speak of a subjective re-inscription of the law as an element in the believer's salvation. Here he means something else: an objective re-inscription of the moral law in the ruined creature, as an act of prevenient grace immediately following the fall. God does it because He is, even at this point, "being reconciled to man through the Son of His love." It is done for all men (S. 29, i, 4). But it is not as in the beginning. Now

man needs God's help to see the law of his own being. God gives this help through conscience, "that true light which enlightens every man that cometh into the world" (S. 29, i, 5; Jn 1:9). And this light is clear enough to condemn all, even those without the written law (Ro 2:12). But to comprehend the height and depth of this re-inscribed moral law, the revealing work of the Holy Spirit, given in salvation, is required (S. 29, i, 6).

Wesley teaches that even this first re-inscription belongs to the giving of the covenant of grace. Christ, by His sacrificial death, ended the covenant of works, and "purchased" for us "a better covenant" (S. 6, intro., 3; Heb 8:8, 10:29, 13:20). Henceforth, the condition of fellowship with God is not obedience but faith, although it must be the faith which works by love (S. 6, i, 1-14). The ambiguity here—a covenant of grace which is yet to include the Mosaic dispensation—can better be discussed below. In so far as this prevenient re-inscription of the law belongs to the covenant of grace, the general characteristic of that covenant would presumably apply: the place of works is not before but after our acceptance with God (S. 30, ii, 3-4). The key difference between the Mosaic and gospel dispensations of the covenant of grace would then concern the method of our acceptance, obedience to the ceremonial law in the one case, in Christ in the other.

3. *The giving of the written law to Moses:* Because man, in spite of the re-inscribed moral law, still did not obey, God chose Israel, and gave her a more perfect knowledge of the law whose principal points "He wrote on two tablets of stone." They were to teach others this law, and thus the moral law was to be made known to all, even those who did not know God (S. 29, i, 5-6). Wesley emphasizes that the decalogue contains the moral law, "the ten commandments being only the substance of the law of nature" (S. 20, i, 2; Ro 2:14, 3:9).

But the law given to Moses also included the ceremonial law. This Wesley understands to be a temporary measure, designed to last until Christ came, to serve as a restraint for a disobedient and stiffnecked people (S. 20, i, 2). The more grievous parts of it were given as a punishment for the national sin of idolatry. However, this ceremonial law in its entirety was also a type of Christ (Gal 3:16, 24, 19, I Tim 1:8).[15]

4. *Jesus Christ's re-establishment, re-proclamation, and full re-inscription of the law:* Whether it differentiates covenants or dispensations, Christ's coming *re-established* the moral law, i.e., put it on a new foundation (S. 29, intro., 3). Both His death and His resurrection were necessary to secure a new relation to the law for us, and to prove His authority as lawgiver (S. 29, intro., 2; S. 6, intro., 3).

At least four elements of this re-establishment may be distinguished in Wesley's several presentations. First, Christ changes the law's relation to us. Neither ceremonial nor moral law is any longer valid as a means of acceptance with God, although Christ does confirm the moral law as having a valid relation to the life of faith (Gal 2:16, Ro 3:31). Second, Christ transforms the demand of the law into a promise: "The very same words, considered in different respects, are parts both of the law and of the gospel: if they are considered as commandments, they are parts of the law; if as promises, of the gospel" (S. 20, ii, 2-3). The re-established law thus becomes a confirmation of hope, that Christians will receive grace upon grace until they are "in actual possession of the fulness of His promises" (S. 29, iv, 4). Third, Christ, in re-establishing the law, makes it an indispensable means of keeping Christians close to Himself.[16] It throws continual light upon remaining sin, and forces the Christian to Christ's cleansing atonement (S. 29, iv, 4, 7, 9). The law is quite literally a "blessed instrument of the grace of God," "our glory and joy, next to the cross of Christ" (S. 29, iv, 8). "He alone gives that pardon and life which the law shows the want of, but cannot give" (Ro 10:4). This point approaches the center of the "full spiritual meaning" of the law about which Wesley speaks so much (II Cor 3:17).[17] Fourth, Christ changes our motive for obedience from the legal principle of fear to the evangelical principle of love (S. 30, iii, 3-4). Christ does this through the atone-ment, where Christ gives to faith the divine love which awakens in man the love of God and neighbor that fulfils the law (S. 31, iii, 3-4). Thereby, Christ makes it possible for us to do what was before entirely beyond our power, namely, to "perform ... a willing and universal obedience" to the law (S. 30, iii, 3).

It may be asked whether Christ gives a new content (love) to the law. Though Christ's fulfilment of the law is an act of perfect love, Wesley probably intends this to be understood as a confirmation of the eternal law of love, which in itself, apart from any explicit relation to Christ, is identical with the eternal law of creation. Strictly speaking, then, Christ reveals what the hidden heart of the moral law has always been. It is, however, open to question whether the moral law's strict demand is main-tained in this new revelation. Love is an obligation "which can never be sufficiently discharged; but yet if this is rightly per-formed, it discharges all the rest" (Ro 13:8-10). In S. 20, iv, 11 Wesley says that Christian acts are "estimated before God only by the tempers from which they spring" (cf. Heb 11:17). Wesley also makes clear that perfection can be understood as purity of intention, and was so understood by him from 1725 onward (W. XI, 444). As will be shown, this preoccupation with the "intention" of a moral act raises a question about the justice of final justification.

Christ, then, not only re-established, He also *re-proclaimed* the law. The "great Author" Himself "condescended to give man-kind [an] authentic comment on all the essential branches" of the law in the Sermon on the Mount (S. 20, i, 4). Moreover, Christ delivered the law in its fulness, with a completeness and depth never known before (S. 31, i, 2; S. 16, intro., 7). That is primarily what is meant when it is said that Christ "fulfilled" the law: namely, that He came to establish it in its fulness, to place in full view what was obscure in it, to declare its purity and spirituality, and this He did both in His words and in His life and deeds (S. 20, i, 3; Mt 5:17).

And, finally, the Christ who re-established and re-proclaimed the law, *re-inscribes* it fully into believing hearts (S. 29, iii, 10). Immediately after the fall, God, reconciled by His Son, had re-inscribed the law on man's heart "in some measure . . . although not as in the beginning" (S. 29, i, 4), and this may be taken as an important element in Wesley's understanding of prevenient grace. But now, given through Christ, and effected through the Holy Spirit, God's promise becomes effective for His believing children, and the law is fully written on their hearts (S. 29, i, 6; S. 20, ii, 3; S. 24, 21). This means that Christ opens their eyes to the true, full spiritual meaning of the law, and gives them inward experience of whatever He has commanded (Heb 8:10). Wesley is speaking of sanctification here (Heb 8:12), and it is true to his intention to say that the believer's sanctification is the point where the law is fulfilled in the usual sense of the word. Faith opens the treasures of God's love; our answering love to Him and the neighbor fulfils the law (S. 20, ii, 3; S. 29, iii, 12). Moreover, this law, written on the heart, is true Christian liberty, not only from Jewish ceremonies and legal justification, but, and that is "infinitely more," from the power of sin (S. 29, iv, 10).

5. *The last judgment by the standard of the law:* Wesley repeatedly emphasizes that the moral law will be the rule whereby Christ will judge the world in the last day (S. 29, iv, 8; Heb 12:25; S. 16, intro., 2). And thus the continuity of the moral order is maintained from age to age.

### c. Christ's Prophetic Relation to the Law

It remains to be emphasized that in all this legal *Heilsgeschichte* there is a surprisingly thoroughgoing Christological aspect, which it is certainly appropriate to ground in the legal aspect of Christ's prophetic work, although important elements belong to the priestly and kingly work as well.

Christ is, first of all, the original "Author" of the law. This is not inferred only on the basis of the prominent Christological element in Wesley's doctrine of creation; it is Wesley's explicit teaching (S. 29, iv, 8; Jn 1:4; S. 20, i, 4; S. 16, intro., 2). The Trinitarian idea doubtless underlies these assertions (Mk 12:29). The only serious qualification here would arise if there were no Christological ground for the assertion which underlies the relation of law and love: "Love existed from eternity, in God, the great ocean of love" (S. 31, ii, 3).

Christ, after the fall, provides the ground for a new covenant which brings all men, quite objectively, into a new relation to the law: the conditional offer of salvation to every man no longer hinges on the law, but on faith in Christ. This reconciliation is, of course, grounded in Christ's priestly act, but its first fruit belongs to the prophetic office: the partial re-inscription of the law in sinful man's heart. Christ is also "the light" which reveals this partially re-inscribed law to men; Wesley can refer to this light both as conscience and, in the words of John 1:9, as the Logos, Himself (S. 105, i, 5; S. 50, i, 2).

Moreover, Christ is the giver of the decalogue to Moses: "It was therefore the Son of God who delivered the law to Moses, under the character of Jehovah" (Ac 7:35, 30, Ro 9:4, but cf. also Heb 1:4). Christ is, likewise, typified by the ceremonial law, if not by the law as a whole.

In His earthly ministry, death, and resurrection, Christ re-established the law, giving it a new relation to our justification (gospel dispensation), a new significance (promise), a new function (to keep us close to Christ), and a new motivation (love). He likewise re-proclaimed the law, showing its full spiritual meaning ("fulfilling it"). And, through the Holy Spirit, Christ performs a kingly re-inscription of the law on believing hearts, thus accomplishing their sanctification and liberation from the power of sin.

And, finally, it is Christ who, in the last day, will judge the world by the law.

On the basis of these findings, it must be flatly asserted: there is no point in the elaborate history of the law where Wesley has not attempted to provide an explicit Christological foundation.

## 4. Comment

It cannot be denied that Wesley's doctrine of Christ's prophetic office, as a whole, puts the emphasis on the law. In part, this impression is unjust, for the Wesleyan Christ is also the preacher of grace, both in his own earthly ministry and through Israel and the church to all ages. But the impression remains, only strengthened by the attempt to emphasize the moral as against the ceremonial law, that in this twofold prophetic ministry of Christ the element which Luther emphasizes, that God's Word is the promise of grace, stands somewhat in the background. Is this Wesley's real intention?

The implicit question can perhaps be more sharply formulated: is the lawgiver Christ the priestly Christ? Wesley goes to great lengths to point out that in Christ alone do we have the revelation of God. It is clear that this exclusiveness applies to the gospel of grace; does it also apply to the revelation of the moral demand?

Wesley wants to say "Yes" to this question. He provides an elaborate Christological foundation for the legal revelation. He wants to assert that Christ's prophetic and priestly works are one mediatorial work of one Mediator. If the Logos reveals the original nature and relations of all things, Wesley insists that He is only revealing what He Himself has created.

But it is precisely Wesley's eagerness to keep the original nature and relations of things in the picture also, alongside the Christological foundation, which gives occasion for question. The assigning of a Christological foundation to the law does not necessarily mean that the law becomes less abstract or speculative; it could mean that a Christ-speculation has been introduced as well. The crucial point about the law-giving Logos, who speaks in the Sermon on the Mount, is that He "knoweth whereof we are made and understands our inmost frame; [He] knows how we stand related to God, to one another, to every creature which God hath made, and consequently, how to adapt every law prescribed to all the circumstances wherein He hath placed us" (S. 16, intro., 2).

What, exactly, does that "consequently" mean? What is the relation between the lawgiver-Logos and the "circumstances" of creation? Are His "knowledge" and "understanding" the active source of the circumstances of creation, or are they, conceivably, only His qualification to be the revealer of a moral order before which both He and we stand? This problem is of crucial importance for understanding Wesley's sanctification doctrine, which turns on the concept of holiness. Does the Wesleyan holiness derive from Christ's revelation of what holiness is, or does it find in Christ a confirmation for an idea of holiness whose content has been learned, possibly only in part, elsewhere? It has often been pointed out how closely the Wesleyan concept of holiness is related to the Puritan ethic. Is the essential Wesleyan message of holiness bound to this Puritan ethic, or is it capable of creative new expressions today? Are the three "General Rules" to continue to be ignored in Methodist churches because of their eighteenth-century illustrations? The creativity of the Wesleyan tradition of holiness depends on the fidelity with which each generation learns anew what holiness means from Jesus Christ, and solely from Him. The question therefore concerns the power and relevance of the central Wesleyan concern for sanctification. Wesley agrees that Christ is the power which effects holiness, but is He also its source?

Wesley answers by saying that to refer to creation is to refer to the work of the same God who reveals the law, and that therefore a thing is right because God wills it, rather than willed because it is right (S. 29, iii, 6-9). But does this necessarily mean that creation is entirely subordinated to the Logos, and especially to the living Word of God, as the foundation of moral obligation? Wesley could also mean that God, having once created what was good, must Himself thereafter come to terms with this entity when He reveals what is good. In so far, then, as creation stands as a semi-independent term between God and man, the holiness which consists in realization of good nature could mean an abstract, code-conforming holiness, based upon some natural perception of what nature is supposed to be, rather than a holiness which is grounded in obedience to God's ever-contemporary, ever-free decision. Such a notion may actually underlie Wesley's curious qualification, in the same passage, that, notwithstanding, "in every particular case," God wills a thing "because it is right, agreeable to the fitness of things, to the relation wherein they stand."

Wesley thus seems to say: in principle, the moral law depends upon God's will in creation; nevertheless, in particular cases— and they are what count in ethics—God, the revealer of the law, looks first of all not to His own free will, but to creation, and conforms His direct command to what is established there. Creation is God's wholly free act; the revealing of the moral law is not in the same sense a free act, but rather a confirmation of a prior act. It may be asked whether such a self-faithfulness is not essential in a God whose command is to be honored. But that puts the matter exactly backwards. God's living will does confirm the created order. But this does not mean that God thereby accredits His will to us, who know from other sources what our nature ought to be. It is rather a wonder and a miracle that God freely, from moment to moment, decides for the continued existence of His creation, and provides for it through the revelation of His will. We do not believe God's command because it confirms nature; we believe that what God commands is a reaffirmation, a re-establishment of the nature we no longer see. There is a way from God's command to the praise of nature; there is no way from a knowledge of nature to an accreditation of God's command. The question is whether we are naturally placed, as men, to know more about the "fitness of things" than Christ through His Word has revealed to us.

Does Wesley's attempt to give a Christological foundation to the law answer this question? As has been shown, Christ originally gives the law, and He gives both reformulations of it, on Sinai and in Galilee. The Christ who does that is most certainly, for Wesley, the same Christ who sacrifices Himself in order to change our relation to the law. Thus far Wesley's position holds: the prophetic and priestly Christs are one, and the law is grounded in the one mediatorial act of Jesus Christ. But it must be added that, once given, this law acquires a kind of status of its own, over against the giver, as the embodiment of the good. Moreover, this strange figure among the original dramatis personae of salvation retains to the end a semi-independent role alongside the priestly work of Christ. That work may alter the law's relation to us, its significance for us, its function in the drama, and even the motivation and means for its fulfilment. But the law's content seems to be fixed, eternal, and immutable, an order with which God Himself must come to terms. Therefore, perhaps, this law remains to the end as the rule of the last judgment. It is not Christ alone who judges there, but Christ and this law. In this form the problem of God's separable justice and mercy will continue to the last day, and there will then be for some, at least, a judgment by this law alone, a judgment in which God's mercy will have no part, while for others there will be a final justification, the justice of which is not beyond question. "Whenever, therefore, God acts as a Governor, as a rewarder, or punisher, he no longer acts as mere Sovereign, by His own sole will and pleasure; but as an impartial Judge, guided in all things by invariable justice" (W. X, 362).

In this light, Wesley's idea of the content of holiness—as distinct from its significance, function, motivation, and relation to our salvation—is such that it can be, in part, abstracted from the person and revelation of Christ, even though its origin may ultimately be in Him, and His is the power which effects it. And to this understanding of the content of holiness corresponds the fact that for Wesley sanctification is not primarily a participation in Christ who, as Paul says, is also our sanctification (I Cor 1:30), but rather such a relation to Christ as allows His Spirit to establish in us a "temper," a more abstract, stylized kind of holiness. Wesley here follows no new path; it is the unhappy path of Protestant orthodoxy in general. Indeed, Wesley here makes his most significant departure from his own most characteristic path: from the cross to holiness. It is in this departure that the danger of a periodic identification of Wesleyan holiness with a puritan, socialist, existentialist, or any other stylized morality is greatest.

It can be argued that this austere picture of the law is used by Wesley primarily in connection with his doctrines of repentance and first justification. It is, indeed, possible that Wesley does permit a Christological redefinition of the law's content in relation to the doctrines of sanctification, perfection, and final justification. Wesley teaches that love fulfils the moral law, and that Christ is the source of this revelation. Moreover, he means by love, not primarily a participation in the being of Christ's love, but an inherent "temper," "affection," or "intention" in man, himself. In the chapter on the priestly work the question is raised whether the severity of the moral law's just demand is not, in fact, diminished in the Wesleyan doctrine of final justification. Here it can only be noted that the moral law retains its semi-independence from Christ in both cases: there is apparently no Christological redefinition of the law of creation in relation to the doctrines of both repentances and first justification; and where there is a redefinition, in relation to the doctrines of sanctification, perfection, and final justification, the independence of the love demanded from the holiness of Christ's active obedience is the root of a far-reaching question about the justice of man's final justification.

Would this picture remain the same if Wesley could see the moral law, and not only the ceremonial law, as a type of Christ, genuinely consummated, fulfilled, and redefined, rather than simply reinforced, in Him? The interest in Wesley's doctrine of the law lies in the fact that he really does intend the law to lead us to Christ, and to keep us there, with Him who gives us "a new commandment." Of this semi-independent moral law, Wesley once writes: "Let it be thy glory and joy, next to the cross of Christ" (S. 29, iv, 8). In practice, if not in theology, this moral law is not an autonomous figure in the drama of salvation, but a servant of the main figure. That does not have to mean what Wesley feared: that the demand for active holiness will be softened. On the contrary, it means open ears, a grateful heart, and ready hands for the One who shows the new forms of love required for each "particular case." Christ's fulfilment of the law is indeed finished, but in such a way that Christ asks each believer to let his every particular act of obedience be made contemporary with and conformed to Christ's own Good Friday and Easter. When Christ is permitted to be the central figure in the doctrine of sanctification, He will, as Wesley also saw, lead us to the law—but only Christ will do it, and only to His law (S. 29, iv, 7).

There remains one final question, concerning Wesley's praise of the law. It is "the immediate offspring . . . of God," "the fairest offspring of the everlasting Father." "What is the law but divine virtue and wisdom assuming visible form?" (S. 29, iii, 3; ii, 6, 4.) "It is God made manifest in our flesh" (S. 29, iii, 12).

This law is an incorruptible picture of the High and Holy One that inhabiteth eternity. It is He whom, in His essence, no man hath seen, or can see, made visible to men and angels. It is the face of God unveiled; God manifested to His creatures as they are able to bear it; manifested to give, not to destroy life—that they may see God and live. It is the heart of God disclosed to man. Yea, in some sense, we may apply to this law what the Apostle says of His Son: it is ἀπαύγασμα τῆς δόξης, καὶ χαρακτὴρ τῆς ὑποστάσεως αὐτοῦ —the streaming forth, or out-beaming of His glory, the express image of His person (S. 29, ii, 3).

Is Christ the only-begotten of the Father? Wesley would vigorously oppose this suggestion, on the ground of Christological doctrine, and point to his assertion that the law is grounded in a created, not a begotten, order. But in this glorification of the law, and this bestowing on it of a semi-independent status, is there not a real danger, certainly not of two Christs, but of limiting Christ in order to emphasize sanctification? Granting the polemical situation which once evoked this heavy emphasis on the law, is it not possible that Wesley's doctrine of sanctification would be strengthened, not weakened, if the law remained throughout the servant of Christ?

1. In light of the wealth of reference to this theme, it seems unnecessarily limiting to say, with Lerch *(Heil und Heiligung,* p. 80), that Wesley used this expression only as a metaphor, on the ground that prophets proclaim while Jesus is Himself the preparer and the content of the good news. But Jesus also proclaims. The fact that He also prepares and is the gospel finds its place in Lutheran and Reformed doctrines of the prophetic office, as well as in Wesley's.

2. Wesley can express this ground in various ways. Characteristic is his assertion that the Son's revealing work parallels that of the Father. At one and the same time the Father shows and does, and the Son sees and does (Jn 5:20), in which sense it is probably best to understand the assertion that Christ's doctrine is "immediately infused" in Him by the Father (Jn 7:16). In one place, Wesley explains this subordination by reference to the two natures: revelation is given by the Father to Jesus in "His holy, glorified humanity, as the great Prophet of the Church" (Rev 1:1), and Jesus then makes it known to His servants. Thus it is God's words that Jesus speaks (Jn 8:47, 3:33, 1:1). Wesley can, then, emphasize that Christ comes into the world as a messenger sent from God, bearing His Word (Ac 10:36, Jn 8:26; S. 20, iii, 1, 7), who, because He descends from heaven, can show us the way to heaven (S. 16, intro., 3). An important Wesleyan theme is also touched when the emphasis is put on Christ as the image of God, who "exactly exhibits the Father to us" (II Cor 4:4, Col 1:15).

3. A partial list of references to Old Testament "types" may be recorded for further study: (a) *Types strictly referring to Christ:* Mt 1:21, 12:39, 26:26, Mk 9:7, Jn 1:29, 8:56, 9:7, 18:1, 19:36, I Cor 5:7, 10:3-4, Gal 3:19, 3:24, Heb 1:5, 5:4, 5:10, 7:1ff., 8:1, 8:2, 9:2, 9:19, 9:22, 9:23, 12:2. (b) *Types of other things:* Lk 1:32, 17:31, 22:16, Ac 2:4, 15:20, Ro 9:8, Col 2:11, Heb 9:9, 9:24, 10:1, Rev 11:19. (c) *Concerning Wesley's understanding of "types":* Lk 24:44, Jn 8:56, Ro 9:6, I Cor 12:8, 14:6, II Cor 3:16, Gal 3:8, Heb 8:5.

4. Wesley notes with approval that the apostles often content themselves with rendering the "general sense" of the Old Testament in their quotations (Mt 2:6). He cautions that the Book of Revelation often speaks figuratively (Rev 21:14, 5:1), and advises that we "neither understand them too literally and grossly, nor go too far from

the natural force of the words" (Rev 21:15). Occasionally, he can claim that Christ does not intend a command to be taken literally, e.g., to wash another's feet, or to give the cloak as well as the coat (Jn 13:14, Mt 5:40-41).

Wesley's rules for interpreting scripture include at least the following. Take the literal sense, if not contrary to other texts, in which case interpret the obscure text by the plain (*Letters*, III, 129. Cf. S. 16, intro., 6 where absurdity is also discussed as a ground for inquiring beyond the literal meaning). Have a constant eye to "the analogy of faith, the connection and harmony there is between [the] grand fundamental doctrines" (W. XIV, 253). Wesley names as "grand fundamental doctrines, original sin, justification by faith, the new birth, inward and outward holiness." Deal with the scripture as a whole (II Tim 2:15). Use the scripture with prayer, since "scripture can only be understood through the same Spirit whereby it was given" (W. XIV, 253).

5. An instructive example of theological depth in Wesley's understanding of scripture is found in the note on how the Book of Revelation came to be written (Rev 1:1-2). The author of this book is Jesus, Himself, who received this revelation from God in "His holy, glorified humanity, as the great Prophet of the Church." (Cf. also the introduction to Romans in the *Notes*.) Jesus makes this revelation known to John by His angel, a "creature" who in Revelation 19:10 declares that he works "by the same Spirit which inspired the prophets of old." This process is summed up in Revelation 2:1 in the words, "Christ dictated to him every word."

Note carefully: (1) This revelation is both received and given by Christ. (2) The doctrine of the Trinity is transparently presupposed in both operations. Revelation is received by the Son, whose subordination is here specifically assigned to His human nature. It is given to John through the Spirit who must, therefore, stand in some procession from the Son. Those Trinitarian relations are implicit here. (3) This background, at least, is presupposed in Wesley's "dictation" theory of scriptural inspiration.

Why this Trinitarian apparatus of revelation? Is Wesley only trying to find an explanation for the text, or is he here reflecting his own doctrine of revelation? It is only fair to presuppose the latter, and press ahead with some questions.

Does it do violence to Wesley's intention to say that Christ's subordination is a safeguard against thinking that Christ is some universal principle of revelation or eternal law? Instead, the ground of revelation is the living relation of Father and Son. What is more, Christ's sub-ordination, as has been seen, belongs to His mediatorial obedience to the Father's eternal decree. This means that revelation is grounded in the dynamic concept of God's will to save, and not only in some static view of the divine nature.

If that inference is correct, is it not appropriate to relate to it Wesley's contention that only in Christ has God revealed Himself to His creatures "at any time" (S. 62, ii, 1)? I.e., there is no other source for revelation than the One who has *received* it in this unique Trini-tarian subordination to the Father. Would this then be the underlying reason for Wesley's concern to give a Christological grounding to his doctrine of prevenient grace and conscience (S. 85, iii, 4; Jn 1:9; S. 105, i, 3, 5), as well as to the universally known moral law (*supra*, pp. 100-101)?

The other side of Wesley's teaching—that Christ also *gives* revela-tion to us through His Spirit—would then signify that our receiving of it is also a living encounter, somehow bound into the living relations of Father, Son, and Spirit. In that case, revelation is not simply learning spiritual truths from a deified source beyond the reaches of critical reason and common sense. As a matter of fact, Wesley inserts at precisely this point a warning against idolizing the "creature" (Rev 19:10). Revelation cannot be abstracted from a living relation with God. Just as Spirit, Son, and Father are one in the Trinity, so what we receive and the way we receive it are indivisibly bound together with what Christ has received and the way in which He has both received it and gives it. In other words, our knowledge of God through scripture is really divine but living knowledge.

If these questions are legitimate on Wesleyan presuppositions, is it then right to fasten on the purely static aspects of his so-called "dictation" theory of inspiration? For Wesley scripture was no static residue of divine "typewriting" as Lawson (*Selections* p. 24) suggests, but a living Word, given by divine condescension into the already imperfect forms of human language, ideas, and conceptions, and therefore requiring responsible, workmanlike interpretation. Could not the highly-colored word "dictation" also be taken to emphasize the encounter in which revelation takes place? And could not human "passivity" in this undertaking (II Pet 1:21) refer to the completeness with which revelation is grounded in grace?

Wesley would not necessarily have asked all these questions, or drawn all these inferences. Indeed, in his haste, he usually gave no hint of such depths to his doctrine of scripture. But the fact is that

Wesley interpreted scripture. It is therefore asked here whether the above questions do violence to any of Wesley's principal presuppositions, and whether they are not legitimate, necessary questions and inferences in the context of present-day Wesley interpretation.

6. The inner witness is usually used in early Methodism to refer to the inner assurance that "I, even, I" have been saved. The reference of this witness here to Christ's Word indicates an objective side of conversion which Wesley himself may have taken more seriously than some of his early and late followers. In describing his own conversion experience Wesley continues the famous words about his heart being strangely warmed, with an immediate reference to the objective ground of the experience: "I felt I did trust in Christ, Christ alone for salvation: and an assurance was given me that He had taken away *my* sins, even *mine*, and saved *me* from the law of sin and death" (*Journal*, May 24, 1738). The accent does not fall alone on the warm heart. It falls with equal if not greater emphasis on the fact that Wesley was now convinced that he, even he, belonged to the world of Romans 8. In this respect, Christ's prophetic work through the Holy Spirit underlies the Methodist doctrine of conversion.

7. In John 14:17 the further explanation is given that fallen man lacks spiritual senses. The restoration of spiritual senses will become important in the Wesleyan doctrine of regeneration (S. 39, ii, 4). Wesley's religious "Lockeanism" has been the subject of comment: C. E. Mason, "John Wesley's Doctrine of Salvation" (unpublished Master's thesis, New York, 1940), pp. 43, 54; Umphrey Lee, *John Wesley and Modern Religion* (Nashville, 1936), p. 56. See Wesley's own late (1781) "Remarks on Mr. Locke's Essay on Human Understanding" (W. XIII, 455-64).

8. One need only struggle with the pages of formal logic in Wesley's polemics to realize that restored reason belongs, for him, to the sanctified life. It is of interest that among the textbooks which Wesley himself produced for the Kingswood school, there is, in addition to English, French, Latin, Greek, and Hebrew grammars, also a Compendium of Logic.

9. Good studies of this theme in Wesleyan theology are surprisingly rare, considering its importance for both justification and sanctification. Lindström (*Wesley and Sanctification*, pp. 75-82) gives a good summary of the main points in Wesley's teaching. Lerch (*Heil und Heiligung*, pp. 44-59) gives, in addition, a most stimulating analysis.

10. Sugden (*Standard Sermons*, ii, 39; i, 399, 408) corrects Wesley

here on the grounds that there is no such distinction in the Mosaic law, and that making the distinction tends to cloud the "typical and prophetic functions" of the ceremonial law. John Lawson, *Notes on Wesley's Forty-four Sermons* (London, 1952), pp. 151-52, 185 also feels that the distinction must be abandoned. Does either of Wesley's commentators realize the extent to which the scriptural foundation for Wesley's doctrine of the law, and therefore of justification and sanctification, is related to this distinction? Notwithstanding, Sugden and Lawson are right to reject the distinction on biblical grounds. What is more, as the following will attempt to show, Wesley's emphasis on the distinction is probably a symptom of a more fundamental problem: the semi-independence of the moral law from Christ, whom the ceremonial law typifies. Lerch *(Heil und Heiligung, p. 50)*, incidentally, has a useful note on the difference between Wesley's and Calvin's uses of this distinction.

11. Lerch, *Heil und Heiligung*, p. 57 (translated).

12. As Sugden points out *(Standard Sermons, i, 276; ii, 46)*, Wesley is here using a moral criterion much used by the Deists. It is all the more curious that in an early reference to those who "ground religion in the eternal fitness of things," Wesley has sharp words for those who, with this "cloud of terms," lay another foundation than the scriptural one for Christian duty! (S. 13, ii, 3 from 1733.)

13. This doctrine of a double covenant is a piece of Puritan speculation (Westminster Confession, Art. VII) which has been deservedly criticized in Wesley. Sugden *(Standard Sermons, i, 131; ii, 65)* takes strong exception ("a theological fiction"), and somewhat more mildly, so does Lawson *(Notes, pp. 55-56)*. Cf. Lerch *(Heil und Heiligung, pp. 44 ff., 30 ff.)*.

14. Cf. Lindström, *Wesley and Sanctification*, p. 73.

15. One of the less clear points in Wesley's doctrine of the law is the precise character of the Mosaic dispensation, and indeed, of the covenants and dispensations in general.

There is some evidence that Wesley intends to follow the outline of the Westminster Confession, Art. VII: two covenants: a covenant of works with Adam, and a covenant of grace with mankind after the fall; and, within the covenant of grace, two dispensations or modes of administration: the Mosaic or Jewish dispensation, and the gospel dispensation (S. 6, intro., 1; Ro 9:4). Wesley often employs, in this connection, a third distinction: within the Mosaic dispensation there are two kinds of law: ceremonial and moral (Gal 3:23-25, Ro 3:20, Ac 13:39, 15:5, I Tim 1:8; S. 29, intro., 2).

But Wesley's usage of the terms "covenant" and "dispensation" is far from precise, as he himself admits (Ro 9:4). Often the terms are plainly synonyms (Gal 5:4, II Cor 3:6). Frequently, throughout the crucial Sermons 29-31, he distinguishes three terms: "the ceremonial law," "the Mosaic dispensation," and "the moral law" (S. 29, iv, 4; S. 30, iii, 2; S. 31, intro., 2). And the problem ceases to be merely terminological when we read that in Christ "the Mosaic dispensation" has been abolished (Heb 8:10, II Cor 3:13, Mt 11:13, I Jn 2:8).

If the "Mosaic dispensation" means simply "the ceremonial law," as it often does, then there is no problem. Wesley emphatically teaches that "our Lord did indeed come to destroy, to dissolve, and utterly abolish" the ceremonial law (S. 20, i, 1). But it is doubtful whether this identification is Wesley's considered intention.

The problem arises because, as indicated above, the Mosaic dispensation, which is abolished, contains the moral as well as the ceremonial law, and the moral law is not abolished. It is a constant element in the entire *Heilsgeschichte,* in both covenants and both dispensations. Wesley, therefore, must intend to say that the believer's relation to the moral law is different under the two dispensations of the covenant of grace. What could that difference of relation be?

The grand distinction is between the moral law as an invalid means of justification, and as a valid guide for sanctification. But this is Wesley's distinction for the two covenants. The term "dispensation" ought therefore to refer to a distinction in the believer's relation to the moral law within the covenant of grace, i.e., within the limits of justification by faith alone.

There are various hints of such a distinction. Wesley's most comprehensive characterization of the two dispensations is given in the note on Hebrews 8:8 where, characteristically, he speaks of the gospel dispensation as a "new covenant"! "It is new in many respects, though not as to the substance of it: (1) being ratified by the death of Christ; (2) freed from those burdensome rites and ceremonies; (3) containing a more full and clear account of spiritual religion; (4) attended with larger influences of the Spirit; (5) extended to all men; and (6) never to be abolished."

In so far as there is a systematic use of terms, it can be formulated thus:

1. *Covenant of works* (applying to Adam alone): moral law as norm, obedience as condition of fellowship with God.
2. *Covenant of grace:* moral law as norm, faith as condition of fellowship with God.

a. *Mosaic dispensation:* moral law as norm, faith in ceremonial mediation, leading to obedience of the letter, as condition of fellowship.

b. *Gospel dispensation:* moral law as norm, faith in Christ-mediation—whose authenticity is attested by spiritual, loving obedience—as the condition of fellowship with God.

Wesley's claim that the Mosaic dispensation is abolished then means: this particular form of mediatorial relation to the moral law is abolished. Hence the inaccurate abbreviation is sometimes possible: the Mosaic dispensation is the ceremonial law. Notice here that the moral significance of scripture is radically relativized: its unique significance is on the religious level, with reference to the form of mediation; on the moral level, scripture merely confirms the moral law, which is consistently present in all covenants and dispensations.

Perhaps a conjecture may be added about Wesley's tendency to use "covenant" and "dispensation" interchangeably. Here again Wesley's two-sidedness may be at work. When Wesley is thinking about justification he wants the sharp distinction of the two "covenants": under the covenant of grace not even obedience to the moral law will justify (Gal 2:16, Ro 3:20, II Cor 3:6; S. 29, intro., 2). On the other hand, he uses "dispensation" to refer to the same distinction when he wants to emphasize sanctification, and especially in scriptural exegesis: (1) When he is thinking about sanctification, or confronting antinomians, he wants a way of speaking about the distinction between the old and new life which emphasizes the continuity of the moral law, while recognizing the believer's changed relation to it. The thought of "dispensations," emphasizing mediation, does this. (2) When he is trying to interpret the New Testament's more negative sayings about the law, he finds the distinction between ceremonial and moral law, embodied in the notion of "dispensations," useful. (Acts 15:5-29 provides an instructive example.) What is rejected is not the law, but the ceremonial relationship to the law.

It must be concluded that Wesley's use of "covenant" and "dispensation" is imprecise: the major distinguishing mark, that we are justified by faith alone, tends to be the differentiation between both covenants and both dispensations.

16. This sentence summarizes Wesley's main teaching about the three uses of the law (S. 29, iv): (1) to convince sinners of sin, (2) to bring the sinner to life, unto Christ, (3) to keep the Christian alive by keeping him with Christ. Lutheran orthodoxy had spoken of four uses: (1) political, or restraint of evil, (2) elenchtical, or manifesta-

tion and reproof of sins, (3) pedagogical, or indirect compulsion of the sinner to go to Christ, and (4) didactic, or direction of moral actions (Schmid, *Doctrinal Theology*, pp. 515-16), the last three of which may be correlated with Wesley's uses, as Lerch *(Heil und Heiligung*, pp. 50-51) points out. Calvin teaches three uses *(Institutes*, II, vii, 6-12): (1) to lead to Christ, (2) to curb sinners, (3) to instruct the elect, of which the first and third correspond to Wesley's three uses. But Wesley elsewhere also teaches a political use (Gal 3:19), and perhaps a further use in the protection of the church (Mt 21:33).

17. A more organic relation between moral and ceremonial law than Wesley often teaches appears in a difficult passage (S. 29, iv, 5) where, significantly enough, Wesley is trying to explain how the law leads us to Christ. He says, in effect, that as the Israelites could not live with the law apart from Aaron's priestly act, so Christians cannot live with the law apart from Christ's priestly act. Wesley emphasizes the parallel: Aaron is "the type of our great High-Priest"; the Israelite relation between ceremonial and moral law is fulfilled in Christ's relation to our sanctification. But this immediately questions the importance of Wesley's distinction between moral and ceremonial law. Indeed, in the light of their organic relation, is not the ceremonial law, like the moral law, fulfilled rather than abolished in Christ? Conversely, is it not possible that the moral law, like the ceremonial law, is a "type of Christ" (cf. Heb 10:1, Mt 11:13, Ro 10:4, II Cor 3:6), i.e., leads to and is fulfilled in Him, with the consequence that the believer finds not only atonement but also the concrete form which his sanctification is to take "in Christ," and not in some moral law abstracted from Him? Such a possibility was ruled out by Wesley, as will be seen in the study of Christ's obedience, because it smacked of the "imputed holiness" of the antinomians. But finding the form of our sanctification in Christ, rather than in an abstract moral law, need not mean that holiness is imputed to a passive believer. The above passage shows that what Wesley considered polemical necessities cut off tendencies in his thinking which might have led him to other, possibly more fruitful, positions.

# CHAPTER FIVE

# The Kingly Work of Christ

THE GRAND THEME of the Wesleyan atonement is Christ's bearing of our guilt and punishment on the cross. This atonement, as the final chapter will show, is Wesley's ultimate ground for man's entire salvation, his sanctification as well as his justification. But, alongside this judicial scheme of thought, there is also in Wesley a pervasive tendency to view Christ's work on Good Friday and Easter, but also today and in the future, in terms of the military metaphor: Christ is a king who has won and wins a victory for us over sin and evil. Much attention has been given to the power of the Holy Spirit in Wesley's doctrine of sanctification. It needs to be more clearly recognized that the sanctifying Spirit is the Spirit of the victorious as well as the suffering Christ.[1]

## 1. CHRIST THE KING

Jesus Christ the King of kings, the Lord of lords: no other creature, certainly not man, can bear the title of king in an absolute sense before God. This theme runs straight through all parts of the *Notes* (cf. as representative: Mt 21:9, Ac 10:36, Eph 1:21, Heb 2:3, Rev 1:5).

Wesley anchors this thought, and several of its corollaries, in the doctrine of the Trinity. Christ, quite apart from His mediatorial kingship, rules eternally with the Father; "ruling" here is obviously another word for Christ's eternal glory (I Cor 15:24-25, 28, Mt 28:18). But He also rules in His mediatorial kingdom, where Christians are His subjects, although Christ refers the glory of this mediatorial service to the Father (I Cor 3:23). What is more, eternal life, the bestowal of which is so important in Christ's kingly work, flows from the union of Father and Son (I Jn 5:20, Jn 6:57). God's sovereign claim

to our love, which is the norm of sanctification, also rests on
this Trinitarian unity of God (Mk 12:29).

It is important to underline the statement that Christ's
Trinitarian relation with the Holy Spirit also underlies His kingly
office. Christ is anointed to this office with the Holy Spirit
(Heb 1:9, Mt 1:16). Later, Wesley will place considerable
emphasis on the work of Christ through the Holy Spirit in the
kingdom, in the church, in our sanctification.

But Christ's kingly office is not only an expression of His
eternal Godhead, for He rules in both natures. Wesley notes
that "Son of Man" is one of the titles for the expected sovereign
of the kingdom (Mt 3:2), and several times he points out that
Christ's body is also in heaven on the throne (Phil 3:21, Rev 1:7,
12-13). But this sovereign power must be bestowed on His
human nature, whereas it belongs to Christ in His divine nature
from all eternity. When this sovereign power is bestowed—
whether in the incarnation, or in the ascension (Jn 19:25,
Lk 19:12)—is not very clear, and one could wish Wesley's
reflections on this point were more clearly connected with the
atonement itself. But there can be no doubt that Christ's kingship
is exercised in both natures. The human nature, in particular,
will be important for Wesley when he thinks of Christ's coming
again as judge.

As a divine-human mediatorial office, Christ's kingship has
a history. David's kingship—the Old Testament kingship, in
general—prefigured it, and found in Christ's sovereignty its
continuation and fulfilment.[2] In his earthly ministry, and especially in His miracles, Christ repeatedly demonstrated His power
over nature and the spirits of men (Mt 8:26, Jn 18:8, 11:41,
Mk 7:34). It is of interest that Wesley connects Christ's miracle-
working power with the Holy Spirit (Mt 12:31), and that in
Christ's name this authority can also be delegated to disciples
(Mk 16:17). However, the grand revelation of Christ's kingship
is not in the miracles but in the cross, resurrection, and ascension.
It is before Pilate, as Wesley emphasizes, that Christ is revealed

to be king (Mt 27:11, Jn 11:50), and the cross is the decisive encounter between Christ, Satan, and sin, before which the kingdom could not be set up (I Cor 15:26, Lk 12:50). The resurrection, which is a victory over death (I Cor 15:26), is the beginning of the kingdom (Lk 22:16, Ac 2:31), and its power will raise men to new life in regeneration, and to eternal life in the general resurrection (Ro 6:5, Eph 1:19, I Cor 15:20). The ascension signifies Christ's elevation to rule from the right hand of the Father (Ac 2:33, Eph 1:21-22), until He comes to judge the world, in a form appropriate to His majesty (Rev 1:7, Heb 9:28). After the judgment, Christ will return the mediatorial kingdom again to the Father, without ceasing to rule eternally with Him (I Cor 15:24).

## 2. CHRIST'S VICTORY

Wesley's connection of Christ's kingship with the atonement is seen much more clearly when he speaks of Christ's victory over His enemies: Satan, sin, and death (I Cor 15:26). These enemies have no right to be in Christ's world. Christ was, from the beginning, the rightful sovereign over all. His victory is not the conquest of a new territory, but the repression of a rebellion (Rev 11:15, 17:14).

This rebellion was, first of all, a rebellion among the angels. Some remained loyal, but others rebelled and became devils (S. 72, intro., 2; i, 3). Notwithstanding, all remained infinitely below the Son in majesty, and are both, good and evil, His servants still (Heb 1:7, 4; Intro. to Col). It is worth noting that Wesley believes that this, and all other knowledge of angels, can properly come only through revelation (S. 71, intro., 4).

Concerning good angels it must be said, first of all, that they are primarily ministering spirits, ministering before God, and sent forth to men (Heb 1:7; S. 71, intro., 4). By nature, they are spirits, i.e., endued with understanding, will, and liberty, which are "the essence of a spirit" (S. 71, i, 1). They, like the evil angels before their fall, are holy, pure, beloved of

God (Jude 6). Being spirits, they can know not only the words
and actions, but also the thoughts of men, and the power of
one angel is sufficient to heave the earth and all the planets
out of their orbits (S. 71, i, 2, 5). They minister to all men
(though preferring believers), in both body and soul: they
cure diseases, inspire divine dreams, deliver us from evil men,
and counterwork evil angels (S. 71, ii, 1-7). Though they
have particular charge over children, Wesley doubts whether
every man has his particular angel, because "this is a point
on which the scriptures are silent" (Mt 18:10, Ac 12:15).

The evil angels, too, are spirits who were created holy
and happy, but left their first estate in rebellion, being filled
with pride and jealousy, probably when God published "the
decree" of Psalm 2:6-7 concerning the kingdom of His only
begotten Son. Then they became devils, and thenceforth they
were doomed to endless destruction; God loves them no more
(S. 72, intro., 2; i, 3; Jude 6). These devils vary in wickedness
(Mt 12:45): some rule in infernal regions; some rule in this world;
some struggle against faith, love, and holiness; but all seem
to be united under one head, Satan, who is their commander,
and who speaks for them (Eph 6:12, 2:2, Col 1:16, Mk 5:9;
S. 72, i, 6).

These miserable creatures are filled with envy of the good
angels who still enjoy the heaven they have lost, and of men,
"those worms of the earth, who are now called to inherit the
kingdom" (S. 72, i, 4). They strive in every way to oppose
God's rule and to lead men to join their rebellion against God.
To this end, Satan "transfused" his own self-will and pride into
our parents (S. 123, i, 1; cf. S. 62, i, 9-10), and became the
"origin of evil" in the world (Mt 13:28, Jn 8:44; S. 62, i, 8). In
evaluating Wesley's "plain answer to the great question concerning the origin of evil," it must be noted that evil entered
creation when Satan made the wrong use of his moral freedom,
causing the fall of angels. This evil is no second original principle,
but a prototype (a reflection?) of human sin, grounded in the

abuse of moral liberty. The devil is "the first sinner in the universe" (I Jn 3:8).

By sin and death, Satan gained possession of the world, so that when Christ came, it was truly "Satan's house" (Jn 12:31, Mt 12:29). Man's guilt gave him up to Satan's power, and man's corruption took Satan's side in temptation. Satan thus enjoyed a right, a claim, and a power over man (Jn 14:30, Ro 6:14). Already strong in himself, Satan was thus armed with man's pride, obstinacy, and self-security (Lk 11:21). He even brings men to act his part for him, and laughs at their feeble efforts to cope with him in their own strength (Mt 16:23, Ac 19:13). Although he is a murderer, and above all a liar to men, he knows how to transform himself and put on the fairest appearance to them (Rev 12:9, II Cor 11:14). He is, in short, the god of all that do not believe (II Cor 4:4).

And yet, in spite of his malice, Satan must also serve God. God sets limits which Satan cannot pass (S. 72, i, 5). God can use the devil as the executioner of His wrath. He can "permit" the devil to strike with disease. He can use Satan to restrain evil-doers with suffering, to be a "messenger of death," and even to be a "destroying angel" (S. 9, ii, 6; I Cor 5:5, 10:10, I Tim 1:20, Lk 12:20). More far-reaching yet is Wesley's observation that the hour of Christ's passion, before which He could not be taken, is "the time when Satan has power" (Lk 22:53, cf. 4:34). An important corrective to this teaching is contained in a remark in Wesley's *Journal*: "The work of God does not, cannot need the work of the devil to forward it" (June 23, 1766). Applied to Wesley's other statements, this could mean: God requires no demonic help for His purposes, but He can cause this rebellion to serve His purpose when it occurs.

There is even evidence for a claim that Wesley, whose Tory appreciation of the state as a restraining ordinance of God is well known, considered political power as such to be demonic power. In a reference to Ephesians 6:13, Wesley makes this statement (S. 72, ii, 1):

They are (remember! so far as God permits) κοσμοκράτορες,—*governors of the world!* So that there may be more ground than we are apt to imagine, for that strange expression of Satan, Matt. iv, 8, 9, when he showed our Lord 'all the kingdoms of the world, and the glory of them;' 'all these things will I give thee, if thou wilt fall down and worship me!' [Parenthesis and italics Wesley's.]

It is too much to claim that this insight was systematically used in Wesley's view of the state, although it is not contradictory to that view as represented in the *Notes* (Eph 1:21, I Pet 2:13, Ro 13:1).

Christ's decisive encounter with the powers of darkness takes place in the cross and resurrection, although it must be remembered that penal satisfaction, not victory, is emphasized when Wesley thinks of the atonement. Still, the two themes, victory and satisfaction, are characteristically present, side by side, in the crucial notes on the passion. God, Himself, looses the powers of darkness upon Christ, while withdrawing the "comfortable discoveries" of His presence, and filling Christ's soul with a terrible sense of the wrath due to the sins He was bearing (Mt 27:46, Lk 22:44).

Christ "triumphed over all His enemies, Satan, sin, and death, which had before enslaved all the world" (Eph 4:8, I Cor 15:26, Mt 27:52-53, Heb 2:14). How? Wesley gives no extended answer, and at this crucial point one must work far too much with inference and conjecture. In one note he says that Christ conquered Satan and sin on the cross, and death in His resurrection, but this assertion is not further explained (I Cor 15:26). Another, perhaps the crucial note, states: "The voluntary passion of our Lord appeased the Father's wrath, obtained pardon and acceptance for us, and consequently, dissolved the dominion and power which Satan had over us through our sins" (Col 1:14). Why is the defeat of Satan a consequence of the Father's pardon? An answer is only implied by Wesley in the suggestion that it is man's guilt which puts him in Satan's power (Jn 14:30). On the basis of these sparse data, it may be conjectured that

Christ's atonement, in securing justification for us, at the same time necessarily implies the breaking of Satan's dominion, at least in principle, since it removes the chief bond—guilt—which Satan has over us. The bond is broken "in principle" because Christ's victory in us remains to be won in our sanctification. If this conjecture is correct, it can be a connection of importance for Wesley's theology, for it implies that the two atonement themes, satisfaction and victory, and consequently also the priestly and kingly-prophetic work, and further justification and sanctification, are not simply parallel, but at heart organically united.[3]

The victory decisively, but not finally, disables Christ's enemies: Satan, sin, and death. Satan is "judged, condemned, cast out of his possession, and out of the bounds of Christ's kingdom"; he is no more able to hurt Christ's people (Jn 12:31, I Cor 15:26). Not only is sin condemned in the cross, but God gives sentence "that sin should be destroyed, and the believers delivered from it"; it also is no more able to hurt Christ's people (Ro 8:3, I Cor 15:26). Death, "the devil's sergeant," is conquered, abolished, destroyed, forever; without sin, which is its sting, death can have no more power; much more, Christ has turned death into a blessing (Heb 2:14, I Cor 15:26, 54, 56, II Tim 1:10; somewhat confusingly, the note on Rev 20:14 indicates that the destruction of death occurs in the last days). Now even Christ's enemies must confess that He is Lord (Phil 2:10-11, Rev 5:13). And the positive scope of the victory is described, according to Ephesians 1:10, as a recapitulation of all angels and men under Christ, their common head.

The victory, won in the atonement, has both retroactive and eschatological consequences. In so far as the miracles of Christ's earthly ministry are victories over Satan, must they not be understood as retroactive consequences of the atonement victory? In the note on Matthew 12:27 Christ explains his healing of the demoniac with a curious reference to the future: "Besides how can I rob [Beelzebub] of his subjects till I have conquered him?" (Cf. Lk 11:20, 10:18, Mt 12:29.)

But the greatest emphasis falls on the eschatological consequences of the victory, for Wesley does not underestimate the provisional remaining power of evil. "The Deliverer is come, but not the full fruit of His coming" (Ro 11:26). Satan has been judged, dethroned, deprived of his usurped power, "yet those who reject the deliverance offered them will remain slaves of Satan still" (Jn 16:11). The evil angels have been bound with chains, "though still those chains do not hinder their often walking up and down seeking whom they may devour" (II Pet 2:4). There remains a state of war between the "Church warring under Christ and the world warring under Satan," but the result of this war is determined: in both heaven and earth God's kingdom stands and that of Satan is being destroyed (Rev 6:9, Mk 9:40, Lk 10:21). Satan is not able to keep those who follow the "drawings" of Christ, nor is the height of Christ's love to be reached by any enemy (Jn 12:32, Eph 3:18). Therefore, the demons live in terror of Him; indeed, because they also believe the propositions of the Christian revelation, they tremble the more at this knowledge of their fate (Jas 2:19).[4]

Because a victory has been won in principle, while the eschatological consequences are not yet fully evident, sanctification has the character of spiritual warfare. This is the Christological context for the central Wesleyan emphasis on the struggle of Spirit with flesh. Christ has been manifested in our hearts to destroy the works of the devil in us, and this He will perform in all that trust in Him, bruising the powers of darkness daily under the believer's feet (I Jn 3:8; S. 4, i, 2). Christ's intercession at God's right hand—a significant reference to the priestly work—guards us from the onslaughts of the evil one (Ro 8:38-39). He does not destroy the whole work of the devil in this life, however. Infirmities—which Wesley did not consider culpable sin—and death are destroyed only in the last days (S. 62, iii, 3-4). "Universal holiness," understood as "the mind that was in Christ," stands, however, as a "general preservative against the devil" (S. 72, iii, 1).

The ultimate victory of Christ over Satan and death comes in the last day (S. 62, iii, 4; Mt 8:29). Satan has already been judged and condemned in the passion-resurrection victory: it is only God's "mysterious wisdom" which has permitted him this interval (Jn 12:31, Rev 20:3). Now, at last, our accuser is to be "taken away," the destroyers are to be destroyed, and the royal government of the world, which has been in the enemy's hands, is to return to its rightful master (Rev 12:10, 11:18, 15). But now it is that "Satan makes his grand opposition to the kingdom of God" (Rev 12:7). And so the great drama of the closing chapters of the Book of Revelation unfolds itself before Wesley's inquiring eyes. First there is the struggle with the "beast," which Wesley, following Bengel, painstakingly presents as the Roman papacy (Rev 13:1).[5] When the "beast" is destroyed, Satan is bound for a millennium, then loosed, to gather his great army with Gog and Magog for the final battle, where, with a great fire from heaven, his force is destroyed. He is finally cast into the lake of fire and brimstone to be tormented day and night, "without any intermission: strictly speaking, there is only night there: no day, no sun, no hope!" (Rev 20:3, 7, 10). And death and Hades are destroyed, for "neither the righteous nor the wicked are to die any more," the one enjoying everlasting blessedness, and the other banished into everlasting torment (Rev 20:14).

It is worth pausing here to make a provisional evaluation of this teaching about Christ's victory.

An obvious problem is how to understand this world of demons, Satan, angels, and final events. The intention behind this language is rather clear: Wesley wants to describe a real victory, the result of which can be seen. It is just possible that at some point in this account—but not too early!—he would utter his warning about reading too literally, or too far from the plain sense. But a programatic demythologization will not do him full justice. He shows few signs of being bothered by this problem.

There is also the problem of how the three aspects of Christ's victory relate to one another: the victory in the atonement, in our sanctification, and in the last day. This is the Wesleyan version of the classical eschatological problem: the relation between the "already" and the "not yet" of the kingdom. However, it must be noted that among the three aspects of Christ's victory, Wesley emphasizes the victory in us. This may account for the impression that much of the emphasis also lies on the final victory. Wesley wants to prevent the believer from relaxing too soon! Further, the atonement victory cannot have for Wesley, as for Calvinism, the effect of confirming the election of the elect. The conditionality of Wesley's offer of salvation requires a certain conditionality in Christ's victory, with this important difference: Christ's ultimate victory is certain, while our salvation is not. Wesley wants the power of Christ's certain victory offered to all men in such a way that its results may become visible in their sanctification. That is the theological reason for the underemphasis on the victory of the cross and resurrection.

It may be asked whether Wesley consistently connects Christ's victory with God's lordship over the demonic powers. At times he seems to speak of this controlled rebellion as an order of creation. The four horsemen of Revelation 6 must be considered demonic powers in Wesley's interpretation. They are "subject to Christ," and yet their subjection is not an event or victory, but a condition which existed from the beginning: "The whole course of the world and of visible nature [is] in all ages subject to Christ, subsisting by His power, and serving His will, against the wicked, and in defence of the righteous" (Rev 6:8). Here the victory theme is obviously dissolved into a general doctrine of providence, although the doctrine of angels is maintained.

It needs to be noted that Wesley's interest in this demonic explanation of evil and disaster remained second to his emphasis on human responsibility for both sin and evil. Either explanation could be given. The demonic interpretation tends to occur in his more speculative moods, and in connection with his curiosity about natural science. The emphasis on human responsibility tends to occur when he is thinking of individual salvation, and preaching for repentance.[6] The emphasis on human responsibility for good and evil in creation is heightened in the doctrine of the political image of God. Wesley can let man in his original state entirely replace angels as the channels of "communication" between the Creator and the whole brute creation, all the blessings of God in paradise flowing through man to the inferior creatures. The fall of man is thus occasion for the bondage of creation, which waits and groans, then, for man's liberation from sin for its own deliverance. Here the victory theme is related to the liberation of creation in and through Christ's sanctifying victory over sin in the heart of man (S. 60, ii, 1; Ro 8:19-21).

It may be observed that this readiness to subordinate the scheme of rebellion-victory to the scheme of sin-grace-judgment, with the latter's heavier emphasis on human responsibility and freedom, attests the basic hypothesis of this volume: the kingly office, in general, is considered to be an aspect of the priestly work of Christ.

### 3. THE KINGDOM

In the interests of clarity, it is well to present a systematic sketch of Wesley's understanding of the kingdom before analyzing it in detail. We find in Wesley the familiar distinction between the kingdom of grace and the kingdom of glory. The kingdom of grace is an inward, spiritual kingdom, with two primary references: the sanctifying of the individual, and the gathering of the church. The kingdom of glory is the eternal kingdom following the last judgment, also with two primary references: the blessedness of the individual, and the heavenly city. The kingdom of grace and the kingdom of glory, taken together, are one kingdom, although Wesley views the kingdom of grace as Christ's mediatorial kingdom, and the kingdom of glory as merged into the prior, everlasting reign of Father, Son, and Holy Spirit.

## a. The One Kingdom of God

At first glance, Wesley's use of the term "kingdom" seems to have a remarkable looseness of meaning. It can mean sometimes eternal glory, sometimes inward religion, sometimes the gospel dispensation, and likewise "a person, or thing, relating to any of those." Thus, "kingdom" can also mean Christ preaching the gospel, or the gospel itself, or the "candidates" of the kingdom, or the "king of heaven, Christ" (Mt 13:24, 21:43, 25:1, 14).

Upon closer analysis, a doctrinal pattern begins to emerge, and this pattern, once seen, is found with remarkable consistency throughout Wesley's writings. The crucial note on Matthew 3:2 touches upon the key concepts, and with its help the following statement of Wesley's doctrine of the kingdom can be given.[7]

1. The kingdom is both a state on earth and a state in heaven. This distinction is found throughout the *Notes*, frequently with the terms "kingdom of grace" and "kingdom of glory" (Mt 5:3, Lk 11:52, Jn 3:3, Jas 1:17, I Jn 5:11, Rev 1:6).

2. Believers do not yet possess the kingdom in its fulness.

3. The state on earth includes both the sanctifying of the individual and the gathering of the church. The note on Matthew 4:17 indicates that these two aspects comprise the content of the phrase "inward kingdom." A warning can thus be taken against over-individualizing one of Wesley's favorite terms. Properly speaking, "inner kingdom" is an equivalent for "kingdom of grace," or "state on earth."

4. The state in heaven likewise includes both future "happiness" for the individual, and a continuation in glory of the "society" which Christ has formed on earth.

5. Both states, taken together, are one kingdom. The kingdom is "not barely" the future state. It is one "society" in both. And Wesley explicitly asserts that the term "generally includes both."

6. Christ's work is essential to the establishment of the kingdom. God "erects" the kingdom; the Son "gathers" the society. In Luke 11:52 we are told that "true knowledge of the Messiah . . . is the key of both the present and the future king-

dom." Wesley can also identify the kingdom with the person of Christ, Himself (Mt 13:24, 25:14).

Missing from the note on Matthew 3:2 are two elements which otherwise have a place in the Wesleyan understanding of the kingdom:

7. The kingdom of grace, Christ's mediatorial kingdom, is only part of Christ's everlasting rule with the Father and the Holy Spirit. In I Corinthians 15:24, 25, 28 it is indicated that Christ has never ceased to participate in the everlasting reign of the Father, even while carrying out His mediatorial commission. In the last day, Christ will return the mediatorial kingdom to the Father, "so far as the Father gave the kingdom to the Son." After the last day, the Son will not "cease to be a king, even in His human nature," for "if the citizens of the New Jerusalem shall reign forever, how much more shall He?" The Trinitarian background for the ultimate reign of God is stressed in I Corinthians 15:28.

8. Christ's everlasting rule with the Father includes the government of all things, and the kingdom of glory is ultimately merged with it. "He is the Lord and disposer of the whole creation, and every part of it" (S. 77, i, 8; cf. I Cor 15:28, Eph 1:21, Mt 28:18). Here, reference should be made to what has already been said about Christ's relation to creation and providence (*supra*, pp. 66-69), to God's dominion over both good and evil angels, and to his government of the world through them (*supra*, pp. 118-19, 125-26), especially to the derivation of state power from God (*supra*, pp. 120-21), and, finally, to God's rule in natural and political catastrophes (*infra*, p. 143). If it is correct to identify this cosmic rule of Christ (S. 77, i, 8) with the Trinitarian rule of God from everlasting to everlasting (I Cor 15:24), then Wesley's doctrine of the kingdom can be comprehensively summarized as follows:

a. The universal rule of Christ in the Trinity is eternal.

b. The kingdom of glory represents the conscious entry of the redeemed into this eternal rule, although both they and the lost were providentially upheld by the rule from the beginning.

c. The mediatorial kingdom of grace would then be God's royal way of bringing fallen men back to their rightful place in His eternal rule. This would account for its strict limitation to the sanctifying of men and the gathering of the "society."

Diagrammatically, this doctrine of the kingdom might be comprehensively summarized as follows:[8]

### THE ONE KINGDOM OF GOD

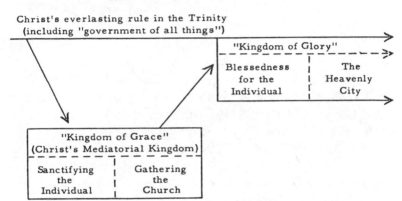

*b. The Kingdom of Grace*

Wesley makes a great number of general characterizations of the kingdom of grace. It is a spiritual, not a temporal or political kingdom (Jn 18:36, 28:23). It is, nevertheless, a kingdom on this earth (Mt 6:10). But it exists in the heart, primarily, as an "internal principle" (Lk 17:21). It has a definite time: its beginning was foretold, and it will have an end (Mk 1:15). It is a kingdom in which Satan's power is being destroyed (Lk 10:21). It is a kingdom of law, and he that breaks its laws is a stranger to it (S. 20, iii, 3).[9] It is a kingdom whose influence can pervade all external circumstances, "as air yields to all bodies, and yet pervades all" (Ac 8:36).

But, as has been indicated, Wesley sees two great aspects to the kingdom of grace: the sanctifying of the individual and the gathering of the church.

## 1) The Sanctifying of the Individual[10]

Wesley begins with the assertion that this sanctification is "the peculiar business of Christ" (Mt 4:17). He purchased this kingdom for us with His blood, and if He does not wash us in His blood and purify us by His Spirit—a reference to both justification and sanctification—we shall have no share in the blessings of His kingdom (S. 16, i, 12; Jn 13:8). The kingdom in our hearts may be described in the terms set forth by Wesley as our being buried with Christ and raised up together with Him (Mt 11:11).

The kingdom of grace comes to a believer's heart when he repents and believes; then Christ begins to exercise His royal power there, conquering and subduing all things to Himself (S. 21, iii, 8). One of Wesley's favorite descriptions of this inner kingdom is that of Romans 14:17: it is righteousness, peace, and joy in the Holy Spirit. Righteousness has two basic aspects: formally, it is the restoration of the image of God; materially, it is the love of God and man which fulfils the law. Peace is Wesley's term for the knowledge or assurance of justification. Joy is the synonym for the Wesleyan blessedness or "happiness," which is the character of eternal life. Together these three are "heaven already opened in the soul; the first springing up of those rivers of pleasure, which flow at God's right hand for evermore" (S. 16, i, 11). And these are Christ's works and gifts in the believer (Rev 3:20).

Wesley draws a strict line, however, between this "proper disposition" for the kingdom, and the later "possession" of it. We are indeed "partakers" of the present kingdom, and "heirs" of the eternal. We partake already of the glory which belongs to the Lord of glory, but until we are entirely changed, we cannot enter that kingdom which is wholly spiritual (Mt 3:2, Rev 1:6, Jas 2:1, I Cor 15:50). Whether this change occurs in perfection before death, as seems implied in Matthew 18:3, or in death as in I Corinthians 15:50, is not entirely made clear in the *Notes*.

## 2) *The Gathering of the Church*

Wesley defines the church in Hebrews 12:23 as "the whole body of true believers, whether on earth or in paradise."[11] In the gathering of this church Christ's work is crucial. The church is the building of which He is the chief cornerstone and foundation (Eph 2:20-21), the flock of which He is "the great shepherd," the sheepfold of which He is "the only lawful entrance" (Jn 10:1ff.), the household, the family, of which He is the "Master" (Rev 6:10, Gal 6:10, I Tim 3:15), and—in by far the commonest metaphor—the "mystical body" of which He is the head (Eph 4:16, 5:22ff.; Intro. to Ac; Mt 16:18).[12] Wesley grounds the founding of the church in God's decree (I Pet 2:4, Jn 10:27-29), and locates its beginning not at Caesarea Philippi, but on the Day of Pentecost, which was the moment foretold when the kingdom of God should come "with power" (Mk 9:1, Mt 16:28).[13] However, the beginning at Pentecost should not obscure a profound continuity between the old and new Israel, in which the key term is Christ, Himself, replacing the temple (Lk 1:33, 2:25, Rev 15:3, Mt 12:5, 8).

This church Christ governs, guides, and guards (Eph 5:23). He protects her from false rulers, guides her decisions and her witness, and guards her members from the evil one (Jn 10:8, 27-29, Mt 18:20, 2:18, Ac 22:18). He labors to remove from the church all impurity of sin, so His church, as His spouse, may be all glorious within, "even in this world"; and to this end He purifies His church with the Word of the gospel (Eph 5:27, Mt 3:12). And Christ's fulness, which He has from God, overflows, so that the whole church is filled with His Spirit, presence, operations, life, truth, holiness, and comfort (I Jn 5:11, Eph 4:10, Rev 1:20).

The church, for her part, undertakes her mission to proclaim this kingdom to the world, under His direction; in this way the subjects of the "society" are gathered (Ac 4:33, 22:18). Although she knows that the world is a foolish, evil, "giddy, unthinking" place (Gal 1:4; S. 19, intro., 1), she also knows that going out of the world is not the way to perfection (I Cor 5:10). God has mixed Christians with sinners so that grace may be communicated to the world (S. 19, i, 7-8; Eph 5:11). The church knows herself appointed by Christ's Spirit, and furnished with His grace and gifts in order to go out and convert sinners (Mt 9:38, Jn 15:16). In this mission, her members are not to conceal their holiness: good works, the result of Christ's victory in men, are meant to be seen, and so to enlarge that victory (Mt 5:16, Mk 1:44; S. 19, ii).[14] But, in so far as this witness is effective, the world will be offended, and the church will be confronted with the "mystery of iniquity," i.e., persecution, through which, by the "mystery of godliness" the kingdom will spread more and more (S. 4, ii, 7-9).[15] Through the missionary church, therefore, Christ's victory is enlarged.

The universal church is now present both on earth and in heaven, as the church militant and triumphant. The church triumphant consists of angels and spirits, the church militant of Jews and Gentiles (Intro. to Eph). The church may be said to be present now in heaven because of her union with Christ who is in heaven (Rev 12:1). By her sentiments, temper, and devotion in heaven, she has some influence in instructing, animating, and encouraging the church on earth (Rev 14:1, Heb 12:22). She nevertheless sighs and prays for the coming of the kingdom, when she shall be fully delivered from all sin and sorrow, and from all her enemies, and be established in a state of perfect and everlasting happiness (Rev 12:2, 22:20, Eph 1:14).[16]

### c. The Last Judgment[17]

The judge of the last judgment is Christ, in His Trinitarian unity with the Father (Jn 5:27, 22, Ac 17:31). Wesley emphasizes that Christ judges in His human nature. A possible reason for this emphasis is that Christ's human nature is thus a norm for perfect obedience, or a standard which discovers and illumines human sin before the judgment seat, in addition to presenting in some sense, even there, atonement for those who believe. When he writes of the last judgment, Wesley's emphasis falls on the former aspect.[18]

There is some kind of anticipation of the final judgment in "temporal judgments" (I Cor 11:29), although Wesley can assert that Christ, Himself, judges no man in His first coming (Jn 8:15). Christ and His angels are now before every door, "hearing every word, marking every thought" (Jas 5:9, I Tim 5:21), but Wesley's emphasis is on the "unparalleled condescension" with which the judge, now, before the end, beseeches us to accept His pardon (II Cor 5:20, Mt 11:21). Christ's judgment, at His first coming, seems to fall on Satan alone (Jn 12:31).

The last day will come abruptly, without previous warning (Rev 16:15, Mt 24:27). The time is known only to Christ's "eternal mind," not to His human nature (I Tim 6:15, Mk 13:32), and its delay until now is explained only through the Lord's long-suffering (II Pet 3:16). Did Wesley expect Christ's immediate return? There is evidence on both sides. He can base his appeals for repentance on the possibility of the Lord's return "before the morning light" (S. 6, iii, 4). But on the night of February 28, 1763, a date when the end of the world had been widely predicted, he records in his *Journal* that he showed his congregation "the utter absurdity of the supposition that the world was to end that night," and concludes, "I went to bed at my usual time, and was fast asleep about ten o'clock." His practical attitude was: be ready! watch! (Mt 25:3-13.)

The judgment begins. Its prelude is the general resurrection of all the dead, both righteous and unrighteous. "All who ever lived and died, since God created man, shall be raised incorruptible and immortal" (S. 48, i, 1; Mt 25:46, I Cor 15:23). At death the data for every man's final judgment is completed, and the soul can even be aware what its eternal portion will be. But there is no judgment at death: judgment comes only in the final day (Heb 9:27; S. 51, iii, 1).[19] Then, "abruptly," Christ appears for the judgment (Col 3:4). With Him are the twelve apostles, except Judas (Mt 19:28). The judgment begins with the church (I Pet 4:17). And when her judgment is finished, the saints join Christ and the apostles in the judgment as assessors of the wicked and spectators of their miseries (I Th 4:17, I Cor 6:2, I Pet 4:17).

Christ's judgment is a judgment of "words, tempers, and works produced as evidence whether you were a true believer or not" (Mt 12:37, I Pet 1:17). "We may, as it were, choose for ourselves whether God shall be severe or merciful to us" (Mt 7:2). But Wesley emphasizes that it is a judgment which penetrates to "the most secret springs of action, the principles and intentions of every heart" (I Cor 4:5; S. 48, ii, 5-12).

The judgment is not only first, but most strict for those on His right hand. Indeed, they have been warned by Jesus Himself to approach this judgment as fearing the one who has the power to cast them into hell (Heb 10:30, 2:5; S. 19, i, 9; Lk 12:5, Mt 10:28). Nevertheless, when they have sought to meet Him being "washed in His blood, and renewed by His Spirit" (W. X, 335), then the Son of Man, Himself, will confess them before the angels, and will deliver them from the eternal vengeance which will come upon the ungodly (II Pet 3:14, Lk 12:8, I Th 1:10; S. 48, ii, 11). For them, glory will be "assigned" by the judge, and they will be allowed to inherit the kingdom of glory (I Pet 1:7, Mt 25:34).

And then the judge shall turn to those on His left hand, examining them likewise by their words and intentions and works. And they will try, even in this day, to justify themselves! (Mt 25:44.) But all their evil works, words, desires, affections, tempers, thoughts, and designs will come to light, and "the dreadful sentence of condemnation" will be spoken against them. They shall be turned into hell, to be punished with everlasting destruction (S. 48, ii, 12; iii, 1). The description of their eternal state continues with reference to the lake of fire, where "they will gnaw their tongues for anguish and pain," cursing God, and where the "dogs of hell—pride, malice, revenge, rage, horror, despair—continually devour them." The eternity of their punishment is emphasized (Mt 25:41, II Th 1:9); "there never can be any alteration of [their] condition, without such a change of the whole man, as would put the natural and settled order of the creation out of course" (*Compend of Natural Philosophy,* v, 223). The essence of their punishment is being cut off from the presence of the Lord, wherein consists the salvation of the righteous (II Th 1:9). Indeed, "the chief of all misery" is their "exclusion from the sight of God" (*Compend of Natural Philosophy,* v, 223). In general, one can say that Wesley does not show a morbid interest in the torments of the damned. After the judgment is over, he is preoccupied with the blessedness of the saints in glory.

## d. The Kingdom of Glory

The scene shifts to the kingdom of glory, but the knowledge of the Messiah remains the key to this kingdom also (Lk 11:52). He has been the author, object, and ground of all our hope (I Tim 1:1). And the light of glory has already, through Him, fallen forward into our hearts and lives (I Pet 1:11, Jas 2:1). Now He appears again in the kingdom of glory (II Tim 4:1).

In itself, the kingdom of glory is the eternal kingdom which will endure through all ages (Rev 19:1). It is a kingdom on earth as well as in heaven, but this must be understood as a new heaven and earth "more glorious than the present heaven and earth" (Mt 5:5, Rev 21:22).[20]

Corresponding to the kingdom of grace, the kingdom of glory has two aspects: the blessedness of individuals, and the heavenly city.

### 1) The Blessedness of Believers

Believers have been made ready for glory by justification and sanctification (Mt 18:3, Col 1:12, II Tim 2:10). Their bodies are now transformed into "the most perfect state, and the most

beauteous form" (Phil 3:21). These bodies are "real bodies,"
incapable of dissolution and decay, and endued with qualities
of a spiritual nature, like those of the angels (Rev 21:15, I Cor
15:42-44). The blessed will be fed by the Lamb with eternal
peace and joy, and being comforted by the Holy Spirit they
shall not suffer or grieve any more (Rev 7:17). They are now
made perfect in a higher sense than was possible in this life,
and, in a remarkable extension of the Wesleyan perfection motif,
they continue in the "other world" to attain higher degrees of
glory (Heb 12:23, Rev 7:9, Mt 19:30). Their happiness consists
in beholding the glory of God (Jn 17:24, Mt 5:8). And they
reign with Christ in glory for ever and ever (Mt 6:10).[21]

## 2) The Heavenly City

The new heaven and earth belong not to this world, not to
the millennium, but to eternity (Rev 21:2). The descriptions
given of it in the Book of Revelation are "undoubtedly figurative,"
yet it is a real city, occupying a "definite and determinate
space" (Rev 21:15). Its foundations bear the names of the
twelve apostles, "figuratively showing that the inhabitants of
the city had built on that faith which the apostles once delivered
to the saints," and they are adorned with precious stones which
"may express the perfect glory and happiness of all the inhabitants," as they reflect the glorious presence of God (Rev
21:14, 19).

The city is prepared for a great number of inhabitants, "how
small soever the number of real Christians may sometimes
appear to be" (Rev 21:15, Jn 14:2, but cf. Lk 18:8 where Wesley's
doubt about the great number is more clearly expressed). A
light throws itself outward from this city, far and near, and
the nations walk by this light. What is more, all that is glorious
from every nation shall be brought into it (Rev 21:24-26).

There is no temple in this city: the Lord God and the Lamb
are its temple, and fill the new heaven and earth, sanctifying it
and all that are in it (Rev 21:10, 22). This absence of the

temple is no incidental detail. Wesley notes it as the principal difference between Ezekiel's and John's descriptions of the new Jerusalem. Wesley's refusal to confuse the church and the kingdom of glory here may have some ground in his emphasis on Christ, Himself, displacing the temple of the old dispensation.

Now the covenant between God and His people is fulfilled in the most glorious manner: they are His people, and He Himself is with them and is their God (Rev 21:3). Through the city, itself, flows the water of life, i.e., "the ever fresh and fruitful effluence of the Holy Ghost," and by it grows the tree of life, i.e., the fruit of the Spirit. And the leaves of this tree are for the healing of the nations, "for the continuing their health, not the restoring of it; for no sickness is there" (Rev 22:1-2).

"Thus ends the doctrine of this Revelation, in the everlasting happiness of all the faithful. The mysterious ways of Providence are cleared up, and all things issue in an eternal Sabbath, an everlasting state of perfect peace and happiness, reserved for all who endure to the end" (Rev 22:5).

### 4. Comment

Wesley's view of Christ's victory has already been discussed; the following remarks concern his doctrine of Christ's kingdom.

The principal question concerning the last judgment must be directed to Wesley's teaching about the priestly work of Christ (Chapter VI): in what sense does the atonement have significance in the final day? In the present context a strong tendency was noted to separate justice and mercy in the judgment act. This was reflected in Wesley's emphasis on Christ's idealized human nature as the law of judgment. The possibility that the law, so understood, could play this role in the last judgment was one of the possibilities left open in Wesley's view of Christ's prophetic work.

Wesley's doctrine of the kingdom lends support to the claim that an essential motif in the Wesleyan version of the eternal decree is not a restoring, but an eternal perfecting. The goal of the Wesleyan eschatology is no church at rest, but a city in which the Son is eternally sanctifying the blessed, and in which the blessed increase in perfection, moving from one degree of glory to another and ruling the less perfect! It is *this* kingdom of glory which is merged with the eternal rule of Christ, i.e., with providence. That means that the line of Christ's eternal rule (in the diagram, p. 129) is not horizontal, but tilted upward:

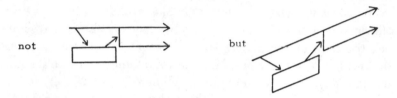

Wesley's perfecting idea underlies his understanding of the entire meaning of existence.

The question may provisionally be put: is the Wesleyan two-sidedness the result of the tension which must result between such a ground-plan of existence, and the fact that this ground-plan—just as the Wesleyan sanctification doctrine itself—has to presuppose Christ's priestly work? The question can be made simpler and more far-reaching: is Christ ultimately a means to the end of this perfecting decree (in which case there will be a two-sidedness), or is the perfecting decree itself somehow an expression of Christ's grace? Does God originally decide to create a perfectible creation because He wants to love it for Christ's sake? Wesley's time doctrine has been his great help in solving this problem thus far. His teaching about the priestly work of Christ will have to be studied to see whether this doctrine of time points to a formal or a real answer.

One further question to this doctrine of the kingdom and the following chapter: where are the damned? Christ, Himself, rules over all at the end of Wesley's eschatology. Even the present creation is not, in principle, excluded from Christ's final rule, as long as Wesley holds open the possibility of some

kind of continuity (restoration) between the old creation and
the new. But the demons and the damned, whose unwilling
service to Christ's rule was an impressive part of Wesley's
victory theme, are summarily judged, thrown into their justly
deserved torment, and forgotten. But does *He* still rule them?
Is it God, Himself, the living God, with whom they have to
do even now? Or do they suffer under a justice and wrath
abstracted from Him—perhaps the wrathful side of that same
abstracted, semi-independent law which loomed so large at the
end of Chapter IV, which cannot be changed without putting
"the natural and settled order of the creation out of course"?
(*Compend of Natural Philosophy*, v, 223.)

Questions press to be asked. Could not the damned, even
here, be under Christ's personal rule? Could they even now
be suffering not only their just reward, but also the unwilling
service of God? Or does God not ultimately and eternally rule
supreme over every part of His creation? It is true that the
unwilling service of evil angels and men has no claim to be
taken seriously; God does not need but only uses their unwilling
service in His kingdom of grace. We recall that God's rule
in the kingdom of grace is for Wesley never one in which
evil is simply negated. God is there the God in whom justice
and love are inseparable, who therefore always overrules evil and
turns it to serve His good purpose. Why should the kingdom
of glory inaugurate a time when this is not so, when rebellion
is only negated by Him, and not overruled and compelled in
spite of itself to praise Him? What does this signify for the
doctrine of God? With the inauguration of this kingdom of
glory, does God Himself suffer a change? Does He then cease
to be the one in whom justice and love are always inseparable,
and become the one in whom there is justice and love for the
blessed, but only justice for the damned?

Furthermore, to the degree that Wesley can be held to the
supralapsarian position that in the fall "mankind ... gained ...
a capacity of attaining more holiness and happiness on earth

than ... would have been possible ... if Adam had not fallen"
(S. 59, i, 1), is it unthinkable that the unwilling service of the
damned is involved in the "capacity" of the new creation to
increase in perfection? Both cases do indeed contain the profoundly problematic thought that the unwilling service of evil
is in some sense necessary. But is the thought less problematic
in the one case, which Wesley seems to affirm, than in the other?
Does Wesley mean that God decides to realize His eternal
perfecting decree by using overruled evil in one part of His
*Heilsgeschichte*, but not in another? Is it possible that the
terms "kingdom of grace" and "kingdom of glory" indicate
the presence of Wesley's familiar problematic two-sidedness in
eschatology also?

The Wesleyan material is remarkably poor in answers to
these questions. That is also a sign that the questions have
pushed beyond Wesley's own thoughts into implications which
are more visible today than they were then, although for that
very reason these implications and the light they can throw on
Wesley's central theme of salvation must be faced.

The impression is difficult to avoid that at the end of
Wesley's eschatology the damned are forgotten. As will be
shown, there is another point in Wesley's theology where a
summary forgetting also occurs: with the past sins and unfulfilled
past obedience of the justified. In the one case God's mercy
forgets; in the other his justice. In anticipation of the final
chapter, the question can be formulated: is not Christ's continuing personal function underemphasized in both places—in
respect to bearing forever the past sins and providing the past
obedience of the justified, and in respect to His personal rule
of the damned—especially after Wesley's heavy emphasis on
Christ's justice in condemning both? This is the reverse side
of the question at the end of Chapter IV: is not Christ's personal
function underemphasized in respect to the law? It must be
emphasized that the problem here is not universal salvation, but
the being and rule of God, and the unwilling service of the

damned. In this form, the theological problem of Wesley's doctrine of the kingdom—i.e., is God's justice somehow semi-autonomous from God's person—can be posed for further study.

1. Lindström (*Wesley and Sanctification*, pp. 71-72) also finds Christ's victory an "ancillary" theme in the Wesleyan atonement. It must be questioned, incidentally, whether, as Lindström claims, this concept is "found chiefly in the earlier sermons." One of its strongest expressions is in S. 62, "The End of Christ's Coming," from 1788. The *Notes*, not earlier than 1754, abundantly support it. Note its importance also in Sermons 71 and 72, "On Good Angels," and "On Evil Angels," both late sermons (probably 1788).

2. The Wesleyan understanding of Christ's kingship in relation to the Old Testament deserves a special study of its own, doubtless in connection with the key term, Messiahship. With this term Wesley emphasizes the continuity of Christ and David. Only a few representative references can be given here: Mt 10:32, 11:4, 16:3, 20, 21, Lk 2:25, Jn 1:1. Concerning the Messiah as the Son of David, see Mt 12:23, 1:6, 21:9, and with special reference to the Messianic fulfilment of the Davidic promise, Mt 1:1, 1:16, 15:22.

3. Obviously, the key term in this conjecture is "guilt." In what sense is man's guilt the key to Satan's power over him?

An answer is suggested, again from sparse data, in Wesley's account of man's fall (S. 62, i, 9-10). Satan's first objective was to lead Eve to disbelieve God, i.e., to doubt that God meant what He said. Only then did Satan face her with the temptation of the pleasantness of the fruit, which she was powerless to resist. Wesley's summary of the fall, then, is as follows: unfaith begot pride, and pride begot foolish desire, which was soon completed in outward sin. At that moment man died! The life-giving relation to God had been broken. "He was full of sin; full of guilt, and tormenting fears."

What is the character of this guilt? Is it not man's memory that the root of his sin was disbelief in God, i.e., man's wilful severance of the one life-giving relationship? Man is aware of his bondage to sin, but he also knows that he chose bondage by an original act of disloyalty to God. The guilt—i.e., the memory—of that sin stands. It cannot be brushed away by man himself. And as long as it stands, it poisons the life-giving fellowship with God. There is no other possibility for man than an endless repetition of the way from pride to self-will, to desire, to outward sin. In short, as long as this guilty memory remains, man is in the power of Satan. The guilty memory can be removed only if the original act of disloyalty which it enshrines is recognized by God for what it is, and the relationship is nevertheless affirmed in spite of that act and its guilt, "as if" (as Wesley liked to say) they had not happened. God's recognizing guilt for what it is, while at the same time reaffirming the relationship with the sinner, is the Wesleyan justification, based on Christ's satisfactory atonement.

This interpretation is obviously an extension of Wesley's thought, although it is not without basis. If it is correct, then the familiar Wesleyan formula, "the guilt and power of sin," must be understood to mean, not two parallel aspects of sin, corresponding to a double view of salvation, but "the guilt, and therefore, in principle, the power of sin." That is to say, although the remaining power of sin must be progressively conquered in sanctification, there is nevertheless, in principle, a definite priority between the two aspects. Guilt is the basis of the power of sin. If this is true, then Wesley's view of salvation from sin is, for all its tendencies toward doubleness, fundamentally a unity.

4. It is well to remember such assertions, for Wesley's interest in Christ's progressive victory in us can lead him to make statements which seem to ignore the fact of an objective victory, already won. Satan is still "prince" of this world; the evil one still "reigns" in it (Jn 17:15, Mt 5:9). He and his angels "govern" the world so as "to most hinder the kingdom of God, and most advance the kingdom of darkness" (S. 72, ii, 1). In fact, Wesley can write an entire sermon about how Christ destroys the works of the devil without once referring to Christ's objective victory on the cross and in the resurrection; the victory is thought of as entirely in us (S. 62, although there is one passing reference to Christ's final victory in the last day).

The point of Wesley's emphasis on the eschatological consequences of Christ's victory is that we should not underestimate the attack which Satan can still launch against both church and believer. Against the church, he sets persecutors to work. He uses distraction to frustrate the work of God. But his "power and policy" and all his "instruments" cannot prevail against the church, and under God his malice can even work to further the gospel (Rev 2:10, Mt 13:19; *Journal*, March 12, 1743; Mk 9:20, Mt 16:18, Ac 19:17). Satan attacks believers by lessening, if not destroying, the gifts of the Spirit, and by inspiring passions and tempers which are the opposite of these. He hates and tries to destroy the love of God and neighbor (S. 72, ii, 6, 8, 5). He dampens the believer's joy, destroys his peace, his righteousness, his holiness, and attacks his faith (S. 37). And, in addition to all this,

Satan is seen as standing before God as our accuser (Rev 12:10).

5. The anti-Roman polemic plays a not inconsiderable role, especially in the latter portions of the *Notes.* The pope is the Antichrist (Rev 13:15, 17:11, but see I Jn 2:18 where the Antichrist, "in St. John's sense," is simply "antichristianism"). He is the "man of sin" referred to in II Th 2:3-4. The "mystery of iniquity" is explained to be "not wholly confined to the Romish Church," but to consist also of human additions to the written word, external religion, and other mediators than Jesus Christ (II Th 2:7).

6. Thus in S. 72, ii, 11 Wesley attributes all manner of "accidents," from overturning carriages to earthquakes, to the agency of the devil. It is of interest to compare with this Charles Wesley's sermon on "The Cause and Cure of Earthquakes" (S. 129), where, in a powerful appeal for repentance, the preacher shakes the hearer's complacency and self-righteousness with urgent illustrations of God's judgment. "God Himself is the author, and sin the *moral* cause of earthquakes, whatever the natural causes may be." "Earthquakes are God's *strange works* of judgment, the proper effect and punishment of sin." And the "cure" for earthquakes is: fear God, repent, believe the gospel. In S. 130 John Wesley deals with the political disaster of the American Revolution in this same vein (cf. "Serious Thoughts Occasioned by the Late Earthquake at Lisbon," W. XI, 1-13; and Mk 3:10).

7. "*The kingdom of heaven* and the kingdom of God are but two phrases for the same thing. They mean, not barely a future, happy state in heaven, but a state to be enjoyed on earth; the proper disposition for the glory of heaven, rather than the possession of it. *Is at hand*—As if He had said, God is about to erect that kingdom spoken of by Daniel . . . , the kingdom of God in heaven. It properly signifies here, the gospel dispensation, in which subjects were to be gathered to God by His Son, and a society to be formed, which was to subsist first on earth, and afterwards with God in glory. In some places of scripture the phrase more particularly denotes the state of it on earth; in others, it signifies only the state of glory; but it generally includes both . . . it was a spiritual kingdom, and . . . no wicked man, how politic, brave, or learned soever, could possibly be a subject of it" (Mt 3:2; cf. the other important note: Mt 13:24).

8. Related conceptions of Christ's kingdom are found in seventeenth-century Reformed orthodoxy; e.g., Alsted, 587 (cited in Heppe, *Reformed Dogmatics,* p. 481): "Christ's kingship is two-fold, essential and personal; the essential, which is also called natural and universal, Christ holds with a glory and majesty equal to the Father and the Holy

Spirit; the personal, which is also called the donative, the economic, and the dispensative, Christ administers as the θεάνθρωπος in a single mode; and it is of grace or of glory; the former is the Church militant, the latter the Church triumphant."

Schmid (*Doctrinal Theology*, p. 370) summarizes the position of Lutheran orthodoxy: "This kingdom of Christ is, in itself only one, and embraces the whole world, the present and the future, with all that it contains. Yet this one kingdom is designated as the kingdom of power, of grace, and of glory. The first is called the *Kingdom of Power*, because it is the kingdom in which Christ exercises His divine power by governing and upholding the world; the second is called the *Kingdom of Grace*, because in this Christ operates through His saving grace; the third is called the *Kingdom of Glory*, because He therein unfolds, in all its perfection, His divine glory before the eyes of all who are there assembled."

Without entering in detail on the complicated differences between the Lutheran and Reformed views, it may be said that Wesley's lies more in the Reformed direction. In his merging of the kingdom of glory into the everlasting rule of the Trinity over all things, he avoids the Lutheran postulation of a separate "kingdom of power," with its temptation of passivity toward the world.

9. It is useful to be reminded that the emphasis on the law in connection with the prophetic office finds its place in the concept of the kingdom, and of the kingly work as a whole. But there are hints of the law's penultimate meaning in the kingdom. In Matthew 11:11, for example, the Baptist is called the least in the kingdom because his was only a legal righteousness.

10. It is simply beyond the scope of this study to give anything like an adequate presentation and analysis of the Wesleyan doctrine of sanctification. The sketch given at this point serves to indicate where this massive doctrine belongs in the study of Christ's work: i.e., within the larger context of the growing kingdom of grace in the believer's heart.

If more than this sketch were attempted, the following connections between Christology and the doctrine of sanctification would have to be shown: (1) how the doctrine of regeneration, which is the gateway to sanctification, is rooted in Christ's victory over death; (2) how our knowledge of this new birth (assurance), which is the active witness of Christ's Spirit in us, also includes the reopening of our eyes to the reinscribed law, an event which plays an important part in Christ's prophetic work; (3) how the common Wesleyan formula for sanctification, "the liberation from the power of sin" is related to Christ's victory; (4) how the fulfilling of the law by way of the commandment to love is the form which Christ's victorious reign takes in our hearts; (5) how the goal of this victorious reign is the restoration in us of the damaged image of God, i.e., that Christ's victory in us is not, so to speak, an aggression but the reconquering of His own possession, and the restoring of it to its intended likeness to Himself; (6) how the theme "in Chirst," as related to sanctification, provides an important link between Christ's victory and our struggle against sin; (7) how the Wesleyan doctrine of perfection exemplifies, and to a certain extent anticipates, Christ's eschatological victory.

If these avenues are by-passed here, it is for the following reasons: (1) All of these points are dealt with elsewhere in this book. (2) The sketch given is, nevertheless, based on one of Wesley's most comprehensive and representative formulas. (3) The fulness with which Wesley developed this doctrine makes the Christological grounding of sanctification the subject for a major study in itself. (4) Wesley's doctrine of sanctification has been exhaustively studied, not once but several times, by competent theologians, and a thorough treatment here could hardly do more than endorse or reaccent existing findings. (5) Except in relatively minor aspects this doctrine has nothing like the problems of the Wesleyan justification, where a certain development of the doctrine in detail will be required.

11. Further Wesleyan definitions of the church can be found in Ac 5:11 (the most comprehensive definition), Jn 10:16, Gal 1:13, 6:16, I Cor 14:4, I Th 3:13. Wesley defines the visible church as "all that name the name of Christ," and the invisible church as "all real Christians," sanctification being the norm (S. 77, i, 9; Mt 13:28, Eph 2:17, Rev 19:8).

12. Wesley places heavy emphasis on the unity of the body: I Cor 1:13, Ac 20:30, Ro 12:5, I Cor 12:12, 20, Eph 1:22, 2:15, 4:4, Phil 2:2, Col 1:18, I Th 4:15. Wesley's profound concern for the unity of the church is otherwise abundantly present in the *Notes:* cf. "Preface" to the *Notes,* 9; Jn 10:16, 11:52, I Cor 3:4, 11:18, Tit 3:10, Jude 19 (these last three concerning heresy and schism). Sermons 34 and 49, intro., also attest Wesley's ecumenical spirit. In this connection, however, Wesley's anti-Catholic polemic cannot be forgotten (*supra,* p. 124).

13. Note the parallelism: the inner kingdom begins in the heart upon conversion. The church begins—the kingdom comes "with power" —when 3,000 are converted at once. It is of interest that Wesley plays

down Peter to emphasize Christ in the founding of the church. Peter's faith was indeed a rock, but Christ pointed to Himself when He said, "On *this* rock I will build My Church"! (Mt 16:18).

14. This theme is emphasized by Wesley. But note Acts 26:24 where Festus cannot see the grace that animates Paul. He sees in Paul's zeal "a mere start of learned frenzy."

15. This theme of Christ's victory through the church's persecution was thoroughly developed by Wesley, who daily experienced what he wrote about. S. 18, iii, 1-13 offers an extended discussion of it. Cf. Ac 2:13, II Tim 3:12, Mt 5:9-12, Col 1:24. The last two references indicate Wesley's view that an increase of one's reward also results from persecution.

16. In the light of this section, it is impossible to agree with Lerch's statement that Christ's kingly office is not brought into relation to Christian *koinonia* under the kingly Head (*Heil und Heiligung*, p. 79, note 43). Lerch doubtless bases his statement on the passages where the kingly office is explicitly spoken of. There, it is true, the emphasis is "strongly individualistic," although Revelation 5:6 and the "Letter to a Roman Catholic" mention Christ's universal rule and victory. In this discussion it has been assumed that Christ's kingly office is immediately connected with His kingdom, and Wesley's abundant teaching about the latter has been applied to the former. If this method is correct, there is a direct connection, such as has been described, between the life of the church and her kingly head.

17. This study has required the splitting up of Wesley's eschatology. Here only the events of the last judgment are presented. In Chapter VI this judgment will be studied again in its character as a second justification. The final victory over Satan has already been discussed. The subsequent kingdom of glory will follow in the next section. The state of the damned is treated in connection with the wrath of God in Chapter VI. A partial justification for this procedure lies in Wesley's own tendency to think of Christ's final functions separately: He comes as "avenger and judge"; He is "the Judge, the Rewarder, the Avenger" (I Cor 10:11, Phil 4:5).

18. The reason for this emphasis on the human nature of Christ the judge is not clear. John 5:27 asserts that He was appointed judge "because He was made man." Acts 17:31 implies that without the resurrection of the body, Christ could not have been judge. Why not? John 5:23 suggests that because the humiliation of his incarnation could be misunderstood, God makes Him judge in order to "demonstrate" the equality of the Son with the Father to both faithful and

unwilling eyes. Philippians 2:10-11 tends to confirm this reading: there likewise the emphasis is that now even His enemies will have to acknowledge Him as Lord, and the additional note is struck that Christ is "not now 'in the form of a servant,' but enthroned" in the glory of God the Father.

The observation that the judge is no longer the humiliated one is underlined in two other, more problematical notes. In Revelation 1:7 Christ appears in the judgment "in a manner worthy of the Son of God," not as before when "it was not like Himself, but 'in the form of a servant.' " And in Hebrews 9:28 we hear a drastic inference: Christ in judgment will appear "not as He did before, bearing on Himself the sins of many, but to bestow everlasting salvation."

But now the emphasis on Christ's human nature has become even more puzzling. Wesley actually intends to emphasize just the opposite of Christ's human nature. It appears to be emphasized in order to give force to the declaration that He whom men have despised is nevertheless Lord and judge of all. That may well be Wesley's homiletical motive. But it creates a serious theological question, for Wesley has weakened his hold on the classic understanding of the role of Christ's human nature in the last judgment: to enable the God-man to bear our sins for us.

In S. 48, ii, 1 Wesley suggests an additional motive for emphasizing the human nature here. The humiliation-exaltation thought is here also used to explain why God committed judgment to the Son of Man. But Wesley now adds that it is also committed to Him because He was the express image of His Father's person. Here lies the suggestion that Christ's idealized human nature, which is the image of God, must be present in the last judgment as the formal standard of human perfection. In this form, the law would indeed be present in the last judgment.

It will not do to confine Wesley to this mold. Although this is one of the hardest problems in Wesley interpretation, it remains true that alongside the judging Christ, the atoning Christ is also present in the last judgment. The second justification, as will be shown, is also by faith. But the above conjecture may help to explain the austere Christ of the Book of Revelation in Wesley's *Notes* (cf. S. 48, iv, 4).

19. It has already been shown that Wesley teaches an intermediate state for the separated souls of the dead between death and judgment (*supra*, pp. 51-52). But his characterization of this state is by no means clear. He speaks a number of times of *"paradise"* as "the place where the souls of the righteous remain from death till the

resurrection" (Lk 23:43, 16:22, II Cor 12:4, Rev 14:13, all of which speak of the immediate resting place of good men). He also speaks of *"Hades"* as the "state" or "receptacle" of separate souls (Rev 6:8, I Cor 15:55; possibly Lk 20:35 belongs here). However, he does not seem to identify Hades as simply the general state into which all go (cf. Rev 1:18). We also hear of a *"hell"* (S. 17, i, 11) where sinners are "reserved" until the last judgment, and from which Wesley doubts they will come out.

We are left to conclude: (1) There is one judgment only, at the last day. (2) Separate souls are kept in an intermediate state until that day. (3) For good men, this state is clearly "paradise," although the entire state may also possibly be called "Hades." And there is also a "hell," not only after, but before the last judgment, in which men may suffer, but not so as to atone for their sins, as in a purgatory. (4) This intermediate state is indeterminate in character, although the separate soul knows of his future state, and this knowledge may account for a certain anticipation of the final result in the intermediate states of "paradise" and "hell." (5) Whatever the intermediate state, there is a general resurrection in order that all may be present at the last judgment where their eternal state will be determined.

20. Does this present creation have to be annihilated to make way for the new? Wesley gives both answers.

In S. 60, iii Wesley explains at length his view of the new creation as a liberation for animals, the coming of a perennial spring, and the possibility that men and animals will each move up a step in the "scale of beings," men occupying the present place of angels, and beasts the present place of men (but cf. Mt 25:34). The new earth will be a "Christian world" (S. 4, iii), which is explained to mean the fulfilment of the Isaiac prophecy and the consumation of the Pauline view of history. There will be no more war, internal disputes, civil discord, oppression, extortion, robbery, rapine, or injustice. There will be no need, for every man will love his neighbor as himself. Men will be joyous, believing, united in one body and one Spirit, and the Lord will reign. In Matthew 19:28 Wesley can speak of this change as a "renovation." It may be noted that "renovation" fits with the supralapsarian aspect of God's eternal decree.

However, Wesley is also capable of explaining in considerable geological and astronomical detail how this old heaven and earth will be destroyed, and a new heaven and earth, "an entire new state of things," will be "raised as it were out of the ashes of the old" (II Pet 3:10-13). "This whole beautiful fabric will be overthrown by that raging element" (fire), "the connection of all its parts destroyed, and every atom torn asunder from the others" (S. 48, iii, 2). Wesley does speculate that matter will not be "totally or finally destroyed," but changed into a material, like glass, over which fire can have no further power, since "it requires the same almighty power to annihilate things as to create, to speak into nothing or out of nothing." However, he believes that we cannot now either affirm or deny this (S. 48, iii, 3).

In line with Wesley's tendency to emphasize the continuity of both the moral law and the kingdom of God, it may be surmised that the former view is closer to his considered intention, although the latter view also has some claim to "standard" status.

21. We have here another confirmation of the supralapsarian aspect of the Wesleyan decree: i.e., God's eternal decision to create a creation of increasing holiness.

The curious Wesley incidentally asks who the subjects of these eternally reigning saints might be, and answers: "The other inhabitants of the new earth. For there must needs be an everlasting difference between those who when on earth excelled in virtue, and those comparatively slothful and unprofitable servants who were just saved as by fire" (Rev 22:4).

# CHAPTER SIX

# The Priestly Work of Christ

IN THE PRIESTLY work of Christ, His sacrifice and intercession, the center of the Wesleyan Christology is reached. Here, as nowhere else, the main themes of Wesley's theology are unified and clarified.

## 1. THE WRATH OF GOD

At the heart of the situation to which Christ's priestly work is addressed are man's offense against God Himself, and the answering wrath of God. Wesley refused to tolerate, even from his honored mentor, William Law, any softening or denial of the wrath of God. If there is no wrath of God, then there is no need of propitiation, and Christ died in vain (Ro 3:25).

Rattenbury suggests that Wesley understood the term "wrath" as a metaphor.[1] Although there is one note which ascribes wrath to God "only in an analogical sense" (Ro 5:9), Wesley's deep seriousness here is better expressed in Revelation 14:11: "God grant thou and I may never try the strict, literal eternity of this torment!" God's wrath in the last days will cover the earth with plagues (Rev 15:1, Ro 2:8; S. 73, i, 1). There is at least one lengthy explanation of the materiality of hell-fire (S. 73, ii, 4-5). In fact, Wesley senses the need for restraint of unbiblical fancies here: "This is too awful a subject to admit of such play of imagination. Let us keep to the written word" (S. 73, ii, 7).

What is God's wrath? It is the legal, just, holy, and good answer of God to wilful sin. It is not arbitrary: it "presupposes sin" (Ro 9:22, Mt 27:46). God invariably loves righteousness and hates iniquity (Jude 6). Because God is infinitely just from all eternity, His anger began to show itself when man had sinned (W. IX, 482). As a just anger, it had to be and is revealed by the law (Ro 1:17). It is, moreover, a "vindictive justice whose essential character and principal office is, to punish sin" (Ro 3:25, Heb 10:31). Wesley has no objection to using the words "wrath," "anger," and "justice" "as nearly synonymous" (W. IX, 481).

This wrath lies upon "whatever is under heaven . . . believers in Christ excepted" (Ro 1:18). It is an eternal vengeance, the sin and punishment of the damned "running parallel throughout eternity itself" (I Th 1:10, II Th 1:8-9, Rev 12:12, Mt 25:46). It is a wrath unmixed with mercy or hope (Rev 14:10-11, Jas 2:13). Wesley even finds room for the thought that it is Christ Himself who in the last day will be the executor of God's wrath (Rev 14:20, 19:15); the prayer "Maranatha" of I Corinthians 16:22 is interpreted to mean, " 'the Lord cometh;' namely, to execute vengeance."

God punishes man doubly, both with the nature of sin itself, and with vindictive justice (Ro 1:24). Both now and in the last judgment God, by withdrawing his "restraining grace," gives sinners up to their sin (Ro 1:23-24, Jn 12:39). But for the unrepentant, God's wrath also brings "vengeance," which completes their destruction (Heb 10:31, I Th 2:16). Then, in the dread "day of vengeance," God will be glorified in the execution of judgment (Ro 2:8, Ac 2:20, Rev 15:8).

One cannot escape the impression, in all this, that Wesley is more interested in describing something which sinners painfully experience than in formulating doctrine. God's wrath is significant in Wesley as the objective side of the experience of fear (S. 7, i, 10; S. 30, iii, 3). When Wesley describes the torments of hell, he describes the punishments felt (S. 73, intro., 4; ii, 2; Mk 9:44). The hardness of this doctrine, much objected to by present-day writers, must surely be understood in the light of its homiletical function: it gave urgency to the appeal for repentance and faith. The theological essence of the matter is perhaps better stated in words like these: "God alone is the center of all created spirits; and consequently, . . . a spirit made for God, can have no rest out of Him. . . . Banishment from the presence of the Lord is the very essence of destruction, to a spirit that was made for God" (S. 73, i, 4).

## 2. CHRIST'S PRIESTLY ACT UPON THE CROSS

### a. The Obedience of Christ

Wesley is apprehensive about the antinomian abuse which can be wrung from the implication that Christ's obedience takes the place of ours. He prefers to speak of Christ's righteousness or merit. But the term "obedience of Christ" is by no means alien to Wesley (Phil 2:8-9, Ro 5:19, Heb 5:7-8, Jn 10:18), and it has the advantage of aiming straight at the central problem of the Wesleyan atonement.

Wesley intends his doctrine of the atonement to be understood within the framework of Anglican and Protestant orthodoxy. The relevant passages from the Thirty-nine Articles are taken over intact.[2] Moreover, in thinking about Christ's priestly act, Wesley habitually uses the traditional scheme of Christ's active and passive obedience. If the following presentation begins with the passive obedience, it is because that is the center of Wesley's doctrine, and much the least ambiguous starting point.

### 1) The Passive Obedience

At every point Wesley emphasizes that Christ's suffering was willed by God. It was no mere accident or incident of history. Though it resulted from the enmity of the "most honorable," "most religious," and "most learned" men of the day (Mt 16:21), it was in the profoundest sense an act of God. God determined the time of the atonement: Christ could not suffer, or be destroyed, or fully manifest His glory before this time came (Jn 7:30, Mk 8:30, 5:43). When that time came, it was not primarily we but God who made Christ suffer. The Father laid our iniquities upon Him (Mt 26:37, I Cor 3:11). The Father treated Him as an enemy, while He bore our sins (Mk

15:34). It was God who loosed the powers of darkness upon Him and filled His soul with a terrible sense of the wrath due to the sins He was bearing (Mt 27:46). But God controlled even the duration and extent of Christ's suffering: Christ's crucifiers could go only so far as was prophesied, "but no farther" (Heb 12:3, Ac 13:29).

Because God willed the cross, Christ's acceptance of the passion had the character of obedience. He chose to remain on the cross voluntarily (Mt 27:50), for "His heart was fixed in choosing the will of His Father" (Jn 12:27). Wesley goes farther and insists that Christ's power to lay down His life and take it again was originally His: He did not receive it as a part of His mediatorial commission. "This commission was the reason why He thus used His power in laying down His life. He did it in obedience to His Father" (Jn 10:17-18). Wesley wants it to be clear that the subject of this act is the God-man.

Though willed by God, and freely accepted by Christ, the suffering was desperately real and painful. It broke in upon Him "with such a violence as was ready to separate His soul from His body" (Mk 14:33, 10:38). Actually feeling the pain belonged to His obedience: He refused the vinegar in obedience, "determining to bear the full force of His pains" (Mt 27:34). And so it came to the shedding of blood. Although the Wesleyans speak a great deal of the blood of Christ, Wesley refuses to hypostasize it into some kind of substance of grace. "His blood" means for Wesley "His bloodshedding," i.e., not a substance, but an act (Ro 5:9).

The meaning of this suffering is terribly simple: it is a punishment directed toward the bearer of our sins (Mt 27:46, Heb 9:28, Ro 3:26). Wesley can describe this punishment in two ways. Christ bears for us, first of all, the curse of the law, i.e., "the curse of God, which the law denounces against all transgressors of it" (Gal 3:13). Again, and more frequently, Wesley refers to Christ's burden as the wrath of God (Lk 22:44, Mt 27:46), exhibited before angels and men "to appease an offended God" (Ro 3:25). In the one instance punishment is defined in relation to the law, in the other in relation to God Himself, corresponding to the twofold answer of sanctification and justification. But here, also, Wesley's sense of priorities is reflected, for it is the personal wrath of God which Christ "most exceedingly feared ... the weight of an infinite justice, the being 'bruised' and 'put to grief' by the hand of God Himself" (Heb 5:7).

Christ is, in one blunt, accurate phrase, "a victim, to be sacrificed" (Jn 17:19).

## 2) The Active Obedience

Concerning the fact of Christ's active obedience, Wesley is perfectly clear. Christ performed a perfect negative and positive obedience. "He never spoke one improper word, nor did one improper action," a "negative" obedience such as "never did, nor ever can, belong to any one that is born of woman save Himself alone." But it was also a "positive" obedience: "He did all things well; in every word of His tongue, in every work of His hands, He did precisely the 'will of Him that sent Him.' ... The whole and every part of His obedience was complete. 'He fulfilled all righteousness!' " (S. 49, i, 3.)

The storm arose over how to evaluate the meaning of this active obedience. Wesley is willing to use the expression: "Christ fulfilled the law" (Mt 3:15-16, Lk 2:21; W. X, 282). But he very explicitly defines the significance of this fulfilment: thereby Christ established, illustrated, and explained the law's highest meaning (Mt 5:17, Ro 3:31; S. 20, i, 3). The active obedience, so far as it has a positive role, has the character of a teaching ministry, closely related to the prophetic office. It reinforces the law's authority in both sanctification and the last judgment.

When pressed, Wesley can also speak of an imputation of the active obedience, but never separately from the passive obedience, and strictly in relation to justification, never in relation to sanctification. But he assigns no discernible role to the active obedience in our justification; indeed, he seems to oppose one, as we shall see. Talk of an imputation of the active obedience must be considered primarily a defensive position in reply to the Calvinist attack, and it is grounded essentially in Wesley's conviction that the two aspects of Christ's obedience are inseparable.

It is worth getting a clearer idea of what Wesley sees at stake here, for it touches most directly the way in which justification relates to sanctification. Wesley sees the antinomians using Christ's active obedience, imputed to them, as an excuse, "a cover" for their own unrighteousness. They make "void that solemn decree of God, 'Without holiness no man shall see the Lord,' by a vain imagination of being *holy in Christ!*" (S. 49, ii, 19-20, italics Wesley's).[3] Wesley can state his position in various ways, depending on whether he is attempting a careful, balanced statement, or simply expressing his own emphasis, or defending his position in the heat of debate. When he is formulating his position with care, or making a gesture of reconciliation toward the Calvinists, he emphasizes the unity of the two obediences as the ground of our justification. This is as far as he wants to go, and the emphasis is clearly on the inseparability of the two obediences, not on the necessity for Christ's active obedience in our justification (S. 49, i, 4). Thus the phrase, "what Christ hath done and suffered," is virtually a habitual formula for him.[4] But this formula is, in Wesley's mind, weighted toward the passive obedience. "Though I believe He hath lived and died for me, yet I would speak very tenderly and sparingly of the former, (and never separately from the latter,) even as sparingly as do the Scriptures" (W. X, 330, 332).

However, when Wesley is simply expressing his own emphasis, without regard to conciliation or polemics, it is the passive obedience alone which has a significant role in our justification. The *Notes* faithfully mirror this emphasis.[5] When this emphasis is not made, Wesley can reply with some astonishment: "So here His passion is fairly left out! Whereas His 'becoming obedient unto death,' that is, dying for man, is certainly the chief part, if not the whole, which is meant by that expression" (W. X, 331).

This deliberate reserve about the active obedience may be illustrated by two more extensive examples. In the sermon where Wesley makes his most careful formulation of the doctrine of imputation, he quotes the Anglican Homily on Salvation to support the orthodoxy of his position (S. 49, ii, 6). As was his custom, he abbreviated the quotation, but, as can be seen in Appendix III, all references to Christ's fulfilling the law, to the justice of Christ, to God's justice having been "fully" satisfied, have also been left out! Again, Wesley describes Christ's active obedience (S. 49, i, 2-4) in precisely the same terms as the obedience required of Adam under the covenant of works (S. 6, i, 2). Moreover, Wesley teaches that the covenant of works was ended by Christ Himself. But when it is inquired how, the answer is: "by the oblation of Himself once offered" (S. 6, intro., 3). In other words, Christ's active obedience is simply coincidental, even in the objective setting-aside of the covenant of works.

But when debate sharpened, Wesley could be driven to the extreme consequence of his position: he denies Christ's active obedience any role in purchasing our redemption, i.e., in justification. "Although I believe Christ fulfilled God's law, yet I do not affirm He did this to purchase redemption for us. This was done by His dying in our stead" (W. X, 386).[6] At times his patience with those who so threaten the life of holiness grows thin. He entitles a tract on the subject, "A Blow at the Root; or Christ Stabbed in the House of His Friends" (W. X, 364-369). In it he can call the doctrine of Christ's imputed obedience the "masterpiece of Satan," the teaching of a reappeared Simon Magus, and those who oppose "either inward or outward holiness, under the colour of exalting Christ" Judases, betraying the Son of Man with a kiss. In his later years, Wesley repented of his conciliatory use of the phrase, "imputed righteousness," because it was constantly misunderstood to mean imputed obedience (W. X, 430).

In summary, it can be said that Wesley follows and sharpens

the tendency toward penal substitution implicit in the formularies of the Anglican church. He so conceives the priestly act of Christ as to provide a basis for removing our guilt alone, while leaving unmodified the demand for our own positive obedience. With such a view of the atonement, Wesley could be and was charged with underemphasizing the role of Christ's active obedience, and he not only accepted that charge, but vigorously defended the position that the suffering and death of Christ are the substance, if not the sum, of His priestly, that is, His substitutionary, work for us.

## b. The Righteousness of Christ

In discussing the obedience of Christ we deliberately focused upon an uncharacteristic concept in order to pinpoint the peculiarity and problem of the Wesleyan atonement. Wesley prefers to speak of Christ's merit or righteousness when referring to the Christological foundation of our salvation. "The righteousness of Christ" is actually the broader term; and it deserves its own analysis, not least because it permits a correlation between the work of Christ and the righteousness of God in the atonement.

Wesley devoted a substantial part of Sermon 49 to a systematic analysis of the righteousness of Christ. For the sake of clarity, a brief outline of the first section can be given here:

Christ's righteousness consists of two parts:

1. His divine righteousness: Wesley does not regard its imputation to be at issue in the debate with the antinomians.
2. His human righteousness: this is imputed as a whole to man. It consists of two parts:
    a. Internal human righteousness: Christ's human image of God.
    b. External human righteousness: Christ's obedience. This, in turn, consists of two parts:
       1) Active obedience: what Christ did. Two aspects can also be distinguished here:
          a) Negative active obedience: He did no sin.

      b) Positive active obedience: He did God's will
          perfectly.
    2) Passive obedience: what Christ suffered.

There are actually four key terms: Christ's divine righteousness,
His human *imago*, and the passive and active obediences. It
should also be noted that Wesley is not altogether clear about
what is imputed. In i, 1, it is the entire human righteousness,
presumably including the internal righteousness, or *imago*, a position somewhat unusual for Wesley. In i, 4, it is the external righteousness which is imputed, i.e., the two obediences. This is
Wesley's more usual position, although if the active obedience is
imputed, it is not unthinkable that Christ's human *imago*, i.e., the
human perfections from which perfect obedience springs, could
be included.

    Before we consider the four concepts in detail, it is necessary
that we pause with Wesley's understanding of "the righteousness
of God." This righteousness consists of two parts: God's essential
righteousness, and God's righteousness in us (Ro 1:17). God's
essential righteousness includes His justice and mercy, both of
which are "eminently shown in condemning sin, and yet justifying
the sinner" (Ro 1:17, 3:25, 21, 10:3). But "the righteousness of
God" can also mean the righteousness whereby a man, through
God's gift, is made righteous (Ro 1:17). This is *God's* righteousness because it is God's gift (S. 24, 21 and 20; Phil 3:9). It is
God's *righteousness* because it is "the image of God" (Ro 14:17,
I Tim 6:11; S. 24, 21 and 23).

    Against this background, the key concepts can be analyzed:

    1. *Christ's divine righteousness* is doubtless identical with
the essential righteousness of God, since in this respect He and
the Father are one (S. 49, i, 1). It must therefore also include
both justice and mercy. This double reference is found. There
is, first of all, the role of Christ's divine righteousness in providing
the background for Wesley's doctrine of Christ's merit, making
Christ "infinitely more precious than any created victim" (Heb
9:14).[7] This role could correspond to the divine mercy. But

another role can be envisaged, corresponding to the divine justice. For if Christ's human *imago* is a copy of the divine righteousness (S. 49, i, 2), then the reverse is also true: Christ's divine righteousness fully participates in the ground of His human *imago*, or, as will be shown, of the moral law which Christ's human *imago* embodies.[8]

2. *Christ's human imago* can also be related in two ways to the righteousness of God. It is, first of all, as a copy of Christ's own divine righteousness (S. 49, i, 2), necessarily a transcript of God's essential righteousness, including both justice and mercy. But Christ's *imago* also serves, in the second place, as a prototype for the progressive conformity to God's righteousness in man.[9] Here again the importance of the Christological presupposition for Wesley's doctrine of God is clearly evident. If God's righteousness is reflected in Christ's *imago*, and man's righteousness is prefigured there, then Christ's *imago* represents the formal point where the two basic elements of God's righteousness are one.

Here a digression is necessary, for the crucial problem about Christ's *imago* concerns its correspondence to, or possible identity with, what Wesley also calls the moral law. It has been noted that Wesley asserts the identity of the law of creation and the law of love without explicit reference to Christ, except that the active obedience confirms the content of both, and presumably reveals their identity also. But the curious notion of Christ's imputed *imago*, inseparable as it is from the active obedience, suggests a Christological center for the doctrine of the law, whereby Christ not only reveals but defines its content.

It can be noted, to begin with, that Wesley uses almost identical language about Christ's *imago* and the moral law.[10] If this correlation can be maintained, then what happens to Christ's *imago* in the passion happens to the law. When Christ's sacrifice re-establishes the law, it is *this* representation of the law, i.e., Christ's humanity, which, crucified and risen, stands as the decisive definition of all law. The new commandment is not only love in the abstract, but that love which is defined by Christ's suffering humanity. More than revelation is involved here. If the humanity of Christ represents the law, then the law is inseparably bound to Christ; Christ's fate is the law's fate; Christ's cross and resurrection are the law's end and fulfilment, and the resurrection of the body is the law's re-establishment as promise to the believer. Here where the law of God ends and begins, law is defined. There is then no longer simply an equation of the law of creation and the law of love. That semi-independent law of creation and that semi-independent law of love are both disclosed to be expressions of *this* essence: the self-giving will of God in the humanity of Christ. While it is not impossible to say, in a derived sense, that the basis of the law is "the fitness of things," or "the great ocean of love" in God, it is more to the point to say that the basis of the law is the love operative in the humanity of Jesus Christ.

On this ground it becomes clear that the obedience demanded of the believer is not simply meticulous conformity to an abstract law of creation, or feeling a "temper" or "affection" of love, but rather a participation in the living Jesus Christ's wondrously creative and unbounded passion to serve the brother, in a way utterly relevant to his concrete situation and need. In Christ the law itself, as Christ's human *imago*, dies and rises again. Christ's risen *imago* is no longer represented by the decalogue and Israel, but by the Word proclaimed and the life of His Body, the church. Now the Christian is invited not only to hear and obey the law, but to share the promised new life with Christ and neighbor, to participate in the "fulfilled" law by walking in the power of the Holy Spirit the path of death and new life of self, for others, with Christ. That is what it could mean that the law, i.e., Christ's risen humanity, confronts believers as the consequence and promise, not the condition, of justification. It is *this* risen humanity which confronts believers as the promise of what the Holy Spirit will write on the heart. *This* risen humanity shows believers not only the demand of love, but the love first given to man, and therefore the love for others whose power is not man's but God's.

In all these respects the moral law turns its promissory face to man, so to speak, in the risen humanity of Christ, imputed to believers in the form of participation in Christ's corporate Body, with its hearing of the Word and its mission of witness and service in the world. Here the law is seen as grace, "costly grace," which at once disciplines and liberates.

It is not claimed here that Wesley made this application of his curious suggestion that Christ's *imago* is imputed to us, although he did teach, in no uncertain terms, the promissory character of the law for believers. It must be remembered also that all depends on a correlation of Christ's human *imago* and the moral law which remains only implicit in Wesley, apart from two exceptions: first, the active obedience which reinforces (but does not redefine) the law; second, and more significant, the "mind of Christ" theme which serves widely as a definition of perfect holiness. Further, it is essential to see. that this unveiling of the law's face depends on its identification, not with Christ's humanity as such, but, as Wesley always insists, with the passion, death, and resurrection of that humanity. Having conceded all that, the question can still be put: is the above identification an illegitimate expression of Wesley's own principles? Is this, as Wesley feared, opposing holiness to exalt Christ?

Returning to the formal analysis of Christ's human *imago*, if that *imago* does in fact represent the moral law, it can then be seen to reflect both aspects of God's essential righteousness. The justice of God is mirrored in the role which Christ's *imago* plays as the law of creation in the doctrines of repentance and the last judgment. The mercy can be seen in the way in which Christ's *imago* defines the law of love in the cross and resurrection.

3. *Christ's passive obedience* can also have a double relation to God's essential righteousness. On the one hand, it exhibits the essential righteousness of God as nothing else does. His justice is shown in the punishment of Christ, who bears our sins, and His mercy is manifested in the atonement's provision of a

"method" for becoming righteous. On the other hand, Christ's passive obedience provides the ground for the progressive conformity to the essential righteousness of God in man. It does this by making possible the renewed fellowship of sinner and God, from which comes the spiritual life and growth in holiness which restores the image of God in man. In Christ's passive obedience, therefore, lies the key to the inner relation of the various aspects of Gods righteousness: it enables a God whose mercy wishes fully to reinscribe His righteousness in man's heart to do so without, presumably, violating the justice which is the other side of His essential righteousness.

What is more, the passive obedience of Christ is the focal point for many of the themes discussed thus far. Not only do the sinner's self-justification and God's mercy confront one another here; this is also the meeting ground for the covenant of works and the covenant of grace, and therefore for the two characters of the law, its condemnation and its promise, or Christ's just *imago* and His merciful *imago*. Finally, this is where God's own attributes of justice and mercy meet and God is reconciled with Himself. It is not too much to say, with such an understanding of God's attributes, that here, in Christ's suffering death, is the place where God's essential righteousness, with its two poles of justice and mercy, is really, wholly righteous. More than any other point, the passive obedience of Christ unites Wesley's theology.

4. There remains the problem of *Christ's active obedience*. Related primarily to the doctrines of sanctification and repentance, its most characteristic role is explaining the law in its fulness, and thus "fulfilling" it. It is very likely, in the light of Wesley's doctrine of the law, that Christ's fulfilment of the law, like the decalogue, must be understood primarily as a republication of the moral law. In so far as the moral law is the transcript of the divine righteousness, Christ's active obedience should set forth God's full essential righteousness, both justice and mercy. However, in and of itself, the active obedience can reveal only

the demand that men be both just and righteous. That means it has only the capacity to reveal sin, and drive us to Christ's passive obedience. In this, the role of the active obedience corresponds to Wesley's first two uses of the law.

This way of saying it is faithful to Wesley's polemically determined doctrine of imputation. But it does not do justice to Wesley's own doctrine of sanctification. For the believer, love fulfils the law, a love which is defined as purity of intention, or, decisively, as "all the mind which was in Christ" (W. XI, 444). But this means that the law has not simply been republished by Christ; it has been decisively redefined. In Christ the secret heart of the law is both grounded and revealed, much as was conjectured above concerning Christ's imputed *imago*. Moreover, against the background of the priestly and kingly work of Christ, this new law confronts us not simply as condemnation, but as promise, corresponding to Wesley's third use of the law. If Christ's active obedience reveals the existence which, though sinful man is incapable of it in his own strength, God has nevertheless promised to him, then there is a sense in which the active obedience, as such, reflects not simply the law but the gospel; not simply the demand for mercy and righteousness, but the merciful character of this demand, as well; not simply the justice and mercy of God's essential righteousness, but that righteousness of God, inseparable from it, "by which a man, through the gift of God, is made and is righteous" (Ro 1:17). It cannot be said that Wesley developed a doctrine of Christ's active obedience adequate to the role which it must, in fact, actually play in the depths of his thinking. When it is understood to play this role, it is significant that a powerful safeguard is at hand against that separating of God's attributes of mercy and justice which threatens Wesley's theology at more than one point.

This much is clear: in order to confront us as grace and not simply as law, there must be some sense in which Christ's active obedience is included in the "in Christ" of sanctification. When His human righteousness is not included in God's gift to man, then it stands simply as a norm against man. The theological result will then be that redeemed man will be held capable of a perfect obedience to God's positive justice, or that this justice will be scaled down to human possibilities, or that this justice will remain unfulfilled, or some combination of these. These consequences lead to a general question: agreeing with Wesley's intention, i.e., agreeing that no unholy life can be a Christian life, were there other ways in which Wesley could have grounded this intention Christologically than by setting aside the imputation of Christ's active righteousness in man's sanctification?

But Wesley also declares that the imputation of Christ's active obedience has some role, together with the passive obedience, in justification, although it is extraordinarily difficult to imagine how it accomplishes all that Wesley claims for it here. Wesley's explicit position is that the active obedience which counts for the believer is his own obedience, not Christ's. Purely as a conjecture, it may be suggested that Christ's active obedience has a necessary role in God's just disposition of the damned.[11] If, in addition, it is true that the justification of believers remains eternally a justification by faith, i.e., if there never comes a time when their own active obedience is judged for itself with all the rigor of God's justice, then there will be a necessity, even if unacknowledged by Wesley, for Christ's active obedience to be imputed for them also. Gods attributes of mercy and justice will harmonize in no other way. This question will be investigated further in the section on justification.

A general conclusion about the priestly act upon the cross can perhaps be drawn at this point. The general doctrine of Christ's righteousness permits one to see deep into the unity of the gospel for Wesley. On this ground, justification and sanctification, as well as the three offices, can all be understood as grace. Consider the Wesleyan gospel as a whole: man stands under the wrath of God and has lost his essence, the *imago dei*. In His priestly act on the cross, Christ substitutes for man in accepting the wrathful but ·ust punishment due to past sins. This is the essential content in

Wesley's first justification: the setting aside of condemnation, and the consequent restoration of life-giving fellowship with God. Then, in Christ's prophetic ministry the humanity (i.e., the law) of Christ which, until then, had condemned man, is transformed into a goal and promise of sanctification, i.e., of the restored *imago dei* in man. And this sanctification will stand as evidence in the final justification for the presence of authentic faith which justifies because it believes in Christ's righteousness. It remains for us to add that the restoration of the *imago dei* in man is thought of, by Wesley, as the work of the Spirit of Christ (S. 49, ii, 12), which, viewed in its cosmic perspective as the destruction of the works of the devil, is the main theme of Christ's kingly work. Here, then, the three offices of Christ can be unified: on the basis of the priestly work, both the prophetic and kingly work can be understood as grace. Let it be clearly said that a decision in Wesley interpretation is demanded here: the prophetic and kingly work, the giving of the law and sanctification, can be understood in a legalistic way, and then the problem of Wesleyan two-sidedness must be faced in all its insolubility. The claim here is that on the ground of the priestly work, the prophetic and kingly offices can also be understood as grace.

### c. The Roles of the Two Natures in the Atonement

Lindström finds that, according to Wesley's thought, the satisfaction given by Christ is given *"qua homo,"* and points out that in this Wesley follows the Anselmic and Protestant-orthodox pattern.[12] This claim probably needs qualification. Although there are passages where Wesley does emphasize the role of the human nature in the atonement, there is here a clear role for both natures. This is the more surprising in the light of his reserve about the human nature and the attenuated personal union. These earlier findings notwithstanding, Wesley insists that both natures are present and active in Christ's atoning act, and indeed, in such a way that the divine nature may ultimately have the crucial role. It is true that full emphasis is given to the human nature of the Reconciler. Lindström cites two passages: in S. 49, i, 1, the fullest statement about Christ's righteousness, Wesley confesses that he does not see that the divine righteousness of Christ is concerned in the doctrine of imputation; and in S. 31, i, 6 Wesley emphasizes that Christ is "our great High-priest, 'taken from among men, and ordained for men.'" To Lindström's passages might be added others from the *Notes:* Eph 1:3, Heb 1:9, I Tim 2:5, and especially Col 1:22 which speaks of our being reconciled by "His entire manhood," and Jn 14:19 where the resurrection applies to the human nature only.

But, of course, Anselm, although he emphasizes the role of Christ's perfect manhood, insists that the subject of the atonement is the "God-man," and in this Wesley certainly follows him (the term occurs, e.g., in Ac 10:36). Wesley frequently goes out of his way to emphasize both natures. The Mediator is "one Christ, very God and very man (Art. II; Phil 2:8, Heb 2:10). He speaks of "the blood of the Son of God" (Ac 20:28, II Cor 5:19). In S. 59, i, 3 it is "the Son of God" who bears our sins in His own body on the tree, and to whose death we are made conformable. It is stressed that the generation of the High Priest is from eternity (Heb 4:14, 5:5). In fact, once, when he was challenged on the very passage which Lindström cites (S. 49, i, 1), with the charge that by eliminating Christ's divine righteousness he was undermining Christ's merit, Wesley replied, with some impatience, that of course he meant "by Christ's human righteousness, . . . that mediatorial righteousness which was wrought by God in the human nature" (W. X, 384).

Wesley may, as a matter of fact, go farther and actually emphasize the divinity of the one who suffers and dies on the cross. The heavy emphasis on the divine nature in general must be remembered here. When He is crucified, then the Jews will know that He is "God over all" (Jn 8:28). Wesley insists that the whole Godhead was in Christ when He took away "that enmity, which could no otherwise be removed than by the blood of the Son of God" (II Cor 5:19). "As Mediator," He has the same "divine nature, perfections, and operations" as the Father (Jn 17:10, II Cor 11:3); it is one grace in Jesus Christ and in God the Father (Ro 1:7). Even in expounding the Second Adam theme, Wesley finds occasion to identify "the second man" as the one who "Himself made the heavens" (I Cor 15:47). Indeed, the human nature is seen as a necessary preparation for the pre-existent Messiah's act of self-offering (Heb 10:5).

Does Wesley agree with Anselm on the person of the Reconciler? In general, yes: the Crucified is necessarily "the God-man." But there is a distinction. In Anselm, God plans the atonement, and the God-man executes it as perfect man, backed by the infinite merit of the divine nature. At the crucial point the atonement is performed, as Lindström says, *qua homo,* with an interruption in the order of grace, God's interest being represented at this crucial point by His justice. In Wesley the *qua homo* is less emphatic and clear. The subject of the atonement is the God-man, seen from the perspective of His divine nature, but provided with a human nature as a necessary instrument for His atoning work, which consists primarily in His death, not so much as man, as for man. In Wesley there is a definite tendency to suggest that the one who suffers and dies is God, even though John 14:19 somewhat inconsistently permits the resurrection to apply to the human nature only.

Is this consistent with Wesley's theology as a whole? It is surprising how consistent it actually is. First, Wesley's dislike of the antinomian understanding of imputed holiness has led him to play down Christ's active human obedience. This agrees with, if it is not actually the root of, Wesley's general reserve about Christ's human nature. Second, Wesley's view of God's punishing wrath requires in the atonement primarily the death of a sacrificial victim, a bearer of punishment. A certain emphasis on Christ's human nature will allow the substitution to take place, but a heavy identification of the Representative Man with our human nature, as demanded by the doctrine of an imputed active righteousness, is not required. Third, the subject of the kingly atonement, studied in the last chapter, must be primarily God Himself. The *Christus victor* and the penal substitution themes are mixed in Wesley, and yet the figure on the cross is one. The *Christus victor* theme, of course, requires an emphasis on the divine nature which Wesley otherwise is not loath to make. Fourth, and most important, there is a real question, as will be shown, whether God's justice is ever really "satisfied" in Wesley's atonement. It is possible that at the crucial point, God's justice abdicates, and God's mercy justifies. In so far as this is true, Wesley is perfectly consistent here in suggesting that God is not in the judge's seat, but, by some prodigy of mercy, is Himself in the dock with us, suffers with us, and dies in fellowship with us. In the Wesleyan justification God is mercifully reconciled with a sinner before the sinner has satisfied the positive demand of God's justice in any way. Is it too much to say that in the Wesleyan atonement God actually dies—at least as the God of that semi-independent moral law—in order to renew and maintain His fellowship with man, and to reveal to man in a new way the heart of the law? The Anselmic tradition, represented in Protestant orthodoxy, considers it the role of the divine nature to supply the efficacy of the human nature's passion. In Wesley, though there are substantial traces of this Anselmic thought, the divine nature is there much more to make tolerable a situation where "justice" is not being done, according to that semi-independent moral law. Could there be a more eloquent testimony that the moral law actually does have penultimate significance, and that Wesley really does mean for the law to lead us to Christ and to keep us there?

Lindström, of course, means that Wesley regards the satisfaction of the *God-man* to be given *qua homo*. Lindström agrees, however, that in the light of Wesley's underemphasis of Christ's active righteousness, "it is clear that the judicial factor cannot be as important in his view of the atonement as it was to the orthodox."[13] It is possible, however, that Lindström's adherence to the Lund perspective on types of atonement theory, as he explains it on page 61, obscures for him the degree to which, in Wesley, too, "God reconciles and is at the same time reconciled." Moreover, for Wesley there is a sense in which the legal order is, if not "overruled," at least transformed, while the order of God's mercy remains continuous. It may be added that unless God is the Reconciler, *qua deus*, the harmonization of His attributes depends upon a human act, which will make a critical Wesleyan theological problem drastic.

### 3. Christ's Priestly Intercession

The second major part of Christ's priestly office is His intercession at the right hand of the Father. Although Wesley often speaks of it, especially in connection with his beloved Epistle to the Hebrews, the significance of this doctrine, as the ground of our being "in Christ," is curiously undeveloped. This may be explained by the fact that the role of Christ as priestly intercessor parallels the role of the exalted Christ which Wesley prefers to express in terms of the kingly office. Nevertheless, the outlines of a doctrine of Christ's intercession are there, and implicitly important for Wesley's doctrine of the church.

The relation of Christ's intercession to the cross is very close: the cross provides the basis for the intercession (Heb 4:14, 9:12). Christ has ascended into the presence of the Father, bearing His wounds with Him, and there they speak for men forever in the ears of God (Rev 5:6, Heb 10:11-12; S. 8, ii, 7). But though the wounds speak, Christ intercedes as one who has a right to be heard, not as a servant, but as a Son (Jn 17:24, I Jn 2:1). The effect of this intercession is mediation: "The gifts of God all pass through Christ to us; and all our petitions and thanksgivings pass through Christ to God" (Ro 1:8, 8:34, Heb 2:17).

Wesley stresses two principal results of Christ's intercession: access to the Father, and all spiritual blessings (I Cor 8:6), a formula which corresponds to the Wesleyan concepts of justification and sanctification. Believers have access to the Father, because Christ presents Himself there together with all believers,

His "younger brethren" (Heb 2:13, 17, Rev 3:5). They now stand before God with unrestrained liberty of speech, "such as children use in addressing an indulgent father, when, without fear of offending, they disclose all their wants" (Eph 3:12). Through the interceding Christ believers can pray to the Father and give thanks to Him (I Cor 1:2, Col 3:17, Eph 5:20). From this intercession, believers receive all spiritual blessings. Foremost among these is the gift of the Holy Spirit, who makes intercession for us in our hearts as Christ intercedes in heaven (Eph 4:10, Rev 7:17, Ro 8:26). Christ's intercession thus results in the appropriation of salvation to believers: justification (Ro 4:25), sanctification and glorification (Ro 8:38-39), and, finally, eternal life (I Jn 5:11).

When Wesley turns his attention more explicitly to our participation in this intercession, he thinks primarily in terms of the Head and Body of Christ. United with Him in one Body, we are raised with Him as our living Head (I Cor 10:17, I Th 4:14). The sufferings of the church, therefore, can be termed the sufferings of Christ, supplied with His strength, spirit, and sense (Col 1:24). Likewise, it is to His Body, the church, that Christ communicates His blessings (I Jn 5:11, Eph 4:10). The "in Christ" theme of Paul is not heavily emphasized by Wesley apart from this context, possibly as part of his reserve against the mystics and antinomians.[14] It is notable that when Wesley speaks of being "in Christ" he often relates it to the Body of Christ (S. 8, i, 1). But Wesley does not intend this reference to the Body of Christ to imply a sacramentalism or ecclesiasticism. Faith, not the means of grace alone, unites us with the Head: "Our Lord ... speaks of no branches but such as are ... united to Him by living faith" (Jn 15:5, I Jn 3:6). The warning against understanding our participation in Christ by sacramental means only is made explicit (Jn 15:6, I Cor 11:24).

For whom does Christ intercede? Wesley notes that in the "high-priestly prayer" Christ prays explicitly for the world, that it may believe (Jn 17:9, 21). And His intercession on the cross "procured forgiveness for all that were penitent, and a suppression of vengeance for the impenitent" (Lk 23:34). However, apart from these instances, Wesley's emphasis is clearly on Christ's intercession for the church (Eph 4:10, Heb 9:12).

In spite of the earlier suggestion about an end to Christ's mediatorial office, Wesley teaches that Christ's intercession lasts forever (Heb 7:1, 24, 28). It is an "unchangeable priesthood," "altogether excellent, new, firm, perpetual" (Heb 7:21, 1).

Two general comments about Christ's priestly intercession can be made at this point. First, this is above all the doctrine which explains our participation in Christ's atoning work, and through that our relation to the entire prophetic and kingly work, as well. This is the place where the gift of the Holy Spirit, with all the implied witness of regeneration and power of sanctification, is clarified. Why, then, the relatively modest development of this doctrine in Wesley? Two answers can be given. First, much which has already been spoken of as Christ's priestly work actually belongs within this doctrine, especially for one who, like Wesley, habitually thinks from the perspective of the exalted Christ. The primary reference of the priestly work in all the passages about the three offices analyzed in Chapter III is, strictly speaking, the exalted Christ's intercessory work. If that is true, then the doctrine of Christ's intercession has not received the attention it deserves in Wesley's theology. Secondly, this is a doctrine through which the proper relation of Christ's active obedience and sanctification could appear. In this context Christ's active obedience could be spoken of in a way which cuts the nerve of antinomianism, with its calculating reliance on the "once-for-all" of Christ's obedience. It may be that Wesley's shyness of the antinomian and mystical abuses of the "in Christ" theme, together with his failure in the standard writings to reflect the importance of the doctrine of the church for his own thinking, in part account for his failure to take the lead in exploring the meaning of the doctrine of Christ's intercession.

A second general comment is this: the doctrine of Christ's

intercession suggests the hidden importance of the doctrine of the church for Wesley's theology. If Wesley did not provide his societies with a doctrine of the church, it was not because he lacked one, or considered it unimportant, but because he presupposed for himself and his movement the Church of England. Wesley never intended his message to lead a man to sanctification apart from participation in a living Christian community, be it Anglican congregation or Methodist society. "Preaching like an apostle, without joining together those that are awakened, and training them up in the ways of God, is only begetting children for the murderer" (*Journal*, June 25, 1763). But the heart of the congregation's life and growth is the risen, interceding Christ. It may be asked whether Wesley's doctrine of salvation can be properly understood apart from the doctrine of the church as the Body of the interceding Christ.

## 4. The Consequence of Christ's Priestly Work: Justification

Justification by faith is "the atonement of Christ actually applied to the soul of the sinner" (S. 1, ii, 7; Ro 4:5). Wesley regarded this doctrine as the foundation of all else: it is "the cornerstone of the whole Christian building" (S. 30, ii, 6). Theologically, it is at once the key and the problem of Wesley's thinking.[15]

### a. God's Justice and Man's Justification

Wesley intends to maintain the Anselmic view that God's justice must be satisfied in the reconciliation of man. In what sense is God's justice satisfied in the Wesleyan atonement and its appropriation?

To begin with, it should be said that Wesley's interests are on the human side of this problem. He is not primarily worried about how God's justice is objectively fulfilled, but about how we, who deserve to be consumed by the divine justice, have been given a way out of the predicament (II Cor 5:21). Nevertheless, he asserts categorically that there is a satisfaction of God's justice

(S. 49, ii, 6; II Pet 1:1). Christ has suffered the punishment which God's justice decreed for us (S. 5, i, 8; S. 49, ii, 6; I Pet 2:24). The merit of this atonement is interposed in the law court of God; justice is satisfied; and sin is remitted (Ro 4:5).

The crucial presuppositions for Wesley's penal substitution theory are the distinction between past and future sins, and the double demand of the law. Justification, both present and final, deals solely with past acts of transgression and the guilt which attaches to them. Apart from this it has no reference to a condition of sin, or in any way to man's future status (S. 1, ii, 3; S. 8, ii, 1-3; Ro 3:25).[16] For its part, the law demands both a positive performing of obedience and a penalty for disobedience (W. X, 281; Mt 5:18; cf. S. 30, iii, 2). In his theory of atonement, Wesley separates the two parts of this demand temporally. Man, as he stands here and now before the judgment of God, is not faced with the double demand with regard to the past, but only with the obligation to bear the penalty for past disobedience (W. X, 324). There is nothing in Wesley about any missing positive obedience in the sinner's past. Indeed, there is an explicit rejection of any talk about a "satisfaction" having to be made to the law itself, as if it were a creditor, once punishment has been borne (W. X, 318). The positive demand of the law is related solely to the future. Thus, with regard to past sins, Wesley can claim that God's justice can be entirely fulfilled by the alternative method of bearing the penalty.

Christ did both obey and die, but His satisfaction of divine justice for us consisted only of His dying. That dying covered our past sin and the penalty of the law. Because God is just, He will pardon men for their past sins on the strength of Christ's penal substitution. That is enough, in Wesley's view, to restore believers to God's fellowship (I Jn 1:9); it is Christ's bearing the weight of God's "infinite justice" for us (Heb 5:7). It must be remembered, however, that the positive demand of the law is still outstanding, and referred to the future. Does Wesley, himself, have any qualms about this interpretation of God's justice? There

are data which at least permit us to raise this question. In quoting
the Anglican Homily on Salvation, he omits phrases which suggest
that the justified believer's debt to the divine justice is "fully" paid
(Appendix III). Sugden points out the peculiarity that Wesley
seems especially anxious to speak of God's mercy as well as God's
justice in relation to justification.[17] In passages where Paul speaks
of God's righteousness as the foundation of justification, Wesley
adds the reference to God's mercy (Ro 3:26; cf. S. 6, intro., 2;
ii, 8). Once he uses the curious phrase, "mercy mixed with justice"
(W. IX, 485). Is it the part of mercy to omit reference to the
positive fulfilment of God's justice in present justification?

How, then, is the law positively fulfilled?[18] The question is
made more urgent by Wesley's claim that, although Christ positively fulfilled the law, there is no imputation of this active obedience to the believer in the place of his own present and future
active obedience. If there is a fulfilment of the law for the
believer, it will be his own fulfilment, worked in him by the
Spirit of Christ (S. 49, ii, 12). The believer is, indeed, clothed with
Christ's righteousness, but by way of the progressive restoration of the believer's own *imago* which conforms to that of Christ
(II Cor 5:3, Mt 22:12). The positive fulfilment of God's righteousness, then, "in its purity," in its "holiness," is possible in the
believer (Ro 3:31, 8:4), by way of love, which is the "sum of all
Christian righteousness" (S. 7, i, 9; Gal 5:14, Ro 13:8). And this
love is not to be understood as the believer's participation in
Christ's love, but as his answer to Christ's love, a human "temper,"
worked in him by the Holy Spirit (Ro 13:8-10; S. 20, iv, 11). But
this love is the key concept of the Wesleyan sanctification. The
conclusion has to be drawn that the positive fulfilling of the law's
demand takes place for Wesley not in justification, but in
sanctification.[19]

Is the "fulfilment" of the law in sanctification a "satisfaction"
of God's justice? It must be remembered that the law is fulfilled
in sanctification according to its "intention," in which, as far as
"intention" is identified with "temper" (S. 20, iv, 11), it is not

entirely clear that a modification of the law's demand does not take place (*supra*, p. 99). In the second justification, on the other hand, which lies on the other side of sanctification, the positive fulfilling of the law is still not judged, as such: there the believer's "intention" to obey is the test, the "evidence," for the presence of justifying faith in the merits of Christ's passive obedience. Only if this "evidence" of faith were to be judged as obedience, and again only if it measured up as perfect positive obedience to the moral law, could a full "satisfaction" of God's justice be spoken of in the Wesleyan doctrine of salvation.

The conclusion must be that only God's condemning justice is "satisfied" in justification. Christ's atonement is a penal substitution only. God's positive justice is never judged as "satisfied," i.e., the positive demand of the law is never, strictly speaking, fulfilled, although it does perform a many-sided function in shaping the believer's sanctification, and its "intention" is fulfilled in the "tempers" of love. In the light of this position, must it not be asked whether Wesley has adequately measured his teaching against the words of his own Article IV: "We are accounted righteous before God . . . ?"

## b. Present Justification

The precise content of the first justification, which Wesley usually calls simply "justification," is that by faith man receives forgiveness of past sins, and acceptance again by God into His fellowship. His favorite formula is "pardoned and accepted" (Ro 3:24, 20, Col 2:14, Tit 3:5; S. 49, ii, 10; S. 5, ii).

Past sins are forgiven for the sake of Christ's blood shed for us, and that means that they are no more remembered to our condemnation. "They are as though they had never been" (Jas 5:20; S. 8, ii, 1). Not sin, not the sinner, but past sins are forgiven: they cannot be forgiven before they happen (W. X, 267, 278-79). This emphasis agrees with Wesley's tendency to regard justification as something that does not happen once for all in the Christian's life. The forgiven sinner is accepted, reconciled, brought again into fellowship with God by the act of Christ which has slain the enmity separating sinners from God (Eph 2:16, II Cor 8:12, Ro 1:17, Jn 1:14). Consistent with the teaching about the fulfilment of the law in sanctification, God here accepts the believer "as if he had been altogether righteous" (Ro 4:3; S. 30, ii, 7).[20] Wesley's main interest in justification seems to be, then, not so much God's justice, as the restored fellowship of the believer with God, which is the nerve of spiritual life and the presupposition for growth in sanctification.

Wesley calls faith the "condition," the only condition, of justification (Ro 4:9, 5:5; S. 50, iii, 1). By faith he means not simply assent to revelation, but trust which is a sure confidence, a fidelity, a reliance, a recumbency on Christ, a fleeing to the wounds of a crucified Savior, and a reliance on His merits (S. 1, i, 5; Mt 23:23, 15:28, II Cor 8:12). Nevertheless, it is not the attitude itself but the object of faith which counts: "Faith justifies only as it refers to, and depends on, Christ" (Heb 11:1). Wesley emphasizes that this faith is a gift (Ac 3:16, Heb 12:2, Jn 6:44, Ro 4:5, Ac 5:31, Eph 2:8). But his most characteristic emphasis is that authentic faith works by love, and cannot subsist without works (Mt 25:3, 34, Rev 20:12, Jas 2:14). It is the fountain of good affections (S. 21, intro., 1). No reading of Wesley is just which overlooks this remarkably rich and active understanding of the fulness of faith. Faith and works are never to be separated, yet faith retains the priority, and they are never to be identified: "Faith hath not its being from works (for it is before them), but its perfection" (Jas 2:22). The sacraments are "tokens" of faith, but where faith is lacking, the sacraments will not save (Mk 16:16; W. X, 192). The real signs of faith are the fruits of faith: peace, hope, love, and power over sin. "Where these are not, that faith is not" (Ro 5:1).

It cannot be overlooked that present justification has a certain conditional and provisional character; just as there was no talk of comfort from the conditional Wesleyan decree, so the peace of justification is not entirely an unqualified peace.

God's eternal vengeance remains a possible end for every
Christian's life, if he makes shipwreck of his faith (Heb 10:38,
I Th 1:10). God's grace is "strong and sweet, yet still resistible"
(Jn 6:44). "Backsliding" out of justification is accordingly a
Methodist possibility (S. 8, ii, 3). This means that the peace
which Wesley associated with justification must also have a
certain provisional character (S. 7, i, 10). Strictly speaking,
we are saved "from the fear, though not from the possibility,
of falling away from the grace of God" (S. 1, ii, 4). And from this
provisionality arises the need not only for the Methodist doctrine
of assurance, by the inner witness of the Spirit, but also for
the final justification, where the result is certain.

### c. Final Justification

The conditional and provisional character of present justification must be evaluated against the breadth of the total doctrine.
Present justification includes only the elements of forgiveness
and reconciliation. The element of judgment, on which the
finality of justification is grounded, in so far as it is present at all,
is deliberately postponed until the final justification.[21]

The factual question must be answered first: in what sense
did Wesley teach two justifications? The question needs to
be explored, for the second justification seemingly played
a secondary if not minor role in Wesleyan polemics, and among
contemporary interpreters of Wesley's theology only Lindström
and Shipley seem aware of its significance.

The earliest reference is probably that of the *Journal* for
December 13, 1739, where Wesley appears to be not at all
sympathetic to the idea of a second justification. Paul and the
Anglican articles refer only to "present remission," our "first
acceptance," when they speak of justification.[22] Nevertheless, in
S. 5, ii, 5, from the same year, Wesley admits that there is a
sense in which the word "justification" can be used, biblically,
to refer to the final judgment, although it is a "distant sense,"
and clearly on the margin of Wesley's thinking.

In the polemical works of 1772-73, however, Wesley defends a twofold justification with vigor. Although the Articles of Religion teach only one justification, Jesus in Matthew 12:37 taught a second, and every Protestant who believes the Bible therefore believes in a twofold justification.[28]

The note on Matthew 12:37 suggests some of the content of the doctrine:

*For by thy words* (as well as thy tempers and works) *thou shalt* then *be* either acquitted or condemned. Your words as well as actions shall be produced in evidence for or against you, to prove whether you was a true believer or not. And according to that evidence you will either be acquitted or condemned in the great day.

There is an explicit reference here to acquittal, i.e., to the element of judgment which was missed in present justification.

In the light of this representative, but not exhaustive, evidence, the following summary statements can be made: (a) There is a twofold justification in Wesley. (b) Present justification is that referred to by Paul and the Anglican articles, final justification that referred to by Christ in Matthew 12:37. (c) Final justification tends to have the character of acquittal under judgment, an element lacking in present justification. (d) It is probable that the idea of a twofold justification grew more important to Wesley as he grew older. (e) Final justification remains, nevertheless, a justification by faith, although works are then adduced to prove the existence of living faith.

The crucial problem, of course, concerns the way in which works and faith are related in this final justification. It is clear that works are much more prominent in the second than in the first justification. Christ then judges every man "according to his works" (Ro 2:11, Heb 10:37, Rev 22:12). It is not the hearers but the doers of the law who are finally acquitted and rewarded (Ro 2:13, Jas 2:12). Moreover, the sentence pronounced in the final justification is irreversible, and its effects remain forever (Heb 6:1, Rev 22:11). But these works do not

lay hold of eternal life; it is rather that the lack of them may
cause God to withhold his grace (I Tim 6:19). "Evil works
merit the reward they receive; good works do not. The former
demand wages: the latter accept a free gift" (Ro 6:23). Wesley
wants it to be perfectly clear that the merit involved in final
justification is solely the merit of Christ (W. X, 320). The
works, with all the stress they receive, are evidences, in Wesley's
decisive note, "to prove whether you was a true believer or not"
(Mt 12:37). They do not justify, or procure justification, "but
prove us to be justified" (W. X, 307). In an especially beautiful
formulation, it is faith that saves us, not love, for "love is
salvation" (Lk 7:50).[24]

Wesley's intention can probably best be grasped here if one
begins with his insistence that authentic faith simply has it in
its nature to beget works (Jas 2:22). The only question is
whether there has been time and opportunity for this begetting
to take place. In first justification this time was lacking, hence,
as in the case of the thief on the cross, it is by faith alone,
without works. In final justification there will have been for
most both time and opportunity. Yet, it remains true that God
in the final day pronounces them righteous not because of
their works, but because of their authentic faith in the merit
of their Redeemer. It must be said that Wesley's evangelical
intention has the final word. And the price of this word is a
qualified satisfaction of the positive demand of God's justice.

There is another occurrence associated with final justification
which marks it off from present justification in a decisive way:
an end is put to original sin. The guilt of original sin has been
removed in present justification (Art. II; W. X, 190), but original
sin remains in the believer, even though it is "gradually killed,
by virtue of our union with Him" (Ro 6:6). Yet, even perfection,
which marks the end of actual sin, does not mark the end of
original sin (S. 8, ii, 5-7; S. 35, i, 1-9). But Christ does put an
end to original sin at the end of the world (W. X, 278). From
this perspective, Christ's work in overcoming sin can be sum-

marized as follows: the guilt of sin, both original and actual, is taken away in justification; the power of sin is taken away in sanctification; actual sin is taken away in 'perfection; and original sin is taken away at the end of the world.

Wesley gives a final warning about the seriousness of this final judgment: he who falls short at the final justification incurs a "greater damnation" (II Pet 2:20). "All blood and righteousness of Christ, unless 'that mind be in thee which was in Him,' and thou likewise 'walk as Christ walked,' will only increase thy damnation" (W. X, 368; Jn 3:3, Ac 2:19, Ro 2:9, Heb 4:2). Therefore, the sure mark of a true or false Christian is whether he longs for or dreads the revelation of this final day (I Cor 1:7, Jn 19:37).

What motivates Wesley in his use of this doctrine? Lindström, who has carefully charted its development, seems to feel that the antinomian challenges of 1740 and 1770 compelled Wesley to find ways of emphasizing the role of works more positively. This doctrine was one result. But Lindström also shows that in the Wesley of 1738 this concern for works is "hardly discernible; it was swept aside by the new and overwhelming conviction of salvation by faith alone,"[25] and moreover, that the Wesley of 1771 admits that the minutes of 1770 were "not sufficiently guarded in the way they are expressed," and that "our works have no part in meriting or purchasing our justification from first to last, either in whole or in part."[26] The labored effort to say that works are not the merit but the condition of final justification is the measure of Wesley's struggle to keep this doctrine of salvation on the foundation of Christ's priestly office. Wesley's doctrine of justification, then, must not be read as a considered, balanced piece of doctrinal instruction; it is much more in the order of a journal of his theological pilgrimage. The impressive thing about it is not its curious complexity, but the point where it ends: in forgiveness and life with God by faith. The great unifying theme is not, after all, the law and its fulfilment; it is rather the merit of Christ. Present justification is by faith in Christ's merits. So long as man is being sanctified he needs the merit of Christ's death. And in the final justification it is the role of works to bear witness that even now the believer stands before God relying on the merit of Christ's death. Wesley's doctrine of double justification is best understood as an affirmation—theologically, a costly affirmation —that the Christ of Wesley's gospel is one Christ, the priest, whose cleansing Word rules from the cross.

## 5. Comment

When the priestly work is considered as a whole, the striking point is that it is conceived almost entirely in terms of the passive obedience. In this emphasis and its consequences, the major problem of the Wesleyan theology arises: is God's justification of man a righteous act, fully just as well as merciful? It is undeniable that there is a certain underemphasis on the justice of God in present justification, and that this underemphasis results in the provisional character and qualified peace of that justification. But the problem goes deeper: in the light of the second justification, it remains a serious question whether God's justice, as Wesley conceives it, is ever fully and positively involved in the relationship of God and the believer. It must not be thought that Wesley had a soft view of God's justice: in the case of the damned, that justice is exhibited in all its hardness, to the last iota, without mercy. What corresponds in the saved to that exhibition of the height and depth of God's justice? One might answer that Christ's active obedience exhibits the full height and depth of the law, and that is true; but Wesley explicitly refuses to allow the believer to participate in this active righteousness of Christ. The believer rather comes forward with his own sanctification, in which the law is realized in "intention," by which Wesley does not mean a participation in Christ's law-fulfilling love, but rather the "temper" of love which grace produces in the heart of the believer. And this "temper," moreover, is not judged; it rather bears witness to the believer's trust that Christ bears his punishment "every moment." And it is this faith which ultimately makes all the difference between the redeemed and the damned. In this emphasis on faith Wesley is at one with the Reformation. Where he is not at one with the Reformation is in the underlying view of grace. Wesley's doctrine of justification is threatened by a view of God's righteousness which oscillates too much between a grace without judgment in the case of believers, and a judgment without grace in the case of the damned.

Wesley tries to defend the justice of God with the claim that it is honored either by obedience or by punishment, so that there is ultimately no difference between the penal and positive demands of God's law. Since Christ suffered the penalty of the law, the justice of God is honored in the case of believers who trust in the merit of Christ's death. In this contention he stands against the main stream of the Protestant tradition. The full humanity of Jesus Christ, including that active obedience which Wesley recognized, but which remained for him a mysterious and undeveloped element, must be allowed to play its necessary role of being the primary revelation of the law (including the relation of law and love), and at the same time the ontological reality, "the new man," within whom, by participation of faith, the believer's positive obedience to the divine command is performed. Such a step, which Wesley rejected too quickly, perhaps, in the heat of debate, would have the effect of taking the law more seriously than Wesley actually does, for the law would then be obeyed in its height and depth as God wills it, and it would be also in believers fulfilled in reality, not simply in "intention." Moreover, if such a step were taken in the context of a developed doctrine of Christ's intercession, with its decisive teaching that "in Christ" means "in the Body of Christ," a theological antidote to antinomianism, at least as promising as Wesley's setting-aside of the active obedience, would be at hand.

It is curious that, having suggested such a far-reaching doctrine of Christ's intercession, Wesley says so little about it in his doctrine of salvation. For here he might have found a sounder defense against the danger of antinomianism. The issue with the antinomians was fundamentally not the extent or character of Christ's obedience, but how we understand the believer's participation in Christ. But the doctrine of Christ's intercession is the doctrine about participation in Christ. The nerve of the antinomianism which Wesley abhorred, especially as he faced it in the formative early forties, was the notion of a private, mystical, quietistic union with a "personal" Savior. It cannot be denied that this heresy defended itself by saying: "Christ has done all: we need do nothing." But the answer should not have been: "Christ has not done all." It should have been: "No man comes to new life alone. We approach God together as brothers of Christ. Take your place in the Body of His people; participate in its worship; its mutual exhortation, admonition, encouragement, and service; and so share the blessings of new life in Christ. Christ has indeed done all: therefore let nothing separate us from those whom He has loved." As a matter of fact, it can be argued that this *was*, in the band societies, the practical answer of the Methodists to antinomianism. The undeveloped possibility lay in the fact that this answer corresponds to the main content of the doctrine of Christ's intercession. Wesley never developed this doctrine's hint that we participate in Christ's active as well as passive righteousness through the Holy Spirit, in the church. Had he done so, he might have found a doctrine of justification which retained the evangelical concern for holiness and good works, without going so far toward a provisional present justification, with its temptation to self-analysis and anxiety, where there should be healthy peace and joy in obedience.

Several questions were asked in earlier chapters which require answer at this point. In the study of Christ's kingly work, it was asked how far the atonement would have significance in the last judgment. When Wesley spoke of the person of the Judge, he drew the picture of an austere Christ confronting men with

God's perfect law embodied in his own perfect human *imago*.
In the light of the doctrine of final justification, however, it must
be said that the faith which justifies in the last day presupposes
the merit of Christ's death. The atonement is present in the last
judgment, but hidden there, for the righteous, under the concept
of "faith." Christ, the High Priest, is presupposed in the last
judgment, although it must be admitted that Wesley has allowed
his Christological (as contrasted with his soteriological) thinking
about this event to be weighted in the direction of the austere
Christ of Wesley's notes on Revelation, who can sometimes judge
without mercy.

A second postponed question asked whether Christ's personal
ministry in bearing the sins of the justified was not underemphasized. While there is a tendency to view Christ's priestly work
so completely from the believer's side that "He bears our sins"
shades off into "They are forgotten," nevertheless, Wesley
also recognizes that Christ's priestly office underlies final as well
as present justification. On this ground it must be questioned
whether Wesley seriously intends to teach that Christ's mediatorial ministry comes to an end. If God's positive justice
is not really satisfied in our justification, is there any other
possibility than an eternal penal substitution for past sins?

A third postponed question asked whether Christ serves
perfection or perfection Christ. More precisely, is Christ ultimately a means to the end of God's eternal perfecting decree,
or did God originally decide to create a perfectible creation
because He wants to love it for Christ's sake? Is Wesley's perfectionism the lord, the partner, or the servant of his gospel?
In the light of the doctrine of final justification, the answer
must be: not for the sake of the perfection of the creature, as
such, but for the sake of what Christ has done, God eternally
accepts His creature. The perfectionism is not absent: it is very
much there, but at the crucial point it serves as the witness to
faith in Christ, indeed so much so that God's positive justice,
which rightly should receive its satisfaction, eternally postpones

its claim. God originally decided to create a good and eternally perfectible creation, because He wanted to restore it and perfect it and love it for Christ's sake. At this fundamental point, Christology is the foundation, and not an appendix, of the theology of Wesley.

Wesley once wrote in his *Journal*: "I think in justification . . . just as Mr. Calvin does. In this respect, I do not differ from him a hair's breadth" (May 14, 1765). Wesley scholars since have echoed Wesley's opinion.[27] In the light of this study it must be said that so far as Wesley begins with a setting-aside of the imputed active obedience, Wesley's opinion of his agreement with Calvin is mistaken.[28] Wesley's way of relating justification and sanctification represents a new emphasis in Protestant theology up to his time. His doctrine of justification is not simply a re-presentation of Reformation doctrine, but a peculiar adaptation of that doctrine, shaped to meet the needs of his doctrine of sanctification. This does not deny that the root of Wesley's understanding of justification lies in his evangelical conversion of 1738. It is probable that without that conversion the doctrine of justification would not have entered significantly into his thinking at all.

In interpreting Wesley's development, we must not say that a passion for sanctification breaks in upon his evangelical concern for justification by faith. Wesley must be read the other way around. Wesley has a legalistic framework of thought from his student days, and suddenly an evangelical concern for justification erupts within it. And the new element begins a lifelong struggle to reshape a theology which is already in large measure shaped. This is why one finds a pervasive moral law of creation, the whole *imago* apparatus, and a final judgment of works without mercy, and then, growing out of the midst of this legal order, a doctrine of justification by faith which refuses to give up the ultimate priority of faith, even at the cost of breaking justification in two and radically underemphasizing a final satisfaction of God's positive justice. For all its problems, this twofold justification, which lays bare the stresses and strains of Wesley's permanently-occurring theological conversion, is the sign of Wesley's determination to give Christ's priestly work first place, and indeed a priestly work which includes the prophetic and kingly work as one. Wesley is not Calvin here: Wesley is much more interesting simply as Wesley, even in his doctrine of justification.

1. Rattenbury, *Evangelical Doctrines*, p. 204.

2. The atonement passages of the Anglican Articles II, XI, XXXI are unchanged in Wesley's II, IX, XX. Whatever the reasons for Wesley's omission of the Anglican Article XI, "Of Christ Alone without Sin," it could not have been his disagreement with its Christological content (S. 62, ii, 5; Ro 8:3, Heb 7:26, II Cor 5:21). It is noteworthy that in neither Anglicanism's nor Wesley's articles on the resurrection is there explicit reference to its role in man's salvation.

3. Wesley paraphrases an example of the doctrine he was opposing, from an unidentified source: "That Christ had done, as well as suffered all; that His righteousness being imputed to us, we need none of our own; that seeing there was so much righteousness and holiness in Him, there needs none in us; that to think we have any, or desire to seek any, is to renounce Christ; that from the beginning to the end of salvation, all is in Christ, nothing in man; that those who teach otherwise are legal preachers, and know nothing of the Gospel" (W. X, 366).

4. Ro 4:9, Heb 5:9, Eph 1:7; S. 5, i, 8; S. 49, ii, 5, 10, 13, 17; W. X, 339, 430. For some of the many variants of the formula, see Ro 8:34, I Cor 2:2; S. 50, i, 3.

5. At baptism, Christ undertook to fulfil all righteousness: "on the cross [He] accomplished what He had undertaken" (I Jn 5:6). The obedience of the Second Adam, by which "many shall be constituted righteous" is "His obedience unto death . . . His dying for us" (Ro 5:19). The Christ of Hebrews says, "*I come to do thy will*—By the sacrifice of Myself" (Heb 10:7), and He "*Learned obedience,* when He began to suffer; when He applied Himself to drink that cup: obedience in suffering and dying" (Heb 5:8).

6. To the proposition, "If it was requisite for Christ to be baptized, much more to fulfill the moral law," Wesley answers, "I cannot prove that either one or the other was requisite in order to His purchasing redemption for us" (W. X, 324). This is no incidental

point: he develops it in an appeal to scripture (W. X, 319ff.), and to experience (W. X, 333).

7. Although Wesley constantly uses the term "merit of Christ," he is considerably more interested in what Christ merits for us than in the nature of the merit itself. Christ's merit "purchases" our justification (Gal 1:4; S. 55, 17; Ro 4:5). But merit also underlies the entire salvation, a term which for Wesley always includes both justification and sanctification (Jn 3:15, 19:30). In no instance does Wesley associate Christ's human perfections with His merit. In general, merit, like obedience, is a term associated with Christ's death (Heb 9:14-15, Ro 7:4, II Cor 8:12). The term suggests for Wesley that the value of Christ's sacrifice arises from the dignity of the divine person who undertakes it (Heb 9:14, Ac 20:28, I Tim 2:6, I Jn 2:1). It must be admitted that this doctrine of merit makes it difficult to understand why Wesley rules out of order the imputation of the divine righteousness of Christ.

8. The apparent difficulty, that the moral law is grounded in the order of creation, is partly met when it is remembered that creation is the penultimate ground of the law. The ultimate ground is the will of the Creator, and, as Wesley adds: "The will of God is God, Himself" (S. 29, iii, 7).

9. In this connection, Wesley's frequent use of the formula, "the mind of Christ," as a description of the goal of sanctification, is significant. Cf. Lerch, *Heil und Heiligung*, pp. 159-61.

10. Christ's human *imago* is "a copy of His divine righteousness, as far as it can be imparted to a human spirit. It is a transcript of the divine purity, the divine justice, mercy and truth" (S. 49, i, 2). In S. 29 the moral law is "a transcript of the divine nature," "divine virtue and wisdom assuming visible form," "God manifested to His creatures as they are able to bear it," "God made manifest in our flesh" (ii, 6, 4, 3; iii, 12).

11. Christ's passive obedience harmonizes the attributes of God only in relation to believers (Ro 3:26). Only in them does God's merciful withholding of judgment reach its goal, namely, that He can be presented with men in whom His righteousness is formed. But Christ also suffered for unbelievers, and their refusal to believe eliminates the condition which permits God to form His righteousness in them. This sets up a contradiction within God's essential righteousness: God's mercy provides Christ's atonement for all men. But this very atonement now becomes the obstacle to the consummation of God's righteous judgment against unbelievers, for God cannot withdraw

Christ's atonement from them without, as well, withdrawing the foundation of His righteousness in believers, or His universal offer of salvation to all men.

It is at least thinkable that in this situation Christ's active obedience has a significance. In the last judgment, Christ's passive obedience will justify believers, for even then their works will only testify to the presence of justifying faith. It covers past sins, and holds open the possibility that believers may yet become fully righteous, inherently righteous, in eternity. Wesley is not afraid to draw the necessary conclusion: there is for believers a possibility of growth in perfection after death.

But another ground must be found for the final disposition of unbelievers, which will harmonize God's attributes in relation to them. In their case, the role of Christ's active obedience could be this: God would have provided not only an atonement, but also, in Christ's active obedience, a perfect satisfaction of the positive demand of His justice, a satisfaction which they will never be able to provide, even by their eternal damnation. Thus, a kind of imputation of the active obedience for, but not to, them—and only for them, not for believers— might occur, an imputation which has no effect on their miserable situation, but which does bring eternal harmony into the essential righteousness of God, as Wesley conceives it.

12. Lindström, *Wesley and Sanctification*, p. 67. He continues: "It is as Man that Christ mediates between God and mankind. In his activity as High Priest Christ is also considered as a representative of mankind."

13. Lindström, *Wesley and Sanctification*, p. 74.

14. Sugden (*Standard Sermons*, i, 162-63) also complains that Wesley's thinking about the phrase, "in Christ," is so shaped by his doctrine of justification that he overlooks the importance of union with Christ in relation to sanctification.

15. The discussion here emphasizes those aspects of the doctrine which are most closely related to Christology. Fuller discussions can be found in Cannon, *Theology*, whose book is primarily a study of this doctrine; Lindström, *Wesley and Sanctification*, pp. 83-104; and Lerch, *Heil und Heiligung*, pp. 83-92. Primary material is reproduced in Burtner and Chiles, *Compend*, pp. 139-92.

16. Cf. Sugden's protest (*Standard Sermons*, i, 167).

17. Sugden, *Standard Sermons*, i, 120-21.

18. The Protestant tradition had insisted that both punishment and positive righteousness must have their proper place in justifica-

tion. The Lutherans, e.g., saw two benefits in justification: remission of sins, and the imputation of Christ's righteousness (Schmid, *Doctrinal Theology*, p. 425).

19. Cf. Lindström, *Wesley and Sanctification*, p. 75: ". . . [Wesley] dissociates the fulfillment of the law from atonement and justification and attaches it instead to sanctification. This explains why sanctification in the sense of fulfillment of the law occupies such an important place in his theology."

20. A peculiarity of Wesleyan preaching is the frequent, if not habitual, reference to God being reconciled to man, rather than, with II Corinthians 5, of man to God (Lk 19:38, Heb 6:11, I Jn 2:5; S. 16, i, 13). It is not necessary or wise to make much of this peculiarity. This, perhaps, can be said: to speak of God being reconciled to man puts the emphasis on God's wrath more than on man's sin as the main reason for separation. This is just what Wesley did. In the Wesleyan justification God is "reconciled" to fellowship with a believer who still remains not altogether righteous.

21. It is possible that Wesley stands in an established stream of Anglican tradition with his doctrine of double justification. A. H. Rees, *The Doctrine of Justification in the Anglican Reformers* (London, 1939), p. 25 claims to find the doctrine in the Anglican formularies and in Latimer and Cranmer. More to the point, David C. Shipley in his article, "Wesley and Some Calvinist Controversies," *The Drew Gateway*, XXV, iv, 195-210, shows how the doctrine of double justification had a definite place in English seventeenth-century nonconformist thought, and especially in that of Wesley's much-loved Richard Baxter. There is some evidence that Wesley associated the teaching with Bishop George Bull's *Harmonia Apostolica* (cf. data cited in Lindström, *Wesley and Sanctification*, p. 210, note 4). Among nineteenth-century Methodists, Richard Watson treats the doctrine with considerable reserve, and prefers not to use the term "justification" in an eschatological context (*Theological Institutes* [New York, 1836 and 1840], II, 262-65). Contemporary scholarship is by no means unanimous on Wesley's use of the doctrine. Lerch (*Heil und Heiligung*, p. 144) remarks, in passing, that both Wesley and Bull "reject this Catholic conception." Cannon gives a useful résumé of the development of the Anglican doctrine of justification, with special attention to Bull's *Harmonia Apostolica*, but, although he shows its tendency to emphasize the role of works in justification, no special note seems to be taken here, or later, of the second justification. Lindström deserves credit for first emphasizing the importance of the twofold justification

as the frame for Wesley's doctrine of sanctification (*Wesley and Sanctification*, pp. 15, 16, 119, 124-25, 198-218).

22. Note that Wesley's objection here is not to a twofold justification, as such, but to using such a doctrine to make works the condition of final acceptance. Justification is by faith, and if Wesley later adds the notion of a second justification, he does not want it to qualify this evangelical position in the slightest.

23. To an opponent who reminded him that he, himself, had endorsed the single justification taught by Paul and the Anglican articles, Wesley replies: "Most true. And yet our Lord speaks of another justification, Matt. xii, 37. Now, I think one and one make two" (W. X, 388-89). Six months later, he made the same point: "I do not deny that there is another justification (of which our Lord speaks) at the last day. I do not therefore condemn the distinction of a twofold justification, in saying that spoken of in our Articles is but one" (W. X, 431). And to the charge: "You hold a twofold justification, one now, another at the last day. So does the Pope of Rome," Wesley answers simply: "And so do all Protestants, if they believe the Bible" (W. X, 444).

24. Lindström shows how William Fletcher, Wesley's right hand in theological debate, makes Wesley's meaning more precise with a distinction between "evidence of works" and "merit of works." "Thy justification," says Fletcher's Christ, "which is purchased by my alone merits, will entirely turn upon the *evidence* of thy works, according to the time and opportunity which thou hast to do them" (cited by Lindström, *Wesley and Sanctification*, p. 212). It is a question for Fletcher of "justification by the evidence of works" (*Ibid.*), a phrase Wesley does not use.

25. Lindström, *Wesley and Sanctification*, p. 205.

26. Lindström, *Wesley and Sanctification*, p. 211.

27. Cannon, *Theology*, p. 88: "In regard to the justifying act itself, Wesley is at one with Luther and Calvin." Cf. Sugden, *Standard Sermons*, i, 112.

28. Calvin, *Institutes* III, xi, 2. Cf., further, the finality of Calvin's justification (*Institutes* II, xvi, 5).

# A Summary Conclusion

THE MANY CONCLUSIONS to which this study points have been indicated as they were suggested. It remains here only to make a general summation of Wesley's main Christological emphases, and to add a word about how Wesley has been read in the course of our discussion.

The principal emphases in Wesley's Christology, as discovered in our investigation, are these:

I. *The Person of Christ:* Wesley places a heavy emphasis upon the divine nature and shows a certain reserve about the humanity, while at the same time tending to idealize it. This distribution of emphasis may correspond, with respect to the deity, to an emphasis on the divine sanction for the law. With respect to the humanity, the underemphasis accords with an atonement of penal substitution, and an exhibition of the ideal *imago dei* as the norm for sanctification. However, in view of final justification, it may also be suggested that the emphasis on the divinity is the ground for the sovereignty of mercy displayed there. This unintegrated situation with respect to the two natures results in a certain natural strain upon the personal union, unrelieved by Wesley's form of the doctrine of communicated properties. The question is thereby raised, how adequately the various aspects of Wesley's soteriological thought, as represented in the Christology, hold together. The incarnation is grounded in a divine decree which has both an infralapsarian aspect, to remedy the fall and harmonize God's attributes, and a supralapsarian aspect, inasmuch as creation, fall, and incarnation are all subsumed under God's decision to create a creation of perpetually increasing holiness. The formal presupposition for the Wesleyan decree in both aspects, as well as for the omnitemporality of Christ generally, is a doctrine of time whereby all time is simultaneously present to God. Although it must be granted that the focus of Wesley's Christology is in the doctrine of Christ's work, the doctrine of Christ's person seriously raises the question whether the Christology is the foundation or the appendix of his theology.

II. *The States of Christ:* The key to Wesley's history of Christ's states is the glory which Christ renounced and regained as a reward for His suffering. Under Christ's humiliation, Wesley includes His birth, circumcision, baptism, ministry, passion, and death. In agreement with his reserve about the human nature, Wesley tends to consider the incarnation as such to be a humiliation. There is no descent into hell, although upon occasion it seems to be replaced by a departure into paradise, an event of uncertain theological significance. Under the exaltation of Christ, which receives considerably greater emphasis, Wesley subsumes the transfiguration (interrupting the temporal sequence; largely associated with the glory of Christ the lawgiver), the resurrection, ascension, and session. Wesley includes under the last-named the effusion of the Holy Spirit, Christ's manifestation in believers, and His coming in judgment. The doctrine of Christ's states is not especially developed by Wesley, and its formulation is subject to more than the usual degree of conjecture. Nevertheless, it provides a perspective within which it is especially clear that the various aspects of Christ's work are a unity, elements of one saving history.

III. *The Work of Christ:* Wesley on occasion distinguishes the mediatorial work of redemption from the non-mediatorial work of creation and providence. But the heavy Christological emphasis in creation as well as the demonstrable continuity between preservation and redemption suggest that, whatever the mediatorial distinction may mean, creation and providence are to be considered works of grace. When he explicates Christ's one mediatorial task of redemption, Wesley habitually uses the doctrine of Christ's threefold prophetic, priestly, and kingly office. It is probable that he considered the prophetic and kingly offices as related to sanctification, and the priestly office to justification. If so, his motive in using the doctrine of the threefold office is probably to emphasize the "complete Christ" of his sanctification doctrine. It is nevertheless significant that he emphasizes the unity of the three offices, and that in his more considered statements the priestly office is seen to be fundamental to the other two. Although Wesley does not exclude ecclesiological, historical, or even cosmological meanings for the three offices, a decided subjective accent is observable: this work is done "for us" and "in us." Moreover, although the offices are grounded in the life, death, and resurrection of Jesus Christ, the habitual perspective is that of the exalted Lord in all three offices.

IV. *The Prophetic Work of Christ:* Wesley insists that Christ alone is the revealer of both the gospel and the law of God, an exclusiveness which he grounds in the doctrine of the Trinity. Christ's evangelical prophecy is first of all a fulfilment of Old Testament prophecies and types, and then continues in the church through the Word of God and the Word-applying Spirit. The heart of revelation is scripture, but Wesley's energetic biblicism is tempered by a certain common-sense hermeneutics. Christ's legal prophecy concerns the revelation of the moral law which, in spite of its elaborate Christological foundation, nevertheless raises problems in its semiautonomous status for the exclusiveness with which Christ is the revealer of God. Though the Logos posits the law in creation, the content of the law is henceforth fixed, and Christ appears as its revealer or as the Mediator who alters man's relation to it. When thinking of justification, Wesley can emphasize that the law's function is to lead men to Christ and to keep them there, but the emphasis is on the sanctifying use of the law, i.e., on Christ re-establishing the moral law and leading men to obey it. There is a possibility that Christ also redefines the moral law as the demand to love, although a question arises about a possible diminution of the law's demand when this love is understood as an inherent "temper," abstracted from participation in the active obedience

of Christ. The ambivalence of this doctrine of the law must be
considered one of the difficult problems in Wesleyan theology.
Here the door is opened for a definition of the good and holy
which, whether puritanical, as in the case of Wesley, or demo-
cratic, socialist, or existentialist, as tends to be the case today,
is not necessarily learned from the revelation of human holiness
in the Man, Christ Jesus. It is not the Wesleyan emphasis
on sanctification but the content or character of that sanctification which is opened to question here. That Wesley found it
possible on occasion to ascribe Christological predicates to both
Jesus and the moral law is a warning sign of one point where
Wesley's two-sidedness threatens to break the fundamental unity
of his message.

V. *The Kingly Work of Christ:* The Trinitarian relation
underlies both the eternal and mediatorial rule of Christ, and
provides the integrating principle whereby Christ's mediatorial
kingdom of grace, which creates and sanctifies the church, after
the last judgment becomes the eternal kingdom of glory, the
heavenly city of the blessed. This doctrine of a twofold kingdom
lends support to the notion that there is a supralapsarian aspect
to the divine decree whereby creation, fall, incarnation, and
redemption serve the motif of perfection. With regard to the
mediatorial work, while the penal substitution motif dominates
Wesley's doctrine of the atonement, the motif of Christ's victory
over Satan, sin, and death is also extensively developed. The
connection between the two motifs lies in the unity of the
mediatorial offices, but also in the notion that it is guilt which
puts man in the power of Satan. Wesley grounds the victory
in the cross and resurrection, but he puts the emphasis on the
eschatological victory yet to be established, doubtless as a
means of emphasizing that the Christian still requires sanctification, i.e., Christ's progressive victory over remaining sin. In so
far as the last judgment is considered in relation to sanctification
and the kingly office, it exemplifies a problematic tension between
the kingly and priestly offices, for the human Christ who judges

in the final day is an austere figure, indeed, about whom the question can occasionally be raised whether he appears there bearing the sins of the world. The question of the relation of atonement and judgment is reinforced by the doctrine of damnation where Wesley tends to define an area of God's activity in which the attributes of mercy and justice are separable. As a whole, the doctrine of Christ's kingly work places the believer's sanctification in a cosmic context, and emphasizes the divine power at work in man; but in and of itself, it raises sharply the question whether Christ is the means to perfection, or, vice versa, whether God perfects a universe because He loves it for Christ's sake.

VI. *The Priestly Work of Christ:* While the kingly office has a cosmic scope, it raises questions about the priestly office. The priestly office, on the other hand, is equally all-embracing in scope, yet it offers a perspective within which the kingly work has its full place and importance. In a word, Christ's passive obedience on the cross is man's penal substitute, the ground for Christ's heavenly intercession, and of both present and final justification. In present justification we are now forgiven and reconciled to God, and in final justification on the last day we are accepted on the basis of true, living faith, i.e., faith which has produced works. Because only the penal demand of the law is met for believers by Christ, while the positive demand is met by the believer himself, in intention only, and only from the moment of first justification, it may be questioned whether the justice as well as the mercy of God is fully the ground of justification. It may be significant against this background that Wesley indicates, in a certain contrast to Anselm, that Christ makes his atonement *qua deus,* for something of the justice of God does give way to His mercy in the case of believers, just as the mercy gives way to the justice in the case of the damned. The theological situation out of which this problem arises is Wesley's decision to resist the Calvinist antinomians by eliminating any significant role for Christ's active obedience in the atonement.

It is suggested that a stronger alternative course would have
been to emphasize the intercession of Christ as that doctrine
which interprets the believer's participation in Christ as participation in the Body of Christ. The congregational Body of Christ,
with its demand and power for mutual admonition, encouragement, and service in Christ, would then have become theologically
what it was practically in the Wesleyan societies, the matrix
of the believer's sanctification. In general, it must be said
that Wesley's twofold doctrine of justification is not simply a
way of making room for the Wesleyan sanctification in the
process of salvation. Its presence is also the decisive clue to
Wesley's intention about the unity of Christ's work and the salvation it brings: here it is seen most clearly that the prophetic
office, together with the law revealed there, and the kingly office,
together with the sanctification revealed there, are aspects
of Christ's priestly office which offers fellowship with God to
authentic faith, i.e., to faith which is instructed and strengthened
by the prophetic and kingly Christ. The doctrines of God's semi-
independent law and of man's sanctification by intention are
seriously problematic: but the crucial point is that they are intentionally made so because Wesley faithfully relates them to his
ultimate ground, the vision of Aldersgate: "I felt I did trust in
Christ, Christ alone for salvation." In this light, Wesley's Christology is not the appendix but the foundation of his theology
and his message of salvation.

In conclusion a word may be said about the way in which
Wesley has been read in reaching this conclusion. The two
guiding principles for this interpretation of Wesley's thought
have themselves been adapted from leading motifs of Wesley's
thinking. First of all, Wesley has been read, as far as possible,
according to his *intention*. Wesley asked no more for any man's
works than that they be judged in this way; it is, moreover,
appropriate to any good hermeneutics to let the text itself, as far
as possible, determine the manner in which it wishes to be understood. Wesley's rule for interpreting Paul must be our rule for

interpreting Wesley: "We must not so interpret the Apostle's words, as to make him contradict himself" (S. 46, iv, 2). Where Wesley has been found obscure, where explicit guidance has been lacking, and especially at the many crossroads of decision in interpreting his thought, recourse has been taken again and again to that moment which Wesley, himself, counted as the beginning of his mature Christian life and understanding, the moment in which he said: ". . . an assurance was given me that [Christ] had taken away *my* sins, even *mine*, and saved *me* from the law of sin and death" (*Journal*, May 24, 1738). The reader must answer for himself: theologically considered, is this Wesley's center or not?

In the second place, Wesley's writings have been read as manifestations of a theological *conversion*. Wesley did not receive on May 24, 1738, at about a quarter before nine in the evening, a brand new theology direct from heaven. Rather the old theology was reborn that night, reconciled to God, and a lifelong process of theological sanctification, so to speak, began. The theology of his student days, of his teaching days and the Holy Club at Oxford; the theology which was profoundly influenced by his mother and her nonconformist background, by Jeremy Taylor, Thomas à Kempis, William Law, the High Church Anglican divines, the mystics, and the Fathers; the theology which drove him to search the scriptures like a miner for inner peace, which sent him across the ocean on a desperate missionary journey to find salvation for his own soul—*this* theology was cut off its old tree and grafted onto a new one. The old branch never lost its character, but the nourishing roots and sap and fruit were new. That is why Wesley's doctrine of good works ends in a final justification by faith; why the moral law ends in a promise to keep the believer near to Christ; why the emphasis on the divine nature is not only a sanction for the law, but a way of praising God's ultimate mercy; why the eternal perfecting decree ends in a creation accepted for the sake of Christ; why the austere last judgment ends in God's justice making way for God's mercy; why at the end of Christ's mediatorial kingdom there remains the profound mystery of Christ's eternal intercession; why the doctrine of the three offices is not simply a form of the problem of twofold salvation, but an assertion of one mediatorial work of grace, grounded in the priestly sacrifice made on the cross. The attempt to read Wesley's theology as the record of a continuing theological conversion has not eliminated the two-sidedness of Wesley. There are, indeed, both the old branch and the new fruit, but the tree is known by its fruit.

# Appendices

## The Numbering of Wesley's Sermons

THE FOLLOWING LIST IS GIVEN to permit users of other editions to find the sermon references in this study. Sermons 1 through 53 are numbered in Sugden's authoritative order, sermons 54-141 according to Jackson's third London edition of 1831.

1. Salvation by Faith
2. The Almost Christian
3. Awake, Thou That Sleepest
4. Scriptural Christianity
5. Justification by Faith
6. The Righteousness of Faith
7. The Way to the Kingdom
8. The First-Fruits of the Spirit
9. The Spirit of Bondage and Adoption
10. The Witness of the Spirit—I
11. The Witness of Our Own Spirit
12. The Means of Grace
13. The Circumcision of the Heart
14. The Marks of the New Birth
15. The Great Privilege of Those That Are Born of God
16. Sermon on the Mount—I
17. Sermon on the Mount—II
18. Sermon on the Mount—III
19. Sermon on the Mount—IV
20. Sermon on the Mount—V
21. Sermon on the Mount—VI
22. Sermon on the Mount—VII

23. Sermon on the Mount—VIII
24. Sermon on the Mount—IX
25. Sermon on the Mount—X
26. Sermon on the Mount—XI
27. Sermon on the Mount—XII
28. Sermon on the Mount—XIII
29. The Original, Nature, Property, and Use of the Law
30. The Law Established through Faith—I
31. The Law Established through Faith—II
32. The Nature of Enthusiasm
33. A Caution against Bigotry
34. Catholic Spirit
35. Christian Perfection
36. Wandering Thoughts
37. Satan's Devices
38. Original Sin
39. The New Birth
40. The Wilderness State
41. Heaviness through Manifold Temptations
42. Self-Denial
43. The Cure of Evil-Speaking
44. The Use of Money
45. The Witness of the Spirit—II
46. On Sin in Believers
47. The Repentance of Believers
48. The Great Assize
49. The Lord Our Righteousness
50. The Scripture Way of Salvation
51. The Good Steward
52. The Reformation of Manners
53. On the Death of the Rev. Mr. George Whitefield
54. On Eternity
55. On the Trinity
56. God's Approbation of His Works
57. On the Fall of Man

58. On Predestination
59. God's Love to Fallen Man
60. The General Deliverance
61. The Mystery of Iniquity
62. The End of Christ's Coming
63. The General Spread of the Gospel
64. The New Creation
65. The Duty of Reproving Our Neighbor
66. The Signs of the Times
67. On Divine Providence
68. The Wisdom of God's Counsels
69. The Imperfection of Human Knowledge
70. The Case of Reason Impartially Considered
71. Of Good Angels
72. Of Evil Angels
73. Of Hell
74. Of the Church
75. On Schism
76. On Perfection
77. Spiritual Worship
78. Spiritual Idolatry
79. On Dissipation
80. On Friendship with the World
81. In What Sense We Are to Leave the World
82. On Temptation
83. On Patience
84. The Important Question
85. On Working Out Our Own Salvation
86. A Call to Backsliders
87. The Danger of Riches
88. On Dress
89. The More Excellent Way
90. An Israelite Indeed
91. On Charity
92. On Zeal

## APPENDIX II

## Some Wesleyan Statements about the Three Offices of Christ

Following is an analysis of six explicit references to the doctrine of Christ's threefold office in the *Notes*, together with three additional representative statements from other sources.

### 1) Note on Matthew 1:16

The word Christ in Greek, and Messiah in Hebrew, signify "Anointed;" and imply the prophetic, priestly, and royal characters which were to meet in the Messiah. Among the Jews, anointing was the ceremony whereby prophets, priests, and kings were initiated into those offices. And if we look into ourselves, we shall find a want of Christ in all these respects. We are by nature at a distance from God, alienated from Him, and incapable of a free access to Him. Hence we want a Mediator, an Intercessor; in a word, a Christ in His priestly office. This regards our state with respect to God. And with respect to ourselves, we find a total darkness, blindness, ignorance of God, and the things of God. Now here we want Christ in His prophetic office, to enlighten our minds, and teach us the whole will of God. We find also within us a strange misrule of appetites and passions. For these we want Christ in His royal character, to reign in our hearts, and subdue all things to Himself.

Several points can be noted in this first and longest statement of the doctrine in the *Notes*. (a) This is the first substantial theological utterance in the *Notes*, a fact made yet more note-worthy by the absence of a demand for reference to the three offices in the text. It is as though Wesley wants this doctrine clear from the first, as a framework for what is to follow. (b) Wesley explicitly connects Christ's three offices with the Old Testament. (c) Without emphasis, there is a clear pre-supposition that the three offices belong together, since they meet in the one Messiah. (d) The subjective character of all three offices is marked: they refer to work accomplished within the individual. This may result from Wesley's effort to make the three offices answer a threefold analysis of sin. Reference to Christ's relation to either church or world or history is missing. (e) The perspective is that of Christ's exaltation. All three offices are being exercised simultaneously by the exalted Christ, although Wesley's definition does not exclude the possibility in other contexts of a reference of prophecy to the earthly ministry and priesthood to the cross. (f) The priestly office is primarily concerned with the relation to God, the prophetic and kingly offices with ourselves. (g) The order of the offices is priest, prophet, king.

### 2) Note on Matthew 11:28-29

*Come to me ... Ye that labor ... And are heavy laden*—With the guilt and power of sin. *And I will give you rest*—I alone (for none else can) will freely give you (what ye cannot purchase) rest from the guilt of sin by justification, and from the power of sin by sanctification. *Take My yoke upon you*—Believe in Me; receive Me as your prophet, priest, and king. *For I am meek and lowly in heart*—Meek toward all men, lowly toward God. *And ye shall find rest*—Whoever, therefore, does not find rest of soul is not meek and lowly. The fault is not in the yoke of Christ, but in thee, who hast not taken it upon thee. (Cf. S. 50, ii, 2.)

Note here: (a) The context of the mediatorial work is quite clear: Christ stands between man and God. (b) The subjective accent is again apparent: Christ's three offices are not effective until they are received. Faith is defined as receiving Christ in His three offices. The result of this faith is justification and sanctification. (c) The three offices are again spoken of from the perspective of Christ's exaltation.

### 3) Note on John 17:3

*To know*—By living, holy faith. *Thee the only true God*—The only Cause and End of all things; not excluding the Son and the Holy Ghost, no more than the Father is excluded from being Lord (I Cor. viii. 6), but the false gods of the heathens. *And Jesus Christ*—As their Prophet, Priest, and King. *This is life eternal*—It is both the way to, and the essence of, everlasting happiness.

(a) Wesley introduces the doctrines of the Trinity and of the three offices. Were both these "threes" some kind of dogmatic shorthand by which he indicated complexes of ideas, long since codified in his own mind? That would indicate the integral relation of both doctrines to his deepest theological interests. Certainly it is clear that the doctrine of the three offices had for him something of the familiarity and clarity of the doctrine of the Trinity. (b) The previous note makes plain that Christ's threefold office is an explication of His mediatorial work. (c) Knowing the Christ of the three offices is the "essence" of eternal life, an indication that the mediatorial work does not end with the world.

### 4) Note on Philippians 3:8

*Yea, I still account both all these and all things else to be mere loss,* compared to the inward, experimental *knowledge of Christ, as my Lord,* as my Prophet, Priest, and King, as teaching me wisdom, atoning for my sins, and reigning in my heart. To refer this to justification only is miserably to pervert the whole scope of the words. They manifestly relate to sanctification also; yea, to that chiefly.

(a) Here is Wesley's short summary of the content of each office. The subjective accent is again noted. (b) The three offices are identified as the content of the Lordship of Christ, i.e., as the meaning of His exalted state. The present participles, "teaching," "atoning," and "reigning" indicate simultaneous present action of Christ in all three offices. (c) One of Wesley's motives in using the doctrine of the three offices so frequently is here disclosed: namely, its association with the "complete Saviour" of sanctification, significantly mentioned only two verses later. The emphasis on "experimental" (experiential) knowledge of Christ in all three offices has the same significance. (d) It is again noteworthy that reference to the three offices is Wesley's necessity, not the text's.

### 5) Note on II John 7

Carefully keep what ye have heard from the beginning, *for many seducers are entered into the world, who confess not Jesus Christ that came in the flesh*—Who disbelieve either His prophetic, or priestly, or kingly office. Whosoever does *this is the seducer*—From God. *And the antichrist*—Fighting against Christ.

(a) To disbelieve any office is to fight against Christ. The sanctification theme again seems to underlie the use of the doctrine. But Wesley safeguards sanctification not by emphasizing the kingly or prophetic offices, but by emphasizing the unity and necessity of all three. (b) To believe the offices is to believe in Christ. (c) Again, it is on Wesley's initiative that the three offices are mentioned.

### 6) Note on Revelation 5:6

For the sake of clarity, Wesley's translation of the text is cited first: "*And I beheld in the midst of the throne and of the four living creatures, and in the midst of the elders, a lamb standing as if he had been slain, having seven horns and seven eyes, which are the seven spirits of God sent forth into all the earth.*"

Wesley's comment:

*And I saw*—First, Christ *in* or on *the midst of the throne;* ... *Standing*
—He lieth no more; He no more falls on His face; the days of His
weakness and mourning are ended. He is now in a posture of readiness
to execute all His offices of prophet, priest, and king. *As if He had been
slain*—Doubtless with the prints of the wounds which He once received.
And because *He was slain,* He is worthy to open the book (verse 9),
to the joy of His own people, and the terror of His enemies. *Having
seven horns*—As a king, the emblem of perfect strength. *And seven
eyes*—The emblem of perfect knowledge and wisdom. By these He
accomplishes what is contained in the book; namely, by His almighty
and all-wise *Spirit....Which*—Both the horns and the eyes. *Are the
seven spirits of God sent forth into all the earth*—For the effectual working of the Spirit of God goes through the whole creation; and that in
the natural, as well as spiritual, world. For could mere matter act or
move? Could it gravitate or attract? Just as much as it can think or
speak.

(a) Unless the doctrine of the three offices were not already
prominent in Wesley's mind, the highly symbolic reference to
wounds, horns, and eyes could hardly have justified its introduction into this note. (b) The context is explicitly that of Christ's
exaltation. It is implied that He was formerly, i.e., in His humiliation, not ready to execute all His offices. Is this a cryptic indication of some historical order in the execution of the offices,
whereby one or more can be more readily executed after the
resurrection? (c) There is a short statement about each office:
the prophet has "perfect knowledge and wisdom"; the king has
"perfect strength"; and the priest intercedes. Because of His death,
He is worthy to open the book which Wesley says (5:1) represents "all power in heaven and earth given to Christ." Here is
Wesley's teaching that the exaltation is a reward for Christ's
suffering, and the connection between the kingly and priestly
offices is thus indicated. (d) Wesley here indicates that through
all three offices Christ accomplishes His role in the last times. (e)
The execution of the kingly and prophetic offices is said to be
identical with the sending of the Holy Spirit. Through the Spirit

the execution of the three offices is related not only to revelation, but to the animation of the whole creation. There may even be an echo here of Wesley's doubt about Newton's gravitation theory: matter does not gravitate, he thinks; it is spiritually moved by Christ Himself (S. 77, i, 6). The presence of this touch indicates that Wesley is not simply following Bengel in this note. (f) This note identifies the three offices not only with personal salvation, but with creation and the fulfilment of history. The subjectivism is therefore an accent for Wesley, not a principle. (g) The order of the offices here is: priest, king, and prophet.

As a check on these findings—for it is not impossible that the *Notes* contain ideas which Wesley would never have written without the stimulation of his sources—three representative statements about the three offices from other sources may be analyzed.

### 7) *"Letter to a Roman Catholic,"* 7 *(W. X, 81)*

I believe that Jesus of Nazareth was the Saviour of the world, the Messiah so long foretold; that being anointed with the Holy Ghost, He was a prophet, revealing to us the whole will of God; that He was a Priest, who gave Himself a sacrifice for sin, and still makes intercession for transgressors; that He is a King, who has all power in heaven and in earth, and will reign till He has subdued all things to Himself.

(a) There is no striking shift from the theological climate of the *Notes*. The statement is a systematic description of the same material. (b) Wesley, in writing this brief credal confession, chooses the doctrine of the three offices to shape his description of Christ's work, a testimony to the importance and role of the doctrine for his own thinking. (c) The mediatorial context is clear: the three offices explicate the one work of the Savior, who was the Messiah foretold by the Old Testament. (d) Anointment with the Holy Spirit is here indicated as the presupposition for Christ's execution of all three offices. (e) The content of each office is defined. Of interest is the traditional double division of the priestly office, and the suggestion that there comes a time when the mediatorial kingdom is given up to the Father. (f) It is noteworthy that the offices are not subjectively conceived here. It is also of interest that He "was" prophet and priest, but "is" king. This may indicate some kind of historical order in the offices.

### 8) Sermon 31, i, 6

It is our part thus to preach Christ, by proclaiming all things whatsoever He hath revealed. We may indeed, without blame, yea, and with a peculiar blessing from God, declare the love of our Lord Jesus Christ; we may speak, in a more especial manner of "The Lord our Righteousness;" we may expatiate upon the grace of God in Christ, "reconciling the world unto Himself;" we may, at proper opportunities, dwell upon His praise, as "bearing the iniquities of us all, as wounded for our transgressions, and bruised for our iniquities, that by His stripes we might be healed:"—but still we should not preach Christ according to His word, if we were wholly to confine ourselves to this: we are not ourselves clear before God, unless we proclaim Him in all His offices. To preach Christ, as a workman that needeth not to be ashamed, is to preach Him, not only as our great High Priest, "taken from among men, and ordained for men, in things pertaining to God;" as such reconciling us to God by His blood, and "ever living to make intercession for us;"—but likewise as the Prophet of the Lord, "who of God is made unto us wisdom;" who, by His word and His Spirit, is with us always, "guiding us into all truth;"—yea, and as remaining a King for ever; as giving laws to all whom He has bought with His blood; as restoring those to the image of God, whom He had first reinstated in His favor; as reigning in all believing hearts until He has "subdued all things to Himself;" until He hath utterly cast out all sin, and "brought in everlasting righteousness."

This is the fullest statement of the doctrine from Wesley's own hand. (a) Wesley's interest in using the doctrine of the three offices to emphasize sanctification is especially plain. (b) Wesley here is obviously protesting against preaching which separates the priestly from the prophetic and kingly offices. In reply, he demands not the prophetic and kingly Christ, but the whole Christ. (c) The content of the offices is again defined. Noteworthy is the mention of the Holy Spirit in relation to the prophetic office, and the connection of lawgiving with the kingly office, although elsewhere lawgiving is connected with the prophetic office. (d) This formulation has a more subjective tone than the preceding one. He is "our" priest; this prophet guides "us"; and the kingly work is concerned with Christians alone. (e) A peculiarity of this statement is the explicit indication that each office is eternal. (f) The order of the offices is: priest, prophet, and king.

### 9) Letter to Samuel Furley, September 15, 1762
### (Letters, IV, 189)

... I know of no persons living who are so deeply conscious of their needing Christ both as prophet, priest, and king, as those who believe themselves, and whom I believe, to be cleansed from all sin; I mean, from all pride, anger, evil desire, idolatry, and unbelief. These very persons feel more than ever their own ignorance, littleness of grace, coming short of the full mind that was in Christ, and walking less accurately than they might have done after their Divine Pattern; are more convinced of the insufficiency of all they are, have, or do, to bear the eye of God without a Mediator; are more penetrated with the sense of the want of him than ever they were before.

Wesley emphasizes the need of the priestly and prophetic offices precisely in the context of the victory of Christ in a believer's heart. It is evident that the emphasis on the "complete Christ" is essential for the right understanding of sanctification as well as of justification.

### APPENDIX III

### Wesley's Editing of the Homily on Salvation

Following is Wesley's editing of a passage from the Anglican Homily on Salvation, first part, in S. 49, ii, 6. *Italics* represent Wesley's version, roman type the omitted portions of the original, *(italics)* in parenthesis, Wesley's additions.

In these foresaid places, the Apostle toucheth especially *three things*, which *must (necessarily) go together in our justification. Upon*

*God's part, His great mercy and grace; upon Christ's part,* justice, that is, *the satisfaction of God's justice,* or the price of our redemption, by the offering of His body, and shedding of His blood, with fulfilling of the Law perfectly and thoroughly; *and on our part,* true and lively *faith in the merits of* Jesus *Christ,* which yet is not ours, but by God's working in us: so that in our justification, there is not only God's mercy and grace, but also His justice, which the Apostle calleth the justice of God, and it consisteth in paying our ransom, and fulfilling of the law: and *so (that) the grace of God doth not shut out the* justice *(righteousness) of God in our justification, but only shutteth out the* justice *(righteousness) of man,* that is to say, the justice of our works, *as to* be merits of *deserving our justification."*—Wesley omits here a lengthy passage, doubtless for reasons of space, since he elsewhere supports the thought that our good works are excluded only from our justification.—*"Our justification* doth *come(s) freely by the mere mercy of God,* and of so great and free mercy, that *(for) whereas* 'all *the world was not able* of themselves *to pay any part towards* their *(our) ransom, it pleased* our heavenly Father of His infinite mercy, *(Him), without any (of) our* desert or *deserving, to prepare for us* the most precious jewels of *Christ's body and blood, whereby our ransom might be* fully *paid,* the law fulfilled, *and His justice* fully *satisfied.* So that *Christ (therefore) is now the righteousness of all them that truly do believe in Him.* He for them paid their ransom by His death. He for them fulfilled the Law in His life. So that now in Him, and by Him, every true Christian man may be called a fulfiller of the Law; forasmuch as that which their infirmity lacked, Christ's justice hath supplied.

Wesley's quotation continues with a passage from the second part of the Homily.

# Bibliography

Listed here are only the works actually cited in this volume. For fuller Wesley bibliographies consult the compilations in the studies of Cannon, Lerch, and Lindström.

## John Wesley's Works

BURTNER, ROBERT W., and CHILES, ROBERT E. (eds.). *A Compend of Wesley's Theology*. New York and Nashville: Abingdon Press, 1954.

CURNOCK, NEHEMIAH (ed.). *The Journal of the Rev. John Wesley, A.M.* 8 vols. London: The Epworth Press, 1909-16. (Cited as *Journal* by date of entry.)

*Explanatory Notes upon the New Testament*. London: The Epworth Press, 1952. (Cited as *Notes* by reference to scriptural passage.)

JACKSON, THOMAS (ed.). *The Works of the Rev. John Wesley, A.M.* 3rd ed., 14 vols. London: Wesleyan-Methodist Book-Room, 1829-31. (Cited as W.)

SUGDEN, EDWARD H. (ed.). *Wesley's Standard Sermons*. 2 vols. London: The Epworth Press, 1921. (All sermons [S.] cited by number.)

*Survey of the Wisdom of God in the Creation, A: or A Compendium of Natural Philosophy*. 4th ed., 5 vols. London: J. Paramore, 1784.

TELFORD, JOHN (ed.). *The Letters of the Rev. John Wesley, A.M.* 8 vols. London: The Epworth Press, 1931.

## Other Sources

BARTH, KARL. *Kirchliche Dogmatik*. Bd. IV: Die Lehre von der Versöhnung. Zollikon-Zürich: Evangelischer Verlag, 1953ff.

*Book of Common Prayer, The.* New York: Oxford University Press, 1938.

CALVIN, JOHN. *Institutes of the Christian Religion.* 2 vols. Translated by H. BEVERIDGE. London: James Clarke & Co., 1953.

CANNON, WILLIAM R. *The Theology of John Wesley.* New York and Nashville: Abingdon-Cokesbury Press, 1946.

*Doctrines and Discipline of the Methodist Church, 1956.* Nashville: The Methodist Publishing House, 1957.

HEPPE, HEINRICH. *Reformed Dogmatics,* ed. ERNST BIZER. Translated by G. T. THOMSON. London: George Allen & Unwin, 1950.

HILDEBRANDT, FRANZ. *From Luther to Wesley.* London: Lutterworth Press, 1951.

LAWSON, JOHN. *Notes on Wesley's Forty-four Sermons.* London: The Epworth Press, 1952.

————. *Selections from John Wesley's Notes on the New Testament.* London: The Epworth Press, 1955.

LEE, UMPHREY. *John Wesley and Modern Religion.* Nashville: Cokesbury Press, 1936.

LERCH, DAVID. *Heil und Heiligung bei John Wesley.* Zürich: Christliche Vereinsbuchhandlung, 1941.

LINDSTRÖM, HARALD. *Wesley and Sanctification.* London: The Epworth Press, n.d. (Preface dated 1946).

MASON, C. E. *John Wesley's Doctrine of Salvation.* Unpublished Master's thesis, Union Theological Seminary, New York, 1950.

MORE, PAUL E., and CROSS, FRANK L. (eds.). *Anglicanism.* London: Society for Promoting Christian Knowledge, 1935.

OUTLER, ALBERT C. "The Methodist Standards of Doctrine." Mimeographed article, Perkins School of Theology, 1958.

POPE, WILLIAM B. *A Compendium of Christian Theology.* 3 vols. London: Wesleyan-Methodist Book-Room, 1880.

RATTENBURY, J. E. *The Eucharistic Hymns of John and Charles Wesley.* London: The Epworth Press, 1948.

————. *The Evangelical Doctrines of Charles Wesley's Hymns.* London: The Epworth Press, 1954.

Rees, A. H. *The Doctrine of Justification in the Anglican Reformers.* London, 1939.

Schmid, Heinrich. *The Doctrinal Theology of the Evangelical Lutheran Church.* Translated by Charles A. Hay and Henry E. Jacobs; 3rd ed., revised. Philadelphia: Lutheran Publication Society, 1899.

Schmidt, Martin. *John Wesleys Bekehrung.* Bremen, 1938.

Shipley, David C. "Wesley and Some Calvinist Controversies," *The Drew Gateway,* XXV, 4 (Summer, 1955), 195-210.

*Sermons or Homilies Appointed to be Read in Churches in the Time of Queen Elizabeth of Famous Memory.* Oxford: The Clarendon Press, 1802.

Spörri, Theophil. *Das Wesentliche methodistischer Theologie.* Zürich: Christliche Vereinsbuchhandlung, 1954.

Telford, John. *The Life of John Wesley.* London: The Epworth Press, 1953.

Turner, George A. *The More Excellent Way.* Winona Lake: Light and Life Press, 1952.

Watson, Richard. *Theological Institutes.* 2 vols. New York: Mason & Lane, 1836 and 1840.

"Westminster Confession of Faith," in Philip Schaff, *The Creeds of Christendom* (3 vols.; New York: Harper & Bros., 1877), III, 600-673.

Wheeler, Henry. *History and Exposition of the Twenty-five Articles of Religion of the Methodist Episcopal Church.* New York: Eaton & Mains, 1908.

# Index